Improving Your Reflective Practice through Stories of Practitioner Research

WITHDRAWAL

Improving Your Reflective Practice through Stories of Practitioner Research shows how research has informed and created effective and valuable reflective practice in early years education, and offers depth to the arguments for a research-orientated stance to this vital field of study.

This thought-provoking text explores and documents a variety of small-scale practitioner research projects from the home and early years settings. The stories are centred around real life for children, families and workers and offer practical ideas and support for early years students around the world. They engage in some of the most current debates in early childhood education today, such as:

- how to support children as individuals
- how young children learn and how parents support their learning
- how to lead and facilitate change in a way that does not take power away from children, parents or workers
- how to support children in taking risks
- how to support parents in returning to learning.

Throughout this book, the 'Pen Green' attitude to practitioner research is actively encouraged. This involves fostering curiosity, being open to the views of others, questioning the 'taken for granted', making the implicit explicit and reflecting on one's daily work. Any practitioner research in early years education and care will draw inspiration from this accessible and supportive text.

Cath Arnold is an Early Years Consultant and leads the MA in Integrated Provision for Children and Families in the Early Years at the world-famous Pen Green Research Base, UK.

Improving Your Reflective Practice through Stories of Practitioner Research

Edited by Cath Arnold

Routledge
Taylor & Francis Group

LONDON AND NEW YORK

First published 2012
by Routledge
2 Park Square, Milton Park, Abingdon, Oxon OX14 4RN

Simultaneously published in the USA and Canada
by Routledge
711 Third Avenue, New York, NY 10017

Routledge is an imprint of the Taylor & Francis Group, an informa business

British Library Cataloguing in Publication Data
A catalogue record for this book is available from the British Library

ISBN: 978–0–415–69729–3 (hbk)
ISBN: 978–0–415–69730–9 (pbk)
ISBN: 978–0–203–11251–9 (ebk)

Typeset in Garamond
by Keystroke, Station Road, Codsall, Wolverhampton

MIX
Paper from
responsible sources
FSC
www.fsc.org   FSC® C004839

Printed and bound in Great Britain by the MPG Books Group

To Patrick Whitaker, who taught for many years on courses at Pen Green and taught these authors as MA participants

Patrick died in June 2010, a fine man, a great teacher and someone who truly believed in human potential

Contents

Notes on contributors

Gill Allen

I was born in the Midlands, an only child in a working-class family, determined to become a teacher when I was 10. During training the early years became my passion as I saw that here the children lead the learning and the whole family is involved. I opened a nursery in my house soon after qualifying, whilst also giving birth to two of my four sons. I have worked in the private, voluntary and maintained sector for 41 years, setting up play facilities in the local hospital using national funding for volunteers, training playgroup staff and sitting on a national training committee for many years. I then returned to the maintained sector as a nursery teacher, also supporting parents and practitioners through informal and formal training.

In 1999 I moved to the south of England to become the headteacher of a maintained nursery school, which gained Early Excellence status in 2003 and became a children's centre in 2006. I gained an MA in Integrated Provision for Children and Families in 2007, which helped to support the development of the centre as a thriving and potentially life-changing learning community, with young children at its heart.

I have been married for 42 years; have four grown-up sons and three young grandchildren. I left my job in 2010 to take the 'gap year' I never had. Rob and I are undertaking a year-long trip around Australia, living close to nature. I look forward to continuing to support learners on my return.

Cath Arnold

Having worked in Early Childhood since my youngest daughter started nursery some 34 years ago, I am still as interested in understanding young children and working with their families as I was back then. However, I have also recently become fascinated with adults and their learning. I now have the good fortune to work as a consultant, and to lead on the MA in Integrated Provision for Children and Families in the Early Years at the Pen Green Research Base. This work provides an extremely stimulating learning community that I currently enjoy being part of.

On a more personal level, I live with my husband in Corby, have three wonderful children and three equally wonderful grandchildren.

Anne Gladstone

My interest in young children's learning and development was awakened with the birth of my own children. After becoming involved with running their playgroup and later helping in the classroom, I returned to university to train as an infant teacher. After a short time teaching in an infant school I moved to the FE sector where I taught childcare workers. I had the opportunity to take up a secondment to a Sure Start Local programme, now a children's centre, where I worked with parents who wished to return to learning, training or work. Through working with colleagues who are infant mental health specialists, I have become extremely interested in the profound effect of early relationships on a child's emotional and cognitive development and the continuing influence of relationships with other people into and through adult life. Of particular interest to me are the links between early experiences of learning and subsequent achievement both in school and in adult life, particularly for families who are experiencing difficulties or who are disadvantaged. I was fortunate to be able to reflect on these issues when I studied for my MA in Integrated Provision for Children and Families at Pen Green. I now work as an independent consultant.

Gina Goody

My life with Bob has been based in central London where we have lived for the past 32 years. Our children, Gemma, Seonaid and Sophie, had the good fortune to attend two excellent schools – Soho Parish School and Camden School for Girls. It was the experience of our daughters at Soho Parish School, under the guidance of a wonderful headteacher, David Barton, and a truly inspirational teacher, Sian Davies, that gave me the confidence to train to teach. When our youngest daughter, Sophie, was three and in the nursery class at Soho, I studied for my BEd. as a mature student at the University of North London, with a specialism in Early Years and English. I worked as an Early Years teacher and Foundation Stage Co-ordinator at St Dominic's in the London Borough of Camden for 13 years. While I was at St Dominic's I studied for an MA in Children's Literature at Roehampton which I completed in 2002. I am now deputy headteacher at Fawood Children's Centre in the London Borough of Brent and in the summer of 2007 I completed my MA in Integrated Provision for Children and Families, which I had been studying for at Pen Green. Bob and I are now grandparents; we have the most delightful grandchildren, Zack and Ayah, and I am seeing the world open out to them in ways that sometimes cause me to tremble.

Elaine Grant

I began my career as a full-time family nanny, during which time I also trained in childcare. After several years, and much enjoyment, I decided to broaden my work experience and took over the running of a struggling local pre-school. From this, I gained a wealth of skills and experience as I strived with other staff to develop the setting.

I have since worked as an Early Years and Childcare Development Officer within Worcestershire, supporting existing childcare settings and the start up of new provision – a challenging but most rewarding role. Following this I moved into family support and the setting up of services for families as an employee of a local Sure Start programme working in the community. This inspired me to complete my MA in Integrated Provision for Children and Families.

My role has since diversified many times and I am now working within children's centres coordinating a family learning and training programme for parents and overseeing a volunteer programme that supports parents to progress, often into training, education and employment. I also submit and manage funding bids to support the learning and development opportunities that we offer.

On a personal note I have a wonderful husband and two amazing children. My family are my passion and priority.

Janette Harcus

I was born in the late 1960s and brought up in north Kent. I began my career path training as a nursery nurse, and went straight on to train as a primary school teacher at Christ Church in Canterbury. I taught in an inner London primary school for six years before retraining as an Early Years teacher and returning to Kent to teach in a large maintained Nursery Unit. For the last seven years I have worked for a National Children's Home (now called Action for Children) Early Years Centre on the south east coast as the teacher/manager for the Nursery Unit.

I completed the MA in Integrated Provision for Children and Families with Pen Green in 2007. I have been fortunate to work with a wide variety of colleagues, families and children over the years who have been the inspiration for my studies and my learning. I have a continued enthusiasm and fascination for young children's learning and increasingly a passion for working with and including parents in the exploration and celebration of young children's 'knowing'. I live near to the coast with my husband, two young daughters and assorted furry creatures.

Clare Knight

For as long as I can remember, I have always wanted to work with young children. I trained as an infant teacher in Birmingham during the mid-1980s and have spent the years since working with children of all ages both in and out of the school environment. In 2001 I was fortunate enough to be appointed as a teacher in charge of a nursery. The nursery is part of a large integrated centre for children and families which became an Early Excellence Centre in 2002/3. I have gained so much from developing and being part of a learning community that tries to embrace all those who become involved, especially children, parents and colleagues. Studying for my MA in Integrated Provision for Children and Families was an inspiring experience and helped me to express my gut feelings about how young children are included and engaged both in and outside of the centre. It is deeply important to me that young children are equal partners in their learning, allowed to make choices and express their own views, and adults are genuinely respectful of this. I believe in the importance of building bridges of shared understanding between the home and nursery cultures.

Away from the centre, I have a marvellous husband and three wonderful sons, twins who are 15 and a younger son who is 13. I am enjoying renovating our Victorian Gothic house, reading, jogging (a pathetic attempt to hold back the years) and cooking for family and friends.

Ana Sevilla

I was born and brought up in central London; I love the diversity and the hustle and bustle of the city and would never consider living anywhere else. My career in Early Years began as a result of my experience of becoming a mother and volunteering at the local playgroup. I have now worked in the Early Years field for many years and have spent time in the private, maintained and voluntary sectors. The experience of studying as a mature student for an Honours Degree in Early Childhood Studies inspired the researcher within me and I then went on to complete an MA in Integrated Provision for Children and Families at Pen Green. I am passionate about inspiring others in believing it is never too late to explore the opportunities of further education. While I was completing my MA, I was working for the Local Authority in an advisory role supporting PVI (Private, Voluntary and Independent Settings) providers. Since then I have moved on and am now employed as a centre manager in an integrated inner city primary school and children's centre. It is a very challenging and rewarding role which I thoroughly enjoy.

At home I live with my partner of 28 years and our two beautiful children – the older they get the greater the worry! My youngest is off to university next year which I hope will give me the opportunity, time and motivation to start my PhD. In my spare time to relax I enjoy cooking, reading and gardening.

Suzanne Taylor

I took a BH (now extinct) in Education and Geography at Froebel: a good opportunity to focus and learn about child development and the environment. Subsequently, during my PGCE at Bulmershe in Reading, I discovered nursery schools and have taught in them or been striving to return to them for the last 20 years. With great satisfaction, in 2007 at Pen Green, I gained my MA in Integrated Provision for Children and Families. From 2003 to 2008, I was an adviser within a Local Authority, enjoying working with practitioners to achieve high quality Early Years provision. Since 2008, I have been head of a nursery school and children's centre – finding myself back at my nursery school roots and enjoying engaging closely with children and families again.

Another strand through the last seven years has been my developing passion for outdoor learning in a natural environment. Building links to Norway has enabled me to take practitioners on study tours to see Norwegian forest kindergartens. I have taken five tour groups now: practitioners all around the country have seen first-hand and shared my excitement for working and learning with children in a natural environment. My next step has been to share this love of learning outdoors with other practitioners through training at Hungerford in West Berkshire.

My wonderful family (husband and two teenage children) support me – even when I am always trying to squeeze extra hours into the day. When I am not working, I love to travel, garden and paint – all seem to help my creative thoughts.

David Westmore

I have worked as an Early Years practitioner in inner London since qualifying as a teacher 20 years ago. During my first teaching practice I found myself in a nursery environment, and remember being fascinated watching a young child's total absorption with water as he washed his hands at a sink. I still retain my joy and enthusiasm in working with young children.

As Deputy of a nursery school in 2001, I was lucky to become involved in the Early Excellence Scheme when we received designation, leading to a broadening and deepening of my knowledge and experience. I took part in a Diploma course in Early Years Leadership, and later the pilot National Professional Qualification for Integrated Centre Leadership (NPQICL). I completed an MA in Integrated Early Years Leadership in 2007.

After 13 years at an integrated centre in Deptford, South East London, where I had the opportunity to work in many roles, including Head of Centre, I am now working as an Early Years Consultant, currently as Interim Head for an integrated centre in south London.

Foreword

It is now more than sixteen years since we first set up the MA in Integrated Provision for Children and Families at Pen Green. Conceptualised over an intense and memorable week in a Cambridge café by Margy Whalley and Tina Bruce, the course has evolved over its eight cohorts – the ninth cohort will embark on their learning journey in September 2012. This MA has been co-constructed from the start by more than 300 participants from the Early Years community. We always refer to 'students' as participants because all of the adult learners on the MA at Pen Green have had rich and spectacularly diverse learning routes before joining the course. Each participant has left their mark on our MA curriculum and on our pedagogical approach. Former students now work as consultants, teach on the MA and on other undergraduate and postgraduate courses at Pen Green and continue to act as critical friends to those of us working in the Research, Training and Development base.

The courses at Pen Green are all developed *by* practitioners (still in practice) *for* practitioners. Whilst our formal links with Leicester University, Hertfordshire University and Middlesex University are vitally important to us, we are deeply committed to a praxeological approach. Practitioner enquiry is at the heart of our work. Research propositions and research questions are generated by families, staff, researchers from the Research Base and participants on our Foundation Degree, BA Hons, EYPS and MA courses. Publications and training materials develop out of our research projects. Practice informs research and research supports practice.

The stories of practitioner research in this volume have already made an impact on research, policy and practice.

Each of these authors has developed a dialectic between their research propositions and robust theoretical frameworks. They have managed to write without too much 'authorial intrusion' and yet have interwoven the personal and the professional highly effectively.

Dr Margy Whalley
Director of Research, Training and Development
at Pen Green Research Base

Introduction

Cath Arnold

Whenever anyone has asked about my profession and I have said that I work with young children, this has frequently evoked an 'Ahhh . . .'. I have then felt the need to explain how intellectually and emotionally demanding working with young children and families can be. The 'Ahhh . . .' seems to me to represent the idea that working with young children is cosy and undemanding and certainly not highly intellectual.

The authors of this book are all currently working at the 'cutting edge' of practice in the Early Years field. They are not only engaged in weaving good practice with children and families each day, but also in reflecting on their own work and studying and writing about what constitutes best practice in the field at this time. Inevitably, they engage in some of the current debates:

- How to support children as individuals
- How young children learn and how parents support their learning
- The Rose Review and its significance for children and families
- How to lead and facilitate change in a way that does not take power away from children, parents or workers
- How to support children in taking risks
- How to support parents in returning to learning.

The 'child's voice' and 'family voice' comes through strongly in most of these accounts. The 'worker voice' is also acknowledged and 'foregrounded' in three of the chapters (Carr, 2001).

Practitioner research

The word 'research' conjures up a vast world of investigation, exploration and examination. Traditionally, research was perceived as finding out or discovering some 'truth' or 'fact' that **could** be discovered, for example, how gravity works or how many people gained five GCSEs in one year. Research was often designed to find out about the physical world and about what we can predict in the world around us. This is often described as being within a 'positivist paradigm'.

Research that involves people seems to be much more complex. Whilst there are still very useful large-scale studies designed to demonstrate certain trends, mostly we find human behaviour less predictable than the behaviour of objects. We are trying to interpret what we see and feel and to gain information from others who are willing collaborators in our settings or homes. This is often described as being within an 'interpretive paradigm'.

The authors of this book were all engaging in study for an MA at the Pen Green Centre for Under-Fives and Their Families. As part of their work, they were engaging in what we refer to as 'practitioner research' or 'practitioner-led enquiry'. This sort of research is small scale and therefore can make no claim to generalisation beyond the people involved. The pattern of the MA means that participants are introduced to certain techniques or methods, which they then try out in their own workplaces. The first method or technique introduced on the course is 'Child Study'. This involves observing a young child alongside their parents over a period of a few weeks, drawing on methods used by Susan Isaacs and others (Isaacs, 1930; Navarra, 1955; Athey, 2007). Some analysis is made and a case study is produced. This is what Stake would describe as an 'intrinsic case study' (Stake, 2000). Stake explains that an 'intrinsic case study is undertaken because the researcher wants a better understanding of this particular case' (2000, p.437).

A second method introduced is practitioner action research, which involves looking at a current concern and working together with others to improve the situation. This method builds on an established tradition of collaborative enquiry designed to reflect on and improve practice in a systematic way (Elliott, 1991; McNiff and Whitehead, 2002).

A third method also involves a 'case study' approach in relation to working with children and families. This may be a single family case study or could involve a small number of families or workers. This is more likely to be what Stake describes as an 'instrumental case study' which 'is examined mainly to provide insight into an issue' (2000, p.437).

A fourth method introduced and used throughout the course and particularly useful when thinking about 'Leadership Learning within Teams' is the use of 'journaling' as a 'documentary tool' (Janesick, 2000, p.392). For some, the act of writing aids reflection and 'gives form to one's thoughts and feelings' (Arnold, 2007, p.142).

Throughout the MA course at Pen Green we hope to encourage participants to develop a kind of 'research stance' towards their daily work. This involves fostering the disposition to be curious; being open to the views of others; questioning the 'taken for granted'; making the implicit explicit; and reflecting on one's daily work.

Ethics

When carrying out any kind of research or practitioner-led enquiry, ethical aspects need to be held in mind at all times. The golden rule is to 'do no harm' to participants, children, parents and colleagues. If all participants feel that they benefit from the enquiry, then we have done what we set out to do. The research literature advises gaining 'informed consent' and this can be quite straightforward at first and more tricky as projects develop. We never quite know exactly what will happen and we need to be alert to anything that participants may not want to be shared. Consent is something to be revisited and thought about at every stage of a research process. Most Higher Education establishments require confidentiality and anonymity but this is sometimes quite hard to achieve completely. Family studies are difficult to anonymise as the author may be parent or grandparent, although some have tried, for example Navarra, who refers to his son as LB (meaning Little Boy) (1955). The main principle is to share power with participants and to listen and to act on what they are telling you at all times (even if that means you have to omit some data from your assignment).

This book

Across this book, the authors have captured some of the complexity involved in working with young children and their families. They have demonstrated that there are no easy solutions to improving the future for young children, but that a great deal can be gained from 'creating a climate of experiment', reflecting on the work, and drawing conclusions or implications for practice.

The authors also show that they are well placed to carry out useful and meaningful research alongside workers and parents and that significant changes in practice have occurred as a result. The book begins with three chapters strongly focussed on young children, containing close and sometimes intimate, observations of children at home and in settings. Elaine Grant (Chapter 1) studied her own child's use of a treasure basket at home and was particularly interested in Millie's schematic explorations (Athey, 2007). In the tradition of Susan Isaacs (1930, 1933), Elaine closely observed Millie over time and made detailed written observations, which she subsequently linked with theory. Elaine gives a fine explanation with examples of Piaget's and Athey's work. She also weaves in a Vygotskian perspective by noticing the interests Millie shared with her important adults. In Chapter 2, Gina Goody gives a moving account of her grandson's use of a particular story as a 'transitional object' at the period around his sister's birth when he himself was feeling bereft (Winnicott, 1971). Gina also makes a strong case for supporting the sharing of stories as the basis for learning to read. There are some powerful messages about how fostering the love of stories supports children's emotions and cognition. Clare Knight (Chapter 3) examines young children's use of a digital camera to record their lives outside nursery to share with adults and peers in the nursery. Clare has coined the phrase 'Bridges of Shared Understanding' to describe what happened when children were given the power and autonomy to share what was important to them at home with nursery workers.

The fourth, fifth and sixth chapters focus on evaluating practice in settings. Suzanne Taylor (Chapter 4) used video observations to help staff in settings in the UK and Norway to think about their attitudes to risk taking. Suzanne used and adapted the method of polyvocal ethnography, which was pioneered by Joseph Tobin in his famous study *Pre-School in Three Cultures* (Tobin *et al.*, 1989). David Westmore (Chapter 5), as leader of a children's centre, considered how workers in his setting were supporting and encouraging the children's role play in the centre. David fully engaged with the staff and has demonstrated admirably, how to effect change in practice.

In Chapter 6, the focus is on involving parents in their children's learning and valuing parents' knowledge of their children. Janette Harcus used an action research approach to investigate how well she and her team knew individual children and families and how they could improve their ways of knowing. Janette has very skilfully woven in theory about 'assimilation and accommodation' (Piaget, 1940), 'construction of self' (Harter, 1999) and 'otherness' (Vandenbroeck, 1999).

Chapters 7 and 8 consider leadership of early years settings. Both authors move a long way from the traditional male paradigm of leading from the front. Ana Sevilla (Chapter 7) interviewed five women leaders of community nurseries in London to discover shared themes in their leadership journeys. Gill Allen (Chapter 8) examined her own leadership by asking her team to give her honest feedback about her leadership.

The final chapter (Chapter 9) is about what supports adults to return to learning and how this is intimately linked with childhood experiences. Unsurprisingly, Anne Gladstone interviewed a small number of parents, who had returned to learning, and found that secure attachment, resilience and social capital were all of importance to parents in their various attempts to return to organised learning. Anne uses the concept of an 'emotional reservoir' to describe the inner strength, gained through positive relationships during childhood and adulthood, that is needed to persist and pursue that second chance to learn and to have the opportunity to gain qualifications.

The book concludes with a discussion of the issues raised and the methods and techniques of investigation used and a glossary of terms.

References

Arnold, C. (2007) Young Children's Representations of Emotions and Attachment in Their Spontaneous Patterns of Behaviour: An Exploration of a Researcher's Understanding, University of Coventry, Unpublished PhD Thesis.

Athey, C. (2007) (2nd Edition) *Extending Thought in Young Children*, London, Paul Chapman.

Carr, M. (2001) *Assessment in Early Childhood Settings: Learning Stories*, London, Paul Chapman.

Elliott, J. (1991) *Action Research for Educational Change*, Buckingham, Open University Press.

Harter, S. (1999) *The Construction of Self*, New York, Guilford Press.

Isaacs, S. (1930) *Intellectual Growth in Young Children*, London, Routledge and Kegan Paul Ltd.

Isaacs, S. (1933) *Social Development in Young Children*, London, George Routledge and Sons.

Janesick, V. (2000) The Choreography of Qualitative Research Design, in Denzin, N.K. and Lincoln, Y.S. (Eds) (2000) *Handbook of Qualitative Research*, London, Sage.

McNiff, J. and Whitehead, J. (2002) *Action Research for Teachers*, London, David Fulton Publishers.

Navarra, J.G. (1955) *The Development of Scientific Concepts in a Young Child – A Case Study*, New York, Stratford Press.

Piaget, J. (1940) The Mental Development of the Child [originally published in *Juventus Helvetica*], in Elkind, D. (Ed.) (1980) *Six Psychological Studies*, Brighton, Harvester Press.

Stake, E.R. (2000) Case Studies, in Denzin, N.K. and Lincoln, Y.S. (Eds) (2000) *Handbook of Qualitative Research*, London, Sage.

Tobin, J.J., Wu, D. and Davidson, D. (1989) *Preschool in Three Cultures*, New Haven, CT, Yale University Press.

Vandenbroeck, M. (1999) *The View of the Yeti*, The Hague, Bernard van Leer Foundation.

Winnicott, D.W. (1971) *Playing and Reality*, London and New York, Routledge.

Chapter 1

Treasuring Millie

Millie's use of treasure baskets

Elaine Grant

In this chapter you will find:

- An observational study by a parent at home of Millie aged 7 months to 13 months.
- An interest in the use of natural materials in order to support Millie's explorations.
- The use of schema theory as a framework to understand Millie's learning.
- What happened when her parents followed Millie's lead.

Introduction/context

This chapter focusses on systematic observations of my first and much treasured daughter, Millie Ann Drew Grant, over a six-month period during the first year of her life.

As Millie's mother I was conscious of the importance of my role as her first educator (Whalley 2001, p.4) and also of the learning environment that I would offer her at home. Even before her birth I was thinking about what this environment might look like. Would she be surrounded by plastic, manufactured, so called 'educational' toys or would I be offering alternative experiences to her?

I therefore wanted to observe Millie's interests at an early age and was particularly interested in schemas and looking for patterns in her play (Athey 1990). Schemas can be defined as:

> patterns of repeatable actions that lead to early categories and then to logical classifications. . . . A schema, therefore is a pattern of repeatable behaviour into which experiences are assimilated and that are gradually co-ordinated. Co-ordinations lead to a higher-level and more powerful schemas.
>
> (Athey 1990, pp.36–37)

Athey's research around schemas drew on the research of Piaget and the work that he carried out from the 1920s to the 1970s. Piaget introduced the concepts of *assimilation* and *accommodation* in relation to schemas:

Sensory-motor intelligence is . . . the development of an assimilating activity which tends to incorporate external objects in its schemas while at the same time accommodating the schemas to the external world.

(Piaget 1962, p.5)

Assimilation describes how new objects or experiences are incorporated into existing schemas. Accommodation defines how schemas are modified to deal with new situations that do not respond to existing schemas and so they are extended or combined (Piaget 1962).

When observing Millie I also wanted to think about natural resources provided in treasure baskets and heuristic play materials in terms of whether these would support her schematic play (Goldschmied and Jackson 2004). I felt that this would help me to provide an environment for Millie which matched her interests, supported her development and would also allow me to research for myself the role of natural materials versus manufactured toys – as I observed Millie's response to both.

However, my overall aim was to prioritise the time to observe Millie and spend time focussing on her – as I quickly realised what a challenge this can be as a parent trying to juggle the business of everyday life. It was important to me to take time out to get to know my daughter more deeply, to be sensitive to her, to understand her thought processes and to enjoy watching her development and learning.

In professional terms, I expected that my study would then impact on my work with other families and children as I developed my observational skills, enhanced my knowledge of schemas, explored treasure basket and heuristic play and also considered how to provide an environment that stimulates and encourages children's schematic play.

I considered the possible benefits to Millie as a result of my conducting this study to be:

- Potential for our relationship to deepen as I have a greater understanding of her.
- Continuation of a strong attachment developing between Millie and myself, and with other main carers; caregiver's understanding of child's mind encourages secure attachment (Fonagy 2001).
- Opportunity to observe and understand Millie's interests.
- Identification of Millie's schemas, with ongoing benefit of then supporting and extending these.
- Involvement of other main carers who are influential in Millie's life (I included them in my observations and analysis).
- Increased knowledge in order to provide a stimulating environment and opportunities for Millie.
- Evidence base from which to plan, as Millie's first educator.
- Informed planning to meet Millie's individual needs.

Farrell (2004, p.20) talks about the need to think about the principle of *beneficence* when researching, whereby the relative benefit of the research is weighed up against the risk to the participant. I therefore felt compelled to think about what could potentially be gained from observing Millie, alongside the potential for this to impact negatively on her, before embarking on my research to ensure that my study was ethically sound.

Approach to the research

I intended to write a case study (Bell 1996, p.8), drawing on detailed and focussed narrative observations and video observations of Millie's play. I began with the hypothesis that treasure baskets/heuristic play is instrumental in terms of supporting and extending children's schemas and from there planned a structure to my research that I hoped would enable this hypothesis to be tested (Bell 1996, p.19).

In terms of supporting children's schematic play, it is important that children have resources available to them that are varied and can be used in different ways, depending on individual interests. They may want several of the same objects, as well as objects that behave in the same way – such as objects which contain or roll.

Children need the freedom to repeat their actions so that they are assimilating new content into their current schemas as well as experiencing accommodation in order for their knowledge to deepen. Access to a range of interesting materials is therefore beneficial to them. Treasure baskets provide a range of open-ended resources, as well as encouraging children to explore their own interests as they are presented with an attractive array of objects, encouraging their natural curiosity. It is possible then that treasure baskets/heuristic play is likely to support and extend schemas through the very nature of the opportunities that they offer.

I kept a personal journal of observations of Millie, recording anything that I felt was significant. This began with preliminary observations when Millie was 7 months old and I introduced her to the treasure basket for the first time. Over a six-month period I continued to keep a diary of observations and collected video clips at the same time. I also included the thoughts of Millie's other close adults. I hoped to achieve a varied set of observations in differing circumstances. I recorded many occasions when Millie was using her treasure basket. In these instances I was mostly true to Goldschmied's theory that baskets should be used at set times when the infant is able to concentrate, without other distractions, and a trusted adult is able to remain close by for reassurance (Goldschmied and Jackson 2004). However, there were some occasions when Millie had access to her treasure basket alongside all of her other toys and whatever else was available to her in her environment – particularly as she became mobile and her basket was more generally accessible to her.

I also then recorded incidents when Millie appeared to be absorbed and concentrating, when she was choosing an activity and being autonomous and when she seemed to be demonstrating patterns (schemas) in her play.

It could be said that I observed Millie when I considered her to be 'involved' in her activity, which Laevers would describe as her benefiting from her environment, in terms of '*deep* level learning' (Laevers *et al.* 1997, p.19).

I was also particularly interested in considering the role of the adult when exploring the process of supporting Millie's schemas, especially in relation to treasure baskets/heuristic play. Goldschmied is clear in her ideas that adults should not interfere or be active in this play. She describes the role of adult as 'emotional anchorage', enabling babies to explore by being nearby (Goldschmied and Jackson 2004, p.101).

My method for collecting video clips was to capture significant moments on tape, which I could then use as evidence alongside my written observations. However, in this study I found this method to be fraught with problems. Millie was generally distracted by the camera, making it difficult to get a natural picture of her behaviour. In addition, having persevered with videoing Millie, when I came to process the video footage I discovered that the microphone had at some point broken on the camera and it was not possible to play back any of the tapes with sound.

For my written observations I had kept notes on a weekly basis, and at the end of each week had processed them and typed them up. I realised that if I had more regularly processed my video footage during the course of my research I would have become aware of the problem with the camera, which would then have minimised the impact.

My results and analysis for my study are therefore taken from my written observations. Focussing on and reviewing my diary entries was an element of my methodology that I found particularly useful. As I observed Millie I found it impossible not to interpret her behaviour and form ideas about her interests. Fawcett talks about the need to 'suspend judgement' (Fawcett 2005, p.4) when carrying out observations but for me I was constantly analysing as I was observing and as I typed up my notes. This meant that as I processed written evidence, I was planning how else I might support Millie's interests, what I might add to her treasure basket accordingly and reflecting on how she might respond.

The project

In this chapter the results being analysed are predominantly taken from a diary of observations of Millie recorded by me over a total period of six months.

My first diary entry documented Millie's initial encounter with a treasure basket and it was noted that this was the longest period – twenty minutes – that I had witnessed Millie concentrating and playing for, up until this point. I recorded a similar period of concentration when Millie next played with her basket. Millie was 7 months and 7 months and 17 days old when these entries were recorded.

During her initial experience Millie chose to explore several items in her basket, with lots of mouthing taking place. This was appropriate for her stage of development, as she got the best sense of what something was like by putting it in her mouth. Millie was demonstrating choice and independence as she did this. When exploring the treasure basket for the second time, there appeared to be a pattern emerging to Millie's actions. I have noted for this observation, how I sat close enough to Millie that she knew I was there but that I was observing rather than being actively involved in her play. My records describe Millie's play:

> She took out set of metal measuring cups that are linked together and shook; this made a noise – seems to enjoy making the noise and repeats several times. Then looked at stainless steel cup with wooden pegs in, again took out pegs one by one: sucks, examines, turns and sucks – 3 in total. Goes back to measuring cups. Millie has recently discovered that banging objects onto something can make a sound – banged measuring cups onto basket and then shook them again. Dropped measuring cups into basket and pulled out metal chain, shook vigorously several times. Went back to measuring cups, examining and shaking. Then pulled out small soft teddy, sucked on foot and ear. Shook teddy and banged on basket. Dropped teddy and picked up chain, shaking and banging on basket.

It was evident that Millie was enjoying:

- Mouthing
- Tapping/banging
- Shaking.

As Millie was finding different objects with which to try out these actions, it could be said that she was assimilating fresh content into her schemas through play with her treasure basket. Further evidence of this is apparent in other observations. It seemed that Millie was interested in the sound that resulted from shaking or banging an object. When she then shook and banged a small teddy bear and no sound was made, Millie dropped this and went back to the metal chain.

The action of banging or tapping, as well as demonstrating cause and effect, could also be described as the dynamic aspect of a Trajectory schema. Piaget (1962, p.26) states that:

> the action and its result constitute a single schema, recognised as such by the child and giving rise as such to repetition.

This suggests that Millie may also have been interested in the action of banging or tapping as well as the possible noise that resulted. Athey (1990, p.31) talks about 'Dynamic Vertical schemas', which infants at first explore with objects, using a 'vertical arm movement' – and later with themselves as they pull themselves up, for instance, to standing.

Athey (1990, p.31) also explains how trajectory behaviour, as well as being repeatable, shows continuity in its development from motor-level to symbolic representation to thought.

As Millie was banging and tapping the objects, she was learning that the resulting noise is 'functionally dependent' on these actions (Athey 1990, p.70). Athey describes how 'Functional dependencies . . . arise from the application of earlier schematic behaviours to environmental events. They develop from the sensory and perceptual information accompanying motor actions and lead to true operations that can be carried out in the mind'.

Piaget (1962, p.7) uses the term 'functional assimilation', whereby a reflex may be unintentionally triggered, but having responded and discovered the result, the infant may repeat the action. Therefore, Millie may not have initially intended to make a sound by banging an object but, having discovered this effect, was then happy to repeat her actions on several different objects.

The next observation describes how Millie had just learned to crawl and was enjoying using this new skill at every opportunity (9 months 24 days). This, I feel, impacted significantly on the results and Millie's cognitive concerns from then onwards. Movement opens up a whole new world to an infant, and changes how they explore and experience their environment. The same entry also documents Millie at a soft play session tapping two shaker instruments together and showing pleasure when I joined in and tapped a rattle on her shaker. This demonstrates how she enjoyed the recognition of her interests. Later on in the day, at home, she tapped two wooden blocks together.

A day later Millie was observed using her treasure basket and predominantly tapping objects. Similarly at 10 months 11 days Millie was sitting in the garden with her treasure basket and the following observation is recorded:

> Millie tapped wooden spatula repeatedly onto container. Continued to explore items in basket. She tapped container and lid together and then tapped wooden egg cup on wooden bowl several times – both of these actions made a noise.

> Examined a shell and accidentally dropped it into a metal bowl, discovered that this made a sound so spent several minutes tapping shell inside bowl, then moving it away with her hand and almost dropping shell before bringing it back and tapping it inside bowl. Also tapped a metal measuring cup onto a metal bowl. Earlier that day had seen Millie playing with a plastic toy potato masher – has crawled off the rug onto the laminate floor and tapped it on the floor several times so that a sound was made.

Again it could be said that Millie did not intend to create a sound by dropping the shell into the bowl but her experience allowed her to assimilate new content into her schema and also to independently create a game that she enjoyed. It is notable that Millie had also been observed that day using other resources in her environment to explore her schema. There is further evidence of such behaviour as at 10 months 15 days Millie was observed:

> sat on bed for several minutes tapping on metal spirals with plastic hairbrush – seemed absorbed with this activity, look of concentration and not being distracted.

At 10 months 18 days, Millie was again observed banging objects from her treasure basket, however she was also now dropping objects into metal and wooden bowls. As well as creating different sounds, this allowed Millie to 'monitor vertical movements of an object' (Athey 1990, p.131). Through practice and experience, Millie had accommodated her schema and was developing her knowledge. Furthermore, this observation described the interest Millie had in a xylophone that her Nana had bought her to support her schema. At 10 months 20 days, Millie was described playing with a wooden xylophone that had also been bought for her at home.

At 10 months 20 days Millie was also observed using a small round mushroom brush from her treasure basket to roll in front of her from one room to another and to follow it. This could be described as a 'straight line trajectory' (Athey 1990, p.135) being explored at a sensory motor level. Athey quotes Piaget's theory that an infant's interest in trajectories is later linked with their operational understanding of lines (Athey 1990, p.135). Millie was moving herself and an object along a trajectory and she was able to experience her schema in this way because she could move.

Athey also talks about toddlers displacing themselves and other objects, and that it is through such displacement that they develop mathematical and scientific concepts (Athey 1990, p.129).

One day later at 10 months 21 days Millie selected a soft ball from her toy box and behaved in a similar way. The observation states:

> Millie selected her ball from a pile of toys today. Dropped it and it rolled towards the kitchen. Millie followed and pushed it again so it rolled through door. I said 'Where has your ball gone?' Millie looked towards the kitchen and crawled through to the ball. She pushed it towards the living room and up a small step into room, then knocked it down again into kitchen. I said 'Where has your ball gone?' again. Millie crawled along kitchen floor and rolled it back again towards living room. She pushed it backwards and forwards by the small step then took hold of stair gate between living room and kitchen and closed it.

It is interesting that Millie ends this sequence of play by closing the stair gate as later that day she was described opening the kitchen drawer and also as liking hinges, opening and closing doors and cupboards. There is the dynamic aspect of a trajectory being demonstrated by the opening and closing of a drawer or door but Millie is also noted here to be taking items out of the drawer and cupboards – which may also demonstrate an interest in containment.

The following observation of Millie at 10 months 24 days also seemed to describe Millie containing:

> Millie sat by her treasure basket with a long oval bowl. Dropped fir cone into it and then took it back out. Found a green plastic cup from her toy basket, put the fir cone into this and tipped it back out again. She took a small teddy from her treasure basket and tried to fit it into cup, it was too big. Millie dropped both items and crawled off.

In this instance Millie was using items from her treasure basket and toy basket to explore containing, until she was not able to contain her teddy bear. As Millie assimilated further content into her schemas she developed her skills and knowledge and was already learning about volume and capacity.

My next observation took place at Nana's house and again demonstrated Millie at 10 months 26 days actively seeking out opportunities in the environment to explore her schemas. It reads:

> Millie smiled at us all and looked pleased. Then crawled over to the brick hearth of the fire and banged the bricks several times, paused for a moment, as if reflecting on the noise that she had just made. Then banged on the fireguard several times, paused and then banged again. Ran the stick backwards and forwards over the bars as she had the xylophone, then resumed banging hard so that a louder noise was created.

> Looked back at us, again seeming pleased as she was smiling. She continued with her games for a few minutes then crawled away.

A day later, also at Nana's house, Millie is described as sitting repeatedly opening and shutting the door of a bedroom cupboard. When some items fell onto the hinge and obstructed this, Millie persisted in moving items one by one until the door would shut again. Millie was engaged in pursuing her own concerns it seemed and, again, could be interested in the cupboard as a container as well as exploring the movement of the door. Athey (1990, p.149) states that young children are obviously fascinated by 'spaces that contain or envelop', and that from around 5 months of age onwards they begin to understand that one object can contain another.

Piaget (1962, p.267) writes that between the age of about 8 months and 1 year, infants are beginning to understand the permanence of objects. He states that 'the child's first behaviours indicate that his universe lacks permanent objects'. From around 8 months onwards, they then begin to look for objects that have vanished as they start to attribute permanence to them. It was interesting, I feel, that Millie was beginning to explore objects contained in spaces where they could not be seen, when she was possibly also learning about object permanence.

At 10 months 28 days I recorded what was the first of many observations of Millie transporting objects, whilst she was also physically transporting herself. She was therefore exploring the dynamic aspect of transporting in various ways:

> Millie carried a wooden xylophone stick into the kitchen in her mouth. Banged on the tiled floor several times then banged on the metal part of the kitchen step several times. Millie later carried a small wooden building block into the kitchen and hit it on to the kitchen floor tiles several times.

Here Millie was combining the action of transporting an object with the vertical trajectory action of banging several times. This resulted in different sounds being made, functionally dependent on the object being used and the surface it comes in contact with – the tiled floor or metal step.

Athey (1990, p.136) writes that 'to the young child things can be banged, thrown, transported, contained, gone through and gone round'.

Through the course of these observations we were witnessing Millie exploring these different concepts in different ways, with varying materials.

Millie was also co-ordinating her schemas or using 'clusters' (Athey 1990, p.160) of schemas as we saw her transporting along a trajectory, where she then used a vertical trajectory in her actions on an object. This enabled Millie to develop her skills and ideas, to understand concepts and to co-ordinate her knowledge. She was experiencing her environment at a higher level.

Athey explains how an infant transporting themselves from one point to another allows them at a sensory motor level to explore points of arrival and departure that will later be represented symbolically – leading to the development of concepts at a thought level (Athey 1990).

Reflecting on Millie's interests in containing, at this point in my diary I documented the fact that I had added various baskets and pots with lids to Millie's treasure basket. I was hoping to provide the resources for Millie that would allow her to develop her patterns of play and was able to add to the open-ended items in Millie's treasure basket, which I felt would allow her to do this.

At 10 months 29 days Millie was observed carrying a shiny bangle from her treasure basket around in her mouth. I wrote the following:

> Millie carried a shiny bangle from treasure basket around the living room in her mouth and then into the kitchen. Realised how many objects I had

been picking up from the kitchen floor – as Millie often brings something in with her when she comes in. Often brings them in her mouth as if she has discovered this as a method of transporting objects and yet still having her two hands to crawl. Have also observed her rolling objects and throwing them in front of her. Millie seems very interested in how she can move from one point to another and is now experimenting with moving her toys from one room to another.

On the same day I also documented how Millie was very interested in climbing up and down the stairs. I noted how, having come down the stairs together on this occasion, Millie looked back up the stairs at the point from where we came. Again Millie had transported herself from a starting to an end point. Athey uses the example of Piaget's child who 'from 9 months, examined the route before and behind him as he wheeled down a long hall' when explaining how infants use trajectories to explore moving between two points (1990, p.135). Piaget feels that this is the child physically experiencing distance, length and speed through the dynamic aspect of this schema (Athey 1990, p.136).

At 11 months 2 days Millie was observed crawling backwards and forwards across the floor five times as if following an invisible line and later at 11 months 27 days was seen making an arc movement with her hands both on the rug and laminate floor. I would describe her as continuing to explore trajectories within her environment.

At 11 months 3 days Millie seemed fascinated by a drawstring bag of props at her rhythm and rhyme group, wanting to look inside and cuddle it – she followed it around the room. The same observation was made at 11 months 17 days, so that a similar bag was made for her for her birthday.

In terms of continuing to explore her schemas, there were repeated observations of Millie continuing to demonstrate patterns to her play – both with her treasure basket and through other activities. For example, Millie transported and contained with her treasure basket at 11 months 3 days. A day later she spent a long time pulling a phone charger backwards and forwards between two bedrooms. At 11 months 7 days I wrote:

> Millie sat for a while with a small plastic pot (cutlery drainer) and a small plastic ball – putting ball in and tipping it out. Concentrating to get ball in and not managing at every attempt.

At 11 months 4 days I describe the game 'Follow the leader', which Millie initiated. This was also observed at 11 months 22 days. During this game either myself or her father or Millie crawled from room to room and the other followed. When Millie led, she looked back repeatedly to check we were following and stopped off at points of interest along the way. Again Millie was exploring trajectories and transporting through play. At 11 months 22 days

Millie stopped at the kitchen drawer during the game and opened it several times before moving on, which interested me as I saw a co-ordination of her schemas and interests in this game.

When Athey (1990, p.189) writes about the results of her research project, she states that:

> children in the different groups were observed representing trajectories with a starting point, several stopping-off points and an end point. This is a common form of representation that probably has its motor roots in early toddling behaviours.

Here we see Millie following this pattern, enjoying both leading and following. Millie began playing this game with her father when she first started to crawl and took great pleasure in him following her. It then became Millie who always initiated this game, and indicated when it was over.

At 11 months 10 days Millie spent time emptying out and putting toys back into her toy basket. Both myself and her father later joined in with this game, which we had not seen before.

At 11 months 11 days I made this observation:

> Still transporting objects, particularly in her mouth. Today plastic cupboard lock taken from inside kitchen cupboard and left on the floor in living room – carried in mouth.

Millie had also rolled a ball from the lounge to the dining room on this day, and followed it. This interest in rolling could demonstrate Millie working out the dynamic aspects of a rotation schema as well as straight line trajectories with objects.

Arnold (2003, p.108) writes that 'understanding rotation and circularity are important aspects of mathematical development'. Athey (1990, p.139) explains how children need to have lots of experiences of the 'movingness' of objects so that eventually they are able to 're-activate cells that were activated during initial perceptions' simply by thinking about the motion. They can then represent circular movements symbolically, through speech and thought.

At 11 months 15 days Millie was observed playing with her treasure basket for almost an hour. However, in this instance both Millie's father and myself were actively involved in the play. I noted that since Millie had been crawling, this was the longest that she engaged in treasure basket play. This finding links with the results of Athey's study where children stayed at activities for longer periods when their parents were involved (Athey 1990, p.63). My observation reads:

> Daddy sat on sofa. Millie stood up on chair and put fir cone from the floor in his hand and then did this again with second fir cone. Looked on floor,

but no more cones so took one back and put it on the floor and then the other. Looked in hand for another, as if now expecting there to be more. Millie picked up wooden ball from treasure basket and rolled it to me. I said, 'clever girl Millie, are we playing roll the ball?' I rolled it back, singing 'I roll the ball to Millie and Millie rolls it back'. We rolled the ball backwards and forwards several times.

At 11 months 17 days I made this observation:

> At home, playing with the treasure basket, Millie took out the wooden ball and rolled it to me. I rolled it back. We did this several times. Millie seems to like games that involve her close adults and uses her Treasure Basket for this as well as other toys.

The following day this note was made:

> Playing with toys. Millie took a red foam ball out of her box and rolled it to me. I rolled it back, singing our rolling ball song. We did this several times.

When I then observed Millie with her treasure basket at 11 months 18 days and 11 months 24 days, she continued to explore her schemas but again wanted to engage adults in her play, rather than us being passive observers:

> Knowing that Millie is starting to contain things, showed her how to put one of her corks into leather purse. She took it out and put it back in. Repeated this over and over again. Then I put cork into a stainless steel container with lid. Millie wanted to put lid on, concentrated very hard to do this and eventually got it on. Tried to pull it off again. Wanted to put lid on and off several times. Millie struggled with this for a while but then got frustrated because it was hard for her. Gave her another pot which fitted lid on easier, Millie did this a couple of times then threw the pot down. Millie then rolled a wicker ball across living room floor, into kitchen and across kitchen floor, following it as it went.

In this example Millie was enjoying activities that matched her interests, but also where one of her closest adults was involved. A week later I wrote:

> Playing with the treasure basket. Millie took the stainless steel ball out and rolled it. She crawled away. Daddy picked up this ball and put it into stainless steel bowl – rolling it around. Millie crawled back, watched this and then went and found two plastic balls in her toy basket. Seems interested again in balls rolling and is actively seeking them out in her environment. Had previously added lots of different kinds of balls to Millie's treasure basket, having observed her rolling and following them.

Here Millie was autonomously choosing the objects that she played with, which included those from her treasure basket as well as other items that matched her interests.

Prevailing schemas

In summary, Millie was observed exploring the following schemas in her play:

- **Vertical trajectories:** banging, shaking, dropping, playing xylophone
- **Straight line trajectories:** throwing, rolling, crawling, climbing, sliding
- **Transporting:** carrying, crawling, ball play, games
- **Containing/enveloping:** pots, cupboards, tunnels, bags, pots
- **Rotation:** rolling, cones, balls.

The dynamic aspects of these schemas were explored, usually at a sensory motor level (Athey 1990).

When engaged in schematic play, Millie often displayed signs of being involved (Laevers *et al.* 1997). She was focussed, enthusiastic, creative, persistent and often showed signs of satisfaction and pleasure.

Reflections/discussion/implications for practice

I feel confident that Millie and our family benefited hugely through the process of this research. We have indeed gained a deeper understanding of Millie's interests and have created opportunities to support these. There are examples given in the written observations, where Millie's treasure basket was added to in order to provide objects that matched her interests. We continue to support Millie to pursue her interests in a variety of ways.

As her main carers, we now feel more able to plan activities and environments that are stimulating for Millie and encourage her to become deeply involved (Laevers *et al.* 1997).

We are committed to continuing to observe and support her schemas and to offering heuristic play opportunities for her. As far as is possible, Millie continues to have open access to her environment and to explore the everyday objects that are around her. As we embrace this ethos of developing a deeper understanding of Millie and supporting her play, it is inevitable, I feel, that we will continue to develop a strong attachment with her and that we will share an ever-deepening relationship. Millie's emotional development is being shaped by such adult interactions and her experiences of adult responsiveness (Gerhardt 2004). Whilst we, as carers, may not always get it right, we feel that we have begun to sharpen our perception of Millie and to endeavour to respond appropriately (Athey 1990, p.142).

Research demonstrates the vital importance of supporting children's schemas as this extends and supports their learning (Athey 1990). It has been demonstrated that 'clusters of schemas . . . become systems of concepts' (Athey 2002, p.8). It is a child's environment and experiences (content) that nourish these patterns of thought (form) (Athey 2002, p.9) and there is also a fundamental impact on children when their parents are involved in the process of identifying and supporting their schemas (Athey 1990).

Piaget (1962, p.269) also explains the importance of environment and experience and how the child is developing ideas and concepts through their encounters:

> sensory-motor adaptation has provided the child with an immediate practical universe, through the gradual establishment of equilibrium between assimilation of objects to his schemas of action, and accommodation of these schemas to the data of experience.

I have observed Millie using her treasure basket on numerous occasions to explore her schemas, and I was able to see her concentrating for longer periods of time with her treasure basket than other toys when she was first introduced to it – before she could crawl. Similarly I have documented Millie demonstrating patterns in her actions when engaged in heuristic play. Treasure baskets and heuristic play provide objects and experiences which are open-ended and encourage creativity, which makes them likely to match the interests of the child in some way. There is also the opportunity to constantly add items and resources that are relevant to the child's schemas, and Goldschmied recommends that treasure baskets evolve in this way (Goldschmied and Jackson 2004, p.97). It could be said then that *treasure baskets have the greatest potential to support children's schemas when adults are actively involved in observing and identifying the child's interests and adapting the items in the basket accordingly*. The principle would then follow when providing resources for heuristic play. Goldschmied herself states that: 'Heuristic play is an approach and not a prescription. There is no one right way to do it' (Goldschmied and Jackson 2004, p.130). Adults are therefore able to think creatively in terms of materials and activities offered to children, depending on their current forms of thought.

I also observed Millie using a variety of other activities and resources that enabled her to use her schemas and witnessed her actively seeking out stimuli in her environment that reflected her interests. At times Millie used both items from her treasure basket and other items together, such as when she was exploring containing, so that she could explore her schemas. She was also able to identify similar properties shared by objects – as on the occasion when she went to her toy box and found two plastic balls having been interested in the stainless steel ball in her treasure basket. Once Millie began to crawl, this obviously allowed her to access a variety of activities and objects around her and her stage of development seemed to influence her interests, in that she enjoyed movement and explored the dynamic aspects of her schemas through, for instance, crawling, climbing, throwing and following both objects and people.

I would therefore conclude that both treasure baskets and heuristic play are valuable experiences for children in terms of the opportunities they offer and the potential to match interests of children as they explore their schemas. However, I am also now more aware of the role that a whole range of other experiences, resources and environments can have in terms of supporting learning and catching the imagination of a child who is actively looking for opportunities to extend their knowledge as they try out their schemas and build up a picture of the world around them.

As we have seen, Goldschmied feels that the adult should not be involved in the play and is more an attentive observer than participant. In terms of treasure baskets, she says that the adult should remain close enough that the infant feels confident to explore but should not interfere (Goldschmied and Jackson 2004, p.101).

However, my observations demonstrate how, particularly in later entries, Millie was active herself in involving adults in her play – including play with her treasure basket. She was in fact engaged for longer periods when an adult was involved.

At 11 months and 18 days Millie and I are noted sitting with the treasure basket and I show Millie how to put a cork into a leather purse, as Millie has been interested in containing. She goes on to do this repeatedly. When I then put the cork in a stainless steel pot, Millie is observed concentrating very hard to get the lid on – which is an achievement as it is difficult for her. Millie then wanted to do this several times – although it was a struggle for her and caused some frustration. Athey (1990, p.76) makes the statement that 'new knowledge is associated with struggle'.

Vygotsky talks about the 'Zone of Proximal Development'. He states that: 'What a child can do with assistance today she will be able to do by herself tomorrow' (Vygotsky 1978, p.87). Vygotsky is referring to the zone of potential learning, demonstrating the difference between what a child will learn independently and what they are capable of with the help of another. I feel that Millie, at times, benefited from the help of an adult so that she took her learning with her treasure basket further.

Rogoff (1990) puts forward the theory of 'Guided Participation', whereby she recognises the importance of children learning from their peers and other adults. She states that children: 'actively seek guidance and participation' in their learning (Rogoff 1990, p.98) and describes children as novices who 'advance their skills and understanding through participation with more skilled partners in culturally organised activities' (Rogoff 1990, p.39).

Rogoff emphasises the importance of the context within which each child is learning, in which they are adapting to a culture and developing a 'shared understanding with those who serve as their guides and companions through . . . joint participation' (1990, p.8). This is relevant when considering that treasure baskets/heuristic play allow children to experience everyday objects, which may well be culturally relevant. It may therefore at times be beneficial for them to experience these with the involvement of a close adult or carer.

Trevarthen quotes much research which demonstrates that children are born wanting to learn in 'companionship' with others and are looking for shared meanings with those around them 'whom they trust and admire' (2002, p.3). He talks about it being in children's nature to be 'eager to learn in conscious collaboration with companions' (Trevarthen 2002, p.3). With this in mind I wonder if it is always interfering to be involved in an infant's exploration of treasure baskets, particularly as I have observed Millie taking pleasure in this involvement at times. Millie demonstrated clearly at times her choice to play in companionship with her close adults; her autonomous choice was not to play independently.

Gopnik *et al.* (1999, p.54) describe how children generally prefer people to objects from birth, but that gradually they also become interested in things around them – and particularly what other people think about these things (Gopnik *et al.* 1999, p.32). This links with Rogoff's idea that children develop a shared understanding with those closest to them about their community and culture. Gopnik and colleagues (1999, p.32) describe a 'cognitive triangle' that develops, involving the child, objects and things and essentially other people. They are reassuring that the infant's growing fascination with other objects in the environment does not detract from their interest in people. In fact, they state that babies are particularly interested in how their loved ones use objects and want to imitate them (Gopnik *et al.* 1999, p.34). This emphasises the importance of offering everyday household items to babies to play with, and also perhaps of sharing the enjoyment of those objects with them at times, considering the thought that 'The babies' new interest in things also leads to a deeper commonality and communication with other people' (Gopnik *et al.* 1999, p.35).

My evidence suggests that open-ended activities and resources are valuable as they enable children to use their schemas. As these patterns of play are observed it is then possible to extend them with a variety of objects and activities. These may include manufactured toys and, particularly as the child becomes mobile, they will actively seek out and use what they find interesting in their environment to explore – a kitchen drawer, a playful adult, a basket of toys, a pile of washing, for example. Therefore, treasure baskets and heuristic play are experiences to be offered as part of a learning environment, which is as open and accessible to the child as much as is safely possible. The most valuable resource, though, could be said to be caring and familiar adults with whom the child is developing close relationships. These people give the child confidence to explore and, importantly, the time to learn with them about the world and a shared culture.

I also feel that the accessibility of the resources to a child is an important issue. Goldschmied (Goldschmied and Jackson 2004) is writing particularly about group settings when she describes how treasure baskets and heuristic play should be activities offered at specific times when other equipment is not available. Whilst with non-mobile and fairly young babies this approach might be used, I feel that children benefit from the consistency of environment that is particularly achievable at home. As we observed with Millie, she sometimes chose to use items from her treasure basket with other toys to explore and as she became mobile her treasure basket was continually accessible to her so that she was able to do this. If children are to be autonomous in their activity, I feel that they should have the confidence to know that resources are available to them if and when they want them – and this applies particularly to objects for heuristic play. Athey (1990, p.59) makes the statement that: 'Continuity is a vital component of conceptual development'.

Through the course of my study, I feel that I have begun the process of learning with Millie and I am now committed to continue with her on this journey. I want to continue to observe and understand how she is learning, identifying her schemas and looking to extend these through activities and resources that match her interests and development as well extending her language. I am also influenced by other theories, such as wanting to learn in companionship with Millie (Trevarthen 2002) and using opportunities to advance Millie's learning through support and participation (Vygotsky 1978; Rogoff 1990).

Reflections and questions

Elaine mentioned language she used when playing with Millie and focussing on Millie's actions.

- What sort of language do you use when playing with very young children?
- What are the sorts of conversations you have with young children?
- How could you use your observation of schemas to plan for children's learning?
- How do you respond when a child wants to engage with you? Are you able to follow their lead?
- Have you noticed babies wanting to engage with you when using the treasure basket?

Applying learning to practice

- When studying, engage with your data as you go along and be aware of when you are interpreting your observations and making plans for the future.
- Use a diary method to record observations and make immediate plans for supporting and extending play.
- The idea of observing a child using the treasure basket and adding to it accordingly, for example, more and different balls when rolling is prevalent, could work in an early years setting as well as at home.

- See treasure basket play as something adults can engage in with children, if a child invites them.

Bibliography

Arnold, C. (2003). *Observing Harry*. Maidenhead: Open University Press.

Athey, C. (1990). *Extending Thought in Young Children: A Parent–Teacher Partnership*. London: Paul Chapman.

Athey, C. (2002). Extending Thought In Young Children. *Early Childhood Practice: The Journal for Multi-Professional Partnerships*. Vol. 4, No. 1, pp. 8–16.

Bell, J. (1996). *Doing Your Research Project: A Guide for First–Time Researchers in Education and Social Science*. Buckingham: Open University Press.

Farrell, A. (2004). Ethical Dimensions of Practitioner-Research in the Early Years. *Early Childhood Practice: The Journal for Multi-Professional Partnerships*. Vol. 6, No. 2, pp. 18–27.

Fawcett, M. (2005). *Learning Through Child Observation*. London: Jessica Kingsley Publishers.

Fonagy, P. (2001). *Attachment Theory and Psychoanalysis*. New York: Other Press.

Gerhardt, S. (2004). *Why Love Matters: How Affection Shapes a Baby's Brain*. East Sussex: Brunner-Routledge.

Goldschmied, E. (1975). Creative Play With Babies. In Jennings, S. (Ed.) *Creative Therapy* (pp. 52– 67). London: Sir Isaac Pitman and Sons Ltd.

Goldschmied, E. (1987). *Infants At Work* (video), London: National Children's Bureau.

Goldschmied, E. and Jackson, S. (2004). *People Under Three: Young Children in Day Care*. Second edition. London: Routledge.

Gopnik, A., Meltzoff, A. and Kuhl, P. (1999). *How Babies Think*. London: Phoenix.

Laevers, F., Vandenbussche, E., Kog, M. and Depondt, L. (1997). *A Process-oriented Child Monitoring System for Young Children*. Leuven: Centre for Experiential Education.

Piaget, J. (1962). *Play, Dreams and Imitation in Childhood*. London: Routledge and Kegan Paul Ltd.

Rogoff, B. (1990). *Apprenticeship in Thinking: Cognitive Development in a Social Context*. Oxford: Oxford University Press.

Trevarthen, C. (2002). Learning in Companionship. *Education in the North: The Journal of Scottish Education*, New Series. No. 10, pp. 16–25.

Vygotsky, L.S. (1978). *Mind in Society*. London: Harvard University Press.

Whalley, M. (2001). *Involving Parents in their Children's Learning*. London: Paul Chapman.

Chapter 2

One child's use of a story as a transitional object

Gina Goody

In this chapter you will find:

- A case study about a 4-year-old boy, called Zack, the grandson of the author.
- Zack's engagement with the picture book *Clown* by Quentin Blake at an emotional period in his life.
- An argument for the importance of picture books to children's affective and cognitive development.
- An explanation of the theories of 'reader response' and 'readerly behaviour'.

Introduction/context

I have always felt passionately about the texts that we offer to children. There are some extremely talented and sensitive illustrators and authors who write with children in mind, and part of my job as an early years educator is ensuring that children are able to choose from a wide range of possibilities, to find the text that is right for them. Part of my delight as a grandmother is to share texts with my grandchildren, Zack and Ayah, purely for the joy of deepening our relationship and sharing experiences together.

Zack's engagement with picture books has confirmed my assumption of how important picture books are in both the affective and cognitive domains of children's development, and how particular texts can take on the significance of transitional objects in turbulent times. In his book *Playing and Reality*, first published in 1971, the child psychotherapist Donald Winnicott explains his theory of the transitional object, which he first introduced in his paper 'Transitional Objects and Transitional Phenomena', published in 1953.

At the time of his sister Ayah's birth, Zack developed a profound attachment to a wordless picture book created by Quentin Blake – *Clown*. I have been able to document his relationship with this text through interpreting it as a transitional object for Zack.

Picture books are usually the first texts and the first form of literature to which children are introduced, in the form of board books, novelty books, pop-up books. They are often the first medium for sharing a story between an adult and a child, or to use the apprenticeship model of reading, between an experienced reader and a less-experienced reader; the first literary space in which one imagination is invited to meet another; the first opportunity for the child reader to become co-author and shape their understanding of a text from their own experience of the world.

In the light of the current debate about the teaching of reading, the importance of texts in the development of young readers should not be underestimated or dismissed. Matching child to text can be very precarious as what is involved is an empowering relationship, which is so much more subtle and creative than being able to use decoding skills. Those of us who have the privilege of working with very young children know intimately 'the special relationship that exists between picturebooks, the child reader and the concept of play' (Lewis, 2001: 77).

James Britton (1977) linked the area of play with the experience of reading in his paper 'The Role of Fantasy' published in *The Cool Web*, a text which has never been matched in its synthesis of authors, educators and critics who were writing a companion piece to the Bullock Report, *A Language for Life*, published in 1975. Britton suggested that the site that unites objective reality and subjective experience, where these two important elements that the reader brings to a text are manifest is located in 'play . . . as an area of free activity lying between the world of shared and verifiable experience and the world of inner necessity – "a third area" as Donald Winnicott has called it' (Britton, 1977: 46).

First readings have enormous significance – as an introduction they are heavily laden with potential – in the same way that meeting someone new has the possibility to be life-changing, so can an introduction to a book. I agree with Cathy Nutbrown that 'books are not just an instrument for learning about words and happenings but can be an essential part of a loving and intimate experience shared by children and adults' (2004: 85). Significantly, this experience cannot be planned for – it is a matter of chance and choice; we have to trust our children to make choices for themselves and to respond supportively when a choice is made even if from our adult perspective we reject their choice as inferior or mismatched. Importantly for our youngest readers, it is far more than lifting words off the page.

Writing in his ethnographical study *The Meaning Makers*, the research undertaken by Gordon Wells demonstrated that there were four domains which nurtured the development of confident, successful readers from their earliest years. According to Wells (1987: 151), these were:

- Looking at a picture book and talking about it
- Listening to a story
- Drawing and colouring
- Writing – or pretending to write.

But the most significant activity was 'listening to stories'.

So I will make a plea that experienced readers working as practitioners with very young children and sharing stories with them, honour the interaction a child brings to a text and do everything possible to promote an engagement which is both literary and emotive.

Approach to the research

In this chapter I look at how texts can assume the significance of transitional objects and offer a site for the working out of anxieties and issues that are troubling for the child on an emotional and psychological plane. I also want to take account of the Winnicottian concepts of the 'facilitating or holding environment', and the wonderfully enabling suggestion of the 'good enough mother'.

When my granddaughter Ayah was born, her brother Zack (4 years 3 months) offered me the opportunity to explore my idea of texts as transitional objects, through developing an attachment to *Clown* by Quentin Blake. During the early weeks of his sister's life, I was able to document Zack's interaction with *Clown*, and observe how this text satisfied Zack's need for a transitional object throughout an intense and emotional period in his life. I also considered theories of reader response and the importance of building up a child's intertextuality, or the way that texts interrelate with each other. Making regular entries in my journal enabled me to build up a case study that linked my observations of Zack with Winnicott's theories. I have analysed the dialogues we shared and made links to relevant theory. Journaling also helped me to include the voice of the child, his actual words and the subtler communications offered through his behaviour.

I have used Winnicottian themes as the basis for a literary analysis of *Clown* and had a chance to play with literary theory in the spirit of the subversive nature of a visual text whose profound and deep structures are contrasted with the lively and imaginative sparkle of the illustrations. The illustrations and the narrative of *Clown* are deceptively simple but the text is multilayered and polysemic, dealing with themes of fidelity and loyalty, attachment and loss, inviting an empathetic and sensitive response from the reader.

I looked at theories of reader response and contrasted this with the so-called 'simple view of reading' being promoted by the Rose Review and now introduced into the Early Years Foundation Stage, with its mistaken emphasis on early reading as primarily a decoding exercise dependent on a highly structured programme of synthetic phonics.

The project

Transitional objects come into their own in times of stress. They originate in filling the gap between the baby and the baby's mother (or other significant caregiver) when the mother is not there. At first the baby does not recognize that s/he is separate from the mother and so the concept of me/not me does not exist. The transitional object helps to comfort the baby when 'me on my own' comes into play, 'me abandoned', 'me totally traumatized', 'me falling apart', and helps to restore a sense of equilibrium which will carry the baby through until the separation is over.

For very little babies you are either there or you're not and they have no way of holding you in mind. They just think you have gone, and this state of acute panic and distress can be reactivated in older infants in times of despair, possibly resulting from a separation from the mother or an echo of that feeling of distress wrought by separation; probably a dramatic separation, but sometimes everyday transitions will trigger an emotional upheaval. Some very young children will find it very traumatic to transition from one space to another, from sitting on the carpet to moving to the nursery garden, so the potential for extreme distress when experiencing transitions involving people and relationships becomes very real and potentially extremely damaging.

The child becomes saturated with despair. As caring and supportive adults we will try any manner of means to comfort and alleviate this powerful level of distress but sometimes children can be inconsolable. They need to work through their grief – it is grief brought on by abandonment – and we can only shelter them by accompanying them and offering a loving gesture when they are ready to accept it. And of course, this level of despair will have resonance for the children that we were and it can be most dreadfully upsetting.

Donald Winnicott is extremely helpful in offering his theory of the transitional object: 'It is not the object, of course, that is transitional. The object represents the infant's transition from a stage of being merged with the mother to a state of being in relation to the mother as something outside and separate' (Winnicott, 1971: 19). In other words, transitional objects give us hope. I am suggesting that both the physical reality of the book and the psychological experience of the text can be interpreted as transitional objects, and that this was the relationship that Zack discovered through his multiple readings of *Clown*.

Journal entry – the evening of 1st August 2006: Zack's first night away from Gemma (Zack aged 4 years 3 months)

Even though Zack had stayed with me before many times, he was extremely distressed on this occasion and far too upset to sleep downstairs. My flat is a split-level maisonette with the bedrooms downstairs in the basement. Going downstairs had connotations of distance and subterranean terror and he had enough to occupy his mind without exploring those chasms of fearfulness. Uncharacteristically, he did not want to have a bath or even to change into his pyjamas. This meant giving up part of himself; I suppose he was experiencing the terror of disintegration. Usually, Zack is in his element in water and will play for hours in the bath if left to his own devices. Not so this night. He cried and cried and kept calling for Gemma. I don't know whether he was more upset about being on his own without Gemma, or troubled that Kays was with her and that he was shut out from them. Winnicott describes another little boy who appeared to share Zack's sorrow:

> This rather healthy little boy was at the age when an appreciation of reality means decreased happiness. . . . The arrival of a new baby brought home to him suddenly a great deal of just that sort of reality which was causing him decreased happiness – namely his position of third person in relation to his parents. This is true whether he was feeling love chiefly towards father or towards mother.
>
> (Winnicott in Shepherd *et al.*, 1996: 99)

Zack agreed to sleep with me upstairs in the sofabed, so while I got this ready, I also managed to grab a selection of books off the bookshelf, as I knew from previous experience with Zack that he loved being read to and that this might be one way that I could calm him.

On less upsetting nights than this one, we often played a game of me getting into bed first and pretending to be asleep which resulted in Zack diving on top of me to wake me up in order to read to him. Not so on this occasion. We got into bed together and he wrapped himself around me and indicated by pointing and sobbing that he wanted me to read all of the books, which I did. That this normally articulate, bright, buzzy little boy could only point and sob was indicative of the depth of his grief. He had lost the power of speech, rendered mute by the separation from his mother.

Selection of books for Zack to choose from:

- *Mr Gumpy's Outing* – John Burningham
- *Harry and the Dinosaurs say "Raahh!"* – Ian Whybrow/Adrian Reynolds
- *In the Night Kitchen* – Maurice Sendak
- *Cloudland* – John Burningham
- *Clown* – Quentin Blake

Cloudland and *Clown* were new to Zack but the other titles were familiar. On that night we shared all of the books and even though he was still very upset and crying, he acquiesced to this reading, and then when I had finished the last book, which happened to be *Clown*, he rolled over and went to sleep, throwing my arm off him quite angrily when I offered to cuddle him, but making sure that I had my mobile phone close by so that he could speak to Gemma the following morning. Some of his emotion had rolled into an anger which he was able to communicate and it was directed towards me, leaving him free to connect lovingly with Gemma when she was available.

At this reading we did not discuss any of the texts; it would have been inappropriate. I read them and he permitted me to read them to him, rather than listening. I was aware of using the stories as a way of calming and comforting Zack almost hypnotically, but I knew that there was no point in trying to distract him from the cause of his grief – his separation from Gemma – because he was too intelligent and sensitive to be fobbed off with anything other than the truth. And at this stage the only facts that I could offer him were inconclusive and therefore not much help at all. We knew she was down the road with his father; we knew she was going to have the baby soon, but we didn't know when. Winnicott says that children are able to cope with the most horrendous situations if they are given the facts. 'Facts are all right because they are facts; what is dreadful is not knowing whether something is a fact or a mystery or a fantasy' (Winnicott in Shepherd *et al.*, 1996: 146). At this stage the birth of his sister was still a fantasy but moving closer to reality all the time.

Journal entry for afternoon of Wednesday 2nd August 2006: Zack's first meeting with Ayah

Ayah was born at 2.20pm and Zack and I visited her at about 4 o'clock. What a relief! When we went into the delivery room, Gemma was holding Ayah. Zack said: 'Give it to Gene!'. He then threw himself into Gemma's arms. What I remember most about this moment is the way Ayah seemed to respond to hearing Zack's voice, as though she was saying to herself: 'Oh there he is, that's the one I've been listening to! I wondered where he was.' I was taken aback by how present Ayah was in the room, and within the family.

Journal entry for evening of Wednesday 2nd August 2006: Zack's second night apart from Gemma

Zack has stayed with me again while Gemma, Ayah and Kays are in the hospital. We are sleeping in the sofabed for the second night but Zack is much, much calmer this evening. He is reasonably amenable to following his usual routine, tea, bath, bedtime and is looking forward to going to fetch Gemma and his sister from the hospital on the following day. We have decided to bring them home in a taxi which has really cheered Zack up, as one of his favourite things is riding in a taxi. We have also decided that we will pop over to his flat in the morning, to fetch more clothes and toys for him, and essential items for Ayah. Zack has chosen his story for the night. It is late and I have suggested that we share just one book at bedtime. Before we settle down for a read he makes a mental inventory of toys that he is going to collect in the morning. He has almost talked himself to sleep, almost hypnotized himself with an interior monologue, but he is just wakeful enough to pick up the book and pass it to me. 'Read it now!' It is *Clown* and Zack listens contentedly, then rolls over and goes straight to sleep.

Journal entry for 15ᵗʰ August 2006

This evening Zack is very keen to talk about Clown's physical ability and how he does 'tricks' to cheer up the children. Zack really studies the illustrations, trying to work out: 'How does he do that? That is really cool!' He breaks the movements down to their foundations in order to analyse them. 'Ah! He's got one foot on the floor and he's upside down!'

Zack is fascinated by Clown's ability to juggle with potatoes, page opening 10 recto. He has been practising with some juggling balls belonging to one of his aunts. Zack is very thoughtful about the toys coming into the children's flat for them to play with. 'They haven't got any toys and the toys need to play with them.' He is aware of the reciprocal need of toys for children/children for toys and how the mutuality of the relationship calls each one into being. Zack also comments on the 'gaze' which is sustained between Clown and the little girl and how Clown does not gaze at adults. We do lots of practice gazing, sustaining eye contact and we talk about holding each other's gaze so that our ideas can communicate. 'I can see me in you. I can see little Zack in your face', he says. Zack thinks for a minute and then says: 'Ayah does sometimes look at me sometimes.'

During this reading Zack has demonstrated his awareness of the function of gaze and the contribution that eye contact makes to communication. He has observed that babies

> use their eyes to scan the environment to gather information; and they use their eyes to convey their feelings and their needs; and they use their eyes to take in the feelings and communications from those around them. Eye contact is one of the core means by which we communicate and build relationships, and it is a key mechanism by which we develop attachments.
> (Trowell in Kahr, 2002: 79)

Zack also chooses *Cleversticks* for tonight's story but finishes with *Clown*.

Journal entry for evening of 18ᵗʰ August 2006

Zack's focus shifts again tonight and he spends a long time scrutinizing page opening 5 verso, working out the relationships between the children in the fancy dress parade and the adults who are taking their photographs. This evening Zack was exceptionally tired and he lay in bed while I took my time getting ready, thinking that he would go to sleep. He nearly dropped off but woke himself up and brought powerful concentration to the text despite his weariness. He was desperate to match the children with their adults and to make connections between them. As soon as the story was over Zack closed his eyes and went to sleep. His determination to share the story before going to sleep made me feel convinced that he was using the text as a transitional object before sleep.

Journal entry from evening of 19th August 2006

Zack's aunt tells him a story tonight. She makes it up weaving Zack into the trajectory of the narrative. It is all about a little boy who goes on a long journey and finds a magical toy to bring back home with him. Zack is delighted to have his very own story and goes to sleep happily tonight. During the day he has taken to watching the two *Toy Story* films. The theme of these films is about toys who have been abandoned or supplanted in a child's affections, and are suffering from fear of rejection. In *Toy Story 1* there is Woody's great fear that Buzz Lightyear will supplant him in the child Andy's affection. In *Toy Story 2* there are themes of being discarded or not being fit for purpose, e.g. Woody is wanted as a collector's item not as a toy for Andy. Zack guards his childness like a wound in identifying with the protagonists. He is responding to themes of separation and loss, and finding ways of dealing with these experiences in his primary world, by experiencing it through the secondary worlds of the narrative fantasies to which he is attracted.

Texts also offer an imaginary space that enables the facilitating or holding environment to be brought into being. As I understand the term 'facilitating environment' it is the physical and emotional space in which the 'good enough' mother holds the child, both literally and figuratively. Donald Winnicott explains his ideas in the following terms:

> If we say 'This child has not been held properly; he has been let down', we mean quite literally that the ground has opened beneath him and there is no security anywhere; there is an infinite drop, which may reappear at any moment and will turn up in nightmares and in his drawings later.
>
> (Shepherd *et al.*, 1996: 145)

The actions of some of the adults portrayed in *Clown* can be read as harmful to children – the indifference to the child who is yanked upwards on leading reins, page opening 4 verso; the materialistic attitude to all things childlike represented by the designer mother on page opening 6; the physical attack on Clown by the savage dog and the threatening behaviour of the dog owner on page opening 7. But the parenting styles predicated by these characters could also be read as 'good enough'. The mother holding the reins has them in order to keep safe hold of her little girl. The designer mummy employs a Norland-type nanny to look after her daughter and to keep her entertained. The skinhead's fury derives from his desire to protect his dog indicating that he will use brute force if necessary. This yearning to protect and cherish our young is a visceral response, an expression of primitive and atavistic emotion.

I feel that the mother of the family who adopt Clown is an exemplification of Winnicott's good enough mother. She could be considered feckless with regard to the wisdom of decisions she has made about leaving her baby with an older sibling in a squalid environment, but she is doing her best. The domestic environment echoes this struggle – at first it is an absolute tip, squalid and revolting, but it has the potential to be cleaned up and made very warm and welcoming.

The little girl's think bubbles on page opening 11 verso and 12 verso encapsulate the extremes of emotion experienced, the highs and lows of family life registered through the expression on the mother's face and her hand gestures. The reality of the domestic idyll is also depicted through the sheltering environment in which Clown and his friends are restored to their legitimate status as objects of play and delight.

Final journal entry, early March 2007, Zack is now 4 years 10 months

I have been away from London working on my dissertation. Zack is helping me to unpack my suitcase. Under my clothes are a pile of books.

'Ah! *Clown*, there it is!' says Zack. 'I wondered where it had gone. I'll put him back.' (I am intrigued by his use of pronouns.)

Zack takes the book from my suitcase and puts it on the floor by the side of my bed. It is as though he feels that *Clown* lives there. Zack, Gemma and Ayah are staying overnight. We are in the front room, deciding where we will sleep. I suggest that we could sleep in the sofabed.

> 'We did sleep in the sofabed before', says Zack.
> 'Yes we did, that was when Gemma went to hospital to have Ayah.'
> 'And I got very upset, I was really crying', says Zack.
> 'Do you know why you were so upset, Zack? Because you were really crying and really missing Gem.'
> 'I thought she was dead . . .', says Zack.
> '. . . and that you would have to stay here with me without Gem?'
> 'Yeah, I didn't think she was coming back because she was dead', Zack says.

I can imagine that Donald Winnicott would explain Zack's fantasy of Gemma's death as stemming from his inability to hold her in mind when juxtaposed with the magnitude of his distress caused by their enforced separation.

> When no understanding can be given, then when the mother is away to have a new baby she is dead from the point of view of the child. This is what dead means.
>
> It is a matter of days or hours or minutes. Before the limit is reached the mother is still alive; after this limit has been overstepped she is dead.
>
> (Winnicott, 2005: 29)

I also feel that as a consequence of going through the experience of having a sibling, which must have felt like being catapulted through the necessary 'transition into childhood' described by Juliet Mitchell (Radio 4, *Woman's Hour*, 26.3.2007), even though terribly traumatic, Zack's experience of the world is wider and his understanding of relationships much greater.

An understanding about the relationship between picture books, young children and readerly behaviour

It has been one of the great joys of my current research to browse through the Bullock Report, *A Language for Life*, published in 1975. I am delighted to be able to source the quote which is probably the most celebrated from the report:

> Ante-natal clinics already have a demanding task, with a range of pre-occupations which must have priority. Nevertheless, we feel that the situation presents too valuable an opportunity to be missed, exemplified in the advice one health visitor gives to every expectant parent: 'When you give your child a bath, bathe him in language.'
>
> (Bullock, 1975: 58)

I am so proud of that anonymous health visitor and hope that she is aware of how her advice has been taken up through initiatives such as Babies Need Books, Bookstart, Booktrust, Talk to Your Baby, but more significantly how her gentle exhortation encapsulates the best practice of early years educators, and families who have been doing just that for generations, every time they sing lullabies or share nursery rhymes, or engage in nonsense ditties or the 'topsy-turvies' of Kornei Chukovsky.

> There is hardly a child who does not go through a stage in his pre-school years when he is not an avid creator of word rhythms and rhymes.
>
> (Chukovsky, 1963: 65)

The origin of these topsy-turvies is the dance of language engaged in by mother and tiny baby as they share nursery rhymes or nonsense language, utterances with sometimes the baby taking the lead and the adult responding. The whole point is that responding to language is an innate way of behaving, whether it is babbling, sharing a nursery rhyme, looking at a picture book or commenting on the structure of a Petrarchan sonnet. This very particular human behaviour has its genesis in babytalk. We share something that can be called a text, however basic – oral or written – and we offer comments or responses; with experience these behaviours can become more solitary but to begin with they are social and collaborative, because they always involve one imagination (the author's) trying to communicate with another (the reader's). What has to be emphasized is that the one is always influenced by the other and this is a reciprocal relationship. The story of *Clown* that I read, or that takes shape in my imagination, will always be different from anybody else's, no matter how close our personal experience.

The reader response theory formulated by Wolfgang Iser is how I make sense of reading. It takes account of the reciprocal relationship between author and reader, who together negotiate a meaning for the text. Gaps and discontinuities are always present in every text for the reader to insert their own cultural experience or to puzzle over. Judith Graham is especially helpful on the contribution of Wolfgang Iser:

> This theory of active reader participation finds its fullest description in the work of Wolfgang Iser. The 'unsaid' (the telling gaps or blanks) in a work of fiction is filled by the reader and in the process the 'said' expands and triggers reflections in the reader. The reader's activity is still controlled by the text but the reader sets the work in motion and becomes a kind of co-author.
>
> (Graham, 1995: 14)

Wolfgang Iser expresses the relationship between text and reader and this is the heart of reader response theory:

> This is why the reader often feels involved in events which, at the time of reading, seem real to him, even though in fact they are very far from his own reality. The fact that completely different readers can be differently affected by the 'reality' of a particular text is ample evidence of the degree to which literary texts transform reading into a creative process that is far above mere perception of what is written. The literary text activates our own faculties, enabling us to recreate the world it presents. The product of this creative activity is what we might call the virtual dimension of the text, which endows it with its reality. This virtual dimension is not the text itself, nor is it the imagination of the reader: it is the coming together of text and imagination.
>
> (Iser, 1974: 278–279)

Zack, when he decided that his route to school passed by a street on *Clown*'s front cover, or when he dared to put his finger in the mouth of the ferocious dog (page opening 7 recto), demonstrated beautifully 'the coming together of text and imagination', and how he was intensely 'affected by the "reality" of a particular text' (Iser, 1974).

The relationship between very young children who are inexperienced readers and play is often commented upon. No wonder really because early years children are learning everything about the world and their place in it through the 'integrating mechanism of play' (Bruce, 2004: 166). Tina Bruce goes on to describe how 'Play helps people's minds to be organized, so that they can become good thinkers, and it also leads to a sense of well-being and good relationships with others' (p.167). I think that this is also one of the functions of a relationship with literature – it offers the world filtered through a multiple of perspectives. Margaret Meek is absolutely tuned into the child's delight in literature when she says that:

> For very young beginners, reading is a kind of play, something you do because you like it. Gradually you discover it's a specially good kind of play, less trouble than dressing up, but just as exciting for imagining you are someone else and somewhere else.
>
> (Meek, 1982: 11)

In their analysis of the roles which readers take, J.A. and S.J. Appleyard describe the first stage of becoming a reader as:

> The Reader as Player. In the preschool years the child, not yet a reader but a listener to stories, becomes a confident player in a fantasy world that images realities, fears and desires in forms that the child slowly learns to sort out and control.
>
> (Appleyard and Appleyard, 1991: 14)

Readerly behaviours and responses are quite difficult to realize in large groups, and I would make the case strongly for the induction of children into the literacy practices of their culture deriving from their first, intimate interaction with their parents and carers. Early years educators should then try and build on this important learning context, which is both social and collaborative. In their early years, children deserve as many one-to-one opportunities as it is possible to give, which will then support them as they widen their circle of engagement. It should not be a hardship to respond to children in this way; it is part of the joy of being with them. It is certainly one of my favourite things. If children do not experience this playing with language and responding to text, for whatever reason, and we should never be judgemental, then as early years educators, it should be part of our established practice.

> 'Good enough' language teachers like 'good enough' parents and carers (Winnicott, 1971: 13) mediate between young children and the wider world of cultural language use, presenting infants with just enough novelty and challenge in secure and unthreatening situations. What constitutes 'just enough' novelty and challenge must be judged in terms of that zone of proximal development demonstrated daily in children's play, pretence and interests for those who have the concern and motivation to observe children closely and respond to them appropriately.
>
> (Whitehead, 1997: 106)

Significance of an holistic approach to the teaching of reading

I believe that children learn to read, rather than are taught to read, and that any amount of targeted teaching will not touch their hearts unless they have a very good reason for wanting to engage their brains in the first place. In my view, becoming a reader depends on the relationship between child and text, the response which a child makes and the intertextuality that parents and practitioners help the child to build up. Of course there is a role for developing alphabetic and phonological awareness, for understanding how language works as a symbol system, but these are only elements of the whole process of becoming literate.

I would like to take this work forward with other children with whom I don't have such a close relationship as I do with Zack. This would involve research around children's readerly behaviours at nursery, and with their parents at home. This is the obvious next step and writing this chapter has confirmed in my thinking the centrality of texts in the development of the whole child.

Becoming a reader is a complicated task and it concerns me that in the Rose Review, reading is described as 'simple' (Rose, 2006: 75). The research that informs the Rose Review suggests that there is a formulaic response that finds exposition through the methodology of synthetic phonics, serving as a magic wand that will bring into being an entirely literate generation.

The 'simple view' breaks reading down into two components: 'decoding and comprehension', and rejects the 'searchlight model' which informed the National Literacy Strategy. The searchlight model attends to a range of cueing systems: syntactic, semantic, graphophonic and contextual. Inexperienced readers bring their developing knowledge about literacy practices to bear by: 'orchestrating these different kinds of information as they learn to read' (Dombey et al., 1998: 2).

There is much in the Rose Review that is deeply relevant to children's language development, particularly with regard to the importance of speaking and listening. However, what troubles me about it, and how its philosophy regarding synthetic phonics is being transferred into practice via the Early Years Foundation Stage and the Primary National Strategy, is that it paves the way for a drill and skill type teaching, which is totally inappropriate for active learners who are intent on making meaning.

It suggests that children's fascination with their environment and the people in it is incidental; it can be put on hold while they get on with the serious business of segmenting and blending, particularly in their early years. It takes limited account of children's different learning styles and it suggests a time scale:

> It would be ridiculous for the review to suggest that phonics teaching should start at the stroke of midnight on every child's fifth birthday.

However, there is ample evidence to support the recommendation of the interim report that, for most children, it is highly worthwhile and appropriate to begin a systematic programme of phonic work by the age of five, if not before for some children, the way having been paved by related activities designed, for example, to build phonological awareness.

(Rose, 2006: 29)

As a methodology, synthetic phonics has not been entirely successful in expanding children's comprehension of texts. The Clackmannanshire study, which has informed decisions implicit in the Rose Review, has been criticized for not being peer-reviewed and for the fact that children's levels of comprehension were not so far advanced as their word identification skills. The dreadful phrase 'barking at print' springs into mind.

From my experience as an early years educator I find that very young children are intensely obliging and social, driven by the desire to communicate; if they feel that they are being cherished and valued, they will try anything to please adults. 'Puh-puh-puh-please, ker-a-ter cat!' They will have a go at all manner of things to indulge the significant adults in their lives, and this is why we have to be cautious about practices which manipulate young minds with promises of a quick fix to a lifelong process, such as synthetic phonics as the royal road to reading.

Surely, one of our aims when educating children to become literate is the development of lifelong readers who will have a love of literature. The Centre for Language in Primary Education (CLPE) staff express their concern about children who can read but choose not to.

We have known for years that many readers who, by age seven or eight, have learned to read the print on the page, do not readily choose to read after this point, and so do not make progress as readers. . . . But children who have not learned what it is about reading that makes other people engage in it for pleasure are, as we know, unlikely to choose to read independently.

(Dombey *et al.*, 1998: 4)

If we think that children who are inexperienced readers will learn best from texts written in a reductive style then we have to consider what is being excluded and why. The relationship between thought and language is crucial; the language children develop empowers their potential for thought. If we inhibit their language then we restrict the power of their thinking, and risk the danger of minimizing their development as literate people.

Finally, what I want to emphasize is the intensity of the relationship that children have with books, and books have with children. Like Clown, seeking out a new home for his toy friends, texts seek out children who will inflect them with meaning. Children, when offered the possibility, will bring their personal experience to the world-of-the-text. In the overcrowded curriculum of primary school, and in the extremely busy environment of the nursery setting, there must be space for a text to become a transitional object if that is the child's desire.

In a recent article in the children's literature journal *The Horn Book*, Tim Wynne-Jones said: 'Words are not simply the building blocks of language; they are the fountainhead of imagination' (2006: 259).

I want children to be independent, fluent and critical readers who bring imagination, intelligence and creativity to the texts they are interacting with so that they are able to have opinions and to use the power of their language and the gift of their imaginations to express themselves fully in any context they encounter. That's what I want. And I do believe that language is power and how language is controlled signifies cultural shaping. If language is used to control and herd people into a functional literacy, then that is going to rip the heart out of their cultural expression by denying their potential for critical literacy. In this sense don't put up with 'good enough' – it just won't cut the mustard.

Reflections and questions

Gina argues for the right of each child to have stories shared with them as often as possible in a one-to-one situation.

- How realistic is that for children attending daycare from an early age?
- How committed are you to sharing stories and picture books with children as often as possible?
- What range of books and stories are available to children from which to choose in your setting?
- How can you foster a love of reading in children?

Applying learning to practice

- As parents and workers, giving children access to a range of books, with pictures and texts will help them to develop a love of reading.
- This might mean visiting the library regularly or making storybooks.
- Sharing books with children in a one-to-one situation gives us access to their emotional as well as cognitive concerns.
- Recognizing young children's 'readerly behaviour' can give us insights into their feeling and thinking.
- Sharing stories is not a one way process but a dialogue.

Bibliography

Primary texts

Ashley, Bernard and Brazell, Derek (1992). *Cleversticks*. London: Harper Collins Publishers Ltd.

Blake, Quentin (1995). *Clown*. London: Jonathan Cape.

Burningham, John (1970). *Mr Gumpy's Outing*. London: Jonathan Cape.

Burningham, John (1996). *Cloudland*. London: Jonathan Cape.

Sendak, Maurice (1970). *In the Night Kitchen*. London: The Bodley Head.

Whybrow, Ian and Reynolds, Adrian (2001) [1999]. *Harry and the Bucketful of Dinosaurs*. London: Gullane Children's Books.

Whybrow, Ian and Reynolds, Adrian (2001). *Harry and the Dinosaurs say "Raahh!"*. London: Gullane Children's Books.

Secondary texts

Applebee, Arthur N. (1978). *The Child's Concept of Story*. Chicago: University of Chicago Press.

Appleyard, J.A. and Appleyard, S.J. (1991). *Becoming a Reader, the Experience of Fiction from Childhood to Adulthood*. Cambridge: Cambridge University Press.

Barnes, Peter (ed.) (1995). *Personal, Social and Emotional Development of Children*. Milton Keynes: Blackwell Publishers in association with The Open University Press.

Britton, J. (1977). 'The Role of Fantasy' in Meek, Margaret, Warlow, Aidan and Barton, Griselda (eds) *The Cool Web: The Pattern of Children's Reading*. London: The Bodley Head.

Bruce, Tina (2001) 'Objects of Transition', *Early Childhood Practice: The Journal of Multi-Professional Partnerships*. 3 (1): 77.

Bruce, Tina (2004). *Developing Learning in Early Childhood*. London: Paul Chapman Publishing.

Bullock, Sir Alan (1975). *A Language for Life: Report of the Committee of Inquiry appointed by the Secretary of State for Education and Science under the Chairmanship of Sir Alan Bullock FBA*. London: HMSO.

Chukovsky, Kornei (1963). *From Two to Five*. Berkeley and Los Angeles: University of California Press.

Dombey, Henrietta, Moustafa, Margaret and the staff of the Centre for Language in Primary Education: Myra Barrs, Helen Bromley, Sue Ellis, Clare Kelly, Deborah Nicholson and Olivia O'Sullivan (1998). *Whole to Part Phonics: How Children Learn to Read and Spell*. London: CLPE.

Doonan, Jane (1993). *Looking at Pictures in Picture Books*. Stroud: Thimble Press.

Graham, Judith (1995). *Pictures on the Page*. Exeter: NATE Publications.

Iser, Wolfgang (1974). *The Implied Reader*. Baltimore, MD: Johns Hopkins University Press.

Kahr, Brett (ed.) (2002). *The Legacy of Winnicott: Essays on Infant and Child Mental Health*. London: Karnac Books.

Lewis, David (1996). 'Going Along With Mr Gumpy: Polysemy and Play in the Modern Picture Book', *Signal*. 80 (May): 105–119.

Lewis, David (2001). *Reading Contemporary Picturebooks: Picturing Text*. London: RoutledgeFalmer.

Meek, Margaret (1982). *Learning to Read*. London: The Bodley Head.

Meek, Margaret, Warlow, Aidan and Barton, Griselda, (eds) (1977). *The Cool Web: The Pattern of Children's Reading*. London: The Bodley Head.

Mitchell, Juliet (26.3.2007). *Woman's Hour*, BBC Radio 4.

Nutbrown, Cathy (2004). *Threads of Thinking: Young Children Learning and the Role of Early Education*. London: Paul Chapman Publishing Limited.

Parker, Rozsika (1995). *Torn in Two: The Experience of Maternal Ambivalence*. London: Virago Press Limited.

Propp, Vladimir (1968). *Morphology of the Folktale*. Austin: University of Texas Press.

Rose, Jim (2006). *Independent Review of the Teaching of Early Reading*. London: Department for Education and Skills.

Rudnytsky, Peter L. (ed.) (1993). *Transitional Objects and Potential Spaces: Literary Uses of D. W. Winnicott*. New York: Columbia University Press.

Shepherd, Ray, Johns, Jennifer and Taylor Robinson, Helen (eds) (1996). *D. W. Winnicott: Thinking About Children*. London: Karnac Books.

Watson, Victor and Styles, Morag (eds) (1996). *Talking Pictures: Pictorial Texts and Young Readers*. London: Hodder and Stoughton.

Wells, Gordon (1987). *The Meaning Makers*. London: Hodder and Stoughton.

Whitehead, Marian R. (1997). *Language and Literacy in the Early Years*. London, Thousand Oaks, New Delhi: Sage Publications.

Winnicott, D.W. (1953). 'Transitional Objects and Transitional Phenomena: A Study of the First Not-me Possession', *International Journal of Psychoanalysis*. 34: 89–97.

Winnicott, D.W. (1977). *The Piggle: An Account of the Psychoanalytic Treatment of a Little Girl*. Harmondsworth: Penguin Books.

Winnicott, D.W. (1990) [1965]. *The Maturational Processes and the Facilitating Environment*. London: Karnac Books.

Winnicott, D.W. (2002) [1958]. *Through Paediatrics to Psychoanalysis: Collected Papers*. London: Karnac Books.

Winnicott, D.W. (2005) [1971]. *Playing and Reality*. London and New York: Routledge.

Wynne-Jones, T. (2006). 'How to Put Words into a Child's Mouth', *The Horn Book*. May/June: 258–260.

Chapter 3

Young children's use of digital cameras to share home at nursery

Bridges of shared understanding

Clare Knight

In this chapter you will find:

- An account of a nursery project involving fifteen families and several workers.
- A real attempt to hear the voices of the children and to make authentic connections between home and nursery.
- One case study to illustrate the project.
- The use of photos taken by children at home to co-construct meaning with workers at nursery.
- A list of themes brought up by the children and a discussion of the questions posed by the adults.

Introduction/context

We probably all have fragments of memory about our early school education. I have some clear impressions of beneficial early learning experiences but also some less positive memories.

I have one vivid impression of my first year at school, filling in reading scheme work books, red books one, two and three. A typical page had a photograph of a girl and boy in their school home corner playing mums and dads. The words on the page (from memory) read: 'Mummy is cooking the dinner. Daddy is reading the newspaper. Draw here . . . [a picture of mummy cooking the dinner]. Write here . . . [copy the sentence].'

These sentences were not about me or my home, I did not recognise them. I hated this reading book so much that one day I scribbled hard on every page. It made me feel much better but caused a terrible fuss.

What I understood from this and subsequent experiences was that:

- The gap between home and school cultures is huge and daunting especially for children.
- Home life and school life have a powerful impact on each other.
- There is a tension between being part of and connecting with a group, and crying out to be acknowledged as an individual.

- Culture is about more than religion, ethnicity, health and gender and must include the 'culture' that is inherited, shaped, added to and passed on again to each child that is part of a family group (be it their biological family or not).
- Parents and especially children must be able to share their opinions, talk about their lives and be heard.

As a teacher in a children's centre I wanted to explore a way of giving children an opportunity to represent themselves, to have some control, to build bridges of understanding with those around them at nursery, and to contribute and share information about themselves and their interests. I wanted the children to contribute to their own profiles at nursery, as well as parents and professionals, so that the documentation would represent their co-construction of meaning. 'Relationships, communications, and interactions sustain our educational approach in its complexity. . . . It is our belief that all knowledge emerges in the process of self and social construction' (Rinaldi 1998: 115).

Throughout this writing my insights and hunches are expressed by the words 'it seems' or 'perhaps'. I cannot be completely sure about the children's thoughts and feelings. This work constitutes my adult interpretation. Ultimately I hope these experiences, in a small way, contribute to the child's ability to speak for him or herself in our nursery.

Facilitating the co-construction; the Album Project

My first step was to ask parents if they would like to make up a mini photo album containing photographs that could tell the story of their child up until they started nursery. Parents were asked to include their children in the process by inviting their child to help select photographs meaningful to them, including pictures of significant family and friends, daily routines, important events, and to scribe for the child if they wanted to include their own words. The success of this project and especially the interest shown by the children led me to the realisation that the children might be interested in using a camera to capture their world outside nursery.

I wanted to know:

- What aspects of house, home life, possessions and surroundings the children would photograph if they could take the camera home.
- What interested them, how they would use the camera and how they would interpret the pictures.
- What interactions each child and I would share when we viewed the photographs together.

I hoped that each child who wanted to take the camera home would be able to choose what they wanted to communicate about, being in control of the camera, and their home life and their surroundings, a context about which the child is expert.

Methodology

My initial way in to developing this project was to conduct a pilot study with four families who wanted to participate. From the pilot study I realised that I would need a lot more information about the child and their home situation to help with the context of the photographs. I decided that all children and families must participate in the Mini Album Project first, which gathers the personal history of the child as previously mentioned, before taking the camera home. I used the group opportunity to enable the parents to regard the camera going home with their child as an extension of the Album Project. I also engaged a member of staff, Jo Morley, who had worked particularly closely with one child in the pilot to help me develop a short leaflet/label which we attached to the camera to give parents some guidance about how to help their child, and how to use the camera when it went home. Fifteen families eventually participated in the project including those who took part in the pilot study.

I decided that a multiple qualitative methodology (Cohen *et al*. 2000) would best serve this project. I gathered participants' personal and family histories in photographs; participant and non-participant interviews; observations; video tape; taped conversations and written notes. This approach has its advantages and disadvantages but seemed more suitable to gathering information on the co-construction of meaning between adult and child.

I like the analogy of a collection of views and opinions as a 'constellation'; each throwing out light of varying intensity, each twinkling with possibility, all merging into one bright significance, intangibly real and captured in a snapshot of time. I wanted my method and resulting project to capture this constellation of views from child, parent and nursery staff.

Taking the camera home

What follows is Aidan's experience of taking the camera home in November 2006.

Aidan's story (aged 4 years)

Aidan started nursery in November 2005. He is the third of four children in the family and his sister Rhianna had previously attended our nursery.

Sharing Aidan's photographs

Aidan was very eager to show me his pictures when he brought the camera back to nursery. He wanted to show me the photographs using the play back button on the camera. He would not allow me to get the Dictaphone when I asked. He said 'No! Now Clare . . . takes too long', so we shared the photographs sitting on the sofa in the nursery and I took pencil notes of his commentary. Aidan had taken fifty-three photographs in total. Aidan took nine pictures of the outside, either from a window looking outside or standing outside. In twenty pictures he referred to who the objects belonged to. He seemed very clear about which possessions were shared and which belonged to him or other family members. Aidan found some of the pictures and our dialogue funny.

Aidan's interests and concerns

Interests

When I compared Aidan's photographs with his key worker's records of his time in nursery (in his profile) and the album he and his mum Maria had made together I could see that some of the pictures he took reflected interests we had observed in nursery. For example Aidan's profile has many pictures of aliens, and characters from space adventure films and programmes such as *Doctor Who* and *Star Wars*. In his album Aidan chose a picture of himself playing with a Dalek and at home with the camera he took pictures of his K9 model. Aidan took two pictures of the long mirror in his parent's bedroom, one with his reflection and one without. He also took pictures of reflections in the paintwork of his car. This seemed to be a continuation of his interest in reflections from his holiday experience of distorting mirrors.

Belongings

Associating an object with a particular person in the home seemed to be a common theme in Aidan's dialogue about his photographs. He mentioned belongings in reference to seventeen photographs, for example:

* 'mummy's bed'
* 'Rhianna's bed'
* 'this her cupboard'
* 'her drawers'.

It seemed important to him to attribute possessions and he was very clear about who the 'Hot Wheels' belongs to and who could touch it: 'This is my Hot Wheels . . . only me can touch this one and my cars . . . it's for me.' Some of his commentary was generally about items in the home which were his, 'our bunk bed . . . I sleep at the bottom'.

Aidan also referred to shared items. He used the word 'ours' spontaneously when he talked about six of the photographs – 'this is our trampoline', 'this is our horse' – and he implied joint ownership when talking about others:

'Guitar . . . like yours Clare.'
'Who can play the guitar?'
'Everyone.'
'Can you?'
'Yes.'

Belonging

I felt Aidan's photographs demonstrated to me his sense of belonging within his family. He could relate family members to their possessions and jobs, for example 'Mummy's washing'. Sometimes his dialogue seemed to be about sorting family members into their place in the home, where they slept, where they sat – 'bean bags. Bradley's sitting here . . . football' – and the rules that governed the use of the home – 'our bunk beds . . . I sleep at the bottom, Bradley sleeps here'. The frequent use of 'our' implies a sense of connection and reflects collective living.

Maria (Aidan's mother) has made large photograph frames for each of the children in the family. Maria adds photographs to the frame when a significant event has happened for each child. Aidan took five photographs of these pictures, two of his own frame and one of each of his sibling's frames. He said:

- 'these are Bradley's pictures'
- 'Rhiannon's pictures'
- 'my pictures'
- 'my pictures again' (laughs)
- 'Liam's pictures . . . Liam . . . one picture in his . . . Bradley and Rhiannon's pictures are full up. Liam's lots of spaces, mine's only few spaces'.

I think Aidan's comparison between the number of photographs in each frame for each of his siblings, showed a sense of time, place and equity for each of the children in the family. Aidan understood that he was older and therefore had more pictures than his brother Liam. Bradley and Rhiannon's frames were full up because they were older. Aidan referred to his younger brother Liam several times as we shared the photographs and Liam sleeping in Mummy's room was mentioned twice. Aidan was locating himself not only with in his environment but also his place within his family.

Anne, Aidan's key worker, recalled that during the autumn term last year, Maria had reported that Aidan was concerned about having friends. Aidan said he did not know if he had any friends at nursery. When Maria brought Aidan into nursery the next day she encouraged Aidan to ask the two children he was beginning to play with if they were his friends. The two children said yes they were his friends. Aidan seemed to be very pleased with this news. Anne thought that because Aidan had not been told these children were his friends, he concluded that he did not have any. She said she sometimes had to support Aidan's verbal understanding of relationship concepts.

Preferences

The last photograph Aidan took was of his favourite tree. He said, 'My favourite tree . . . because I can climb it'. It seems Aidan associated the tree with capability and challenge. He has climbed and conquered the tree, which gives him great satisfaction. This was the only time Aidan expressed a clear verbal inclination. His dialogue implied strong partiality in conjunction with the photograph of his Hot Wheels – 'it's for me'. Maria said Aidan had asked for the Hot Wheels as a Christmas present.

My experience of sharing the photographs with Aidan

I enjoyed the experience of sharing photographs with Aidan. Each picture allowed me to share the moment and the view when Aidan pressed the shutter. There was a feeling of togetherness as we sat together on the sofa in the book area of the nursery. I was not in control of the situation. Each photograph was a surprise and I wanted time to consider it and digest it. However Aidan did not allow me this luxury. I knew I was supposed to ask deep and searching questions but they ended up seeming rather inane, unproductive and repetitive. I felt it was wrong for me to interrupt his dialogue with poor questions.

Control

Sharing the photographs felt like a process of collaborative guided learning for Aidan and me. However our roles were reversed. Aidan became the teacher and guide, in control of the situation. He had the knowledge of the photographs and of his family environment. He was the expert.

Aidan started asking me questions – 'Hey Clare, do you know what this is?' If I asked a question that he considered to be rather stupid he felt in control enough to treat it with the contempt it deserved – 'not *real* Clare, he's not moving, silly!' However, Aidan also checked occasionally to make sure we still had a shared understanding by relating some of the objects in his house to me – 'guitar . . . like yours Clare'.

Aidan held the camera and dictated the speed at which we looked at the pictures. If they did not hold his interest then he labelled them and moved on to the next picture quickly; sometimes he would label a picture and then look at it intently – for example, of one photograph, 'Mummy's washing', I asked, 'Are there any of your clothes in the basket?' Aidan: 'Don't know . . . yes . . . trousers see?' (Aidan pointed to the trousers). I thought that having this control gave Aidan the opportunity to talk about his home as he perceived it.

I felt Aidan enjoyed having control over the camera and the objects or people he could see through the lens. In five of the photographs (1, 2 and 25 to 27) Aidan arranged the objects before he took the picture, controlling what and how the objects looked through the screen. Maria reported that he had arranged Bradley's scarf on the floor before he took the picture.

Being at the centre and creating

Having control over the camera seemed to give Aidan the opportunity to experiment and create different images with the camera; viewing things differently but at the same time being at the centre of what was happening. Maria said that Aidan enjoyed looking through the camera using the LCD screen. He spent a long time moving about the house framing shots, going up very close to objects and pulling away, then moving in close again. He seemed to have enjoyed changing the angle of his shots and looking at objects and people in a different way. When he was showing me his pictures he was particularly pleased with the photo of his feet: 'down at my feet . . . my feet!'.

He was also pleased when the photograph created a mystery or caused laughter. In photograph 29 he had taken a picture of his reflection in the mirror using the camera. Aidan told me, 'this me in Mummy's [bedroom] mirror, see me . . . taking a picture', then of photograph 30 he said dramatically, 'Now . . . gone!' He moved quickly on to talking about his brother's cot and I did not ask him about his reflection disappearing. I felt he wanted to let the mystery and the magic 'live'. Explanation may have ruined the effect for him and for me. I think the two photographs were deliberately taken using knowledge about reflections that he had been experimenting with on holiday and at other times. Aidan seemed to enjoy playing with the 'now you see it, now you don't' scenario. He tried a similar experiment with K9 except in this sequence he moved K9 from the foreground to the middle and then it vanished. It reminded me a bit of the flick books we used to make as children. If I could flick the photographs fast enough I could see K9 moving away.

I sensed Aidan's efforts to entertain me while looking at the photos. He was aware of me as his audience and created moments to engage me by either asking a question or drawing my attention to something in particular such as the bean bags. We laughed together at my absurd questions and ignorance: 'Hey Clare, can you see who that is?' Me: 'No who is that?' Aidan: 'K9 of course.' We laughed and Aidan looked at me with incredulity. We also laughed at photos that had not worked out as planned: 'Liam's head (laughing) Liam, wrong way silly' (laughing and talking to the photograph).

Building bridges to a shared understanding

I felt that laughing together was a way we built an understanding. I think that both laughing at the same picture connected us. We laughed when the other laughed, even if we would not necessarily have done so in different circumstances. The act of laughing together seemed to create a bond and I heard Aidan trying the same talk that had made us laugh when he shared his pictures with other children.

It seemed to me that Aidan's dialogue consisted of a lot of verbal bridge building, to help me comprehend the new world I was looking at. He labelled most of the photographs succinctly for me: 'Labels categorise objects and events in ways specific to the language of the child's culture' (Rogoff 1990: 70). Aidan was using these labels to guide me into a position of understanding about his home, a place that I had little experience of, for example, 'going down the steps from the little room'. 'The little room' referred to by Aidan was described by his mum as a conservatory but it is referred to as 'the little room' at home. Aidan's label was perfect for me to imagine its dimensions and position. Aidan had taken words, labels and sentences and made them his own by employing them to express his meaning, and using them for his purpose. Most of Aidan's language consisted of everyday words but he used them to tell his story.

My experience, what did I learn?

Sharing the photographs with each child was an enlightening experience and each set of photographs were very much a reflection of the individual child and their home culture. The photographs and the conversations that I shared with Aidan and the other children revealed common themes such as an interest in belongings and belonging. Each individual experience of sharing a child's photographs provided new insight into the concerns and interests of the rest of the group.

So what did we talk about?

Sharing each set of photographs was an absorbing and fresh experience. Aidan and the other children – Zak (3.4 years), Elliot (4.2 years), Rhianna (3.5 years), Joshua (3.5 years), Alex (4.1 years), Lily (3 years), Tommy (3.9 years), Molly (4 years), Harvey (3.9 years) and Jonathon (4 years) – shared information about:

- Their families, their names and relationships
- Their pets
- Their possessions and objects of interest to them
- The rules and routines in the home
- The environment around their home such as the garden
- Places of interest
- Family celebrations such as a birthday and Christmas.

Some information was volunteered and some given in response to a question. It seemed to me that in talking about their lives outside nursery that they used 'outside nursery words' too. The photographs facilitated the use of home words in nursery and perhaps vice versa. It seemed to me to be another way of exchanging home and school language and enabling 'young children to construct bridges between home and school' (Gregory 2005: 223). The combination of personal pictures, dialogue and non-verbal communication seemed proficient at creating meaning.

To ask or not to ask?

What questions to ask and when was a huge issue for me during this project for several reasons:

- The children must be facilitated to have *their* voice.
- Some of the published material I had explored about listening to children contained child interviews where the adult asked very specific questions (Clark and Moss 2001). My concern with regard to this project was that a field of narrow, pre-determined questions would not allow the children to tell me what they wanted.
- Too many questions might be viewed as probing by the child and make them feel uncomfortable.
- Inappropriate or numerous questions might inadvertently move the balance of control towards the adult.
- Inappropriate or too many questions might disrupt the flow of the child's meaning making.
- Too few or no questions from the adult might be interpreted by the child as lack of interest.
- Children's communication and interaction styles are various and my approach needed to reflect this (Flewitt 2005).

My aim was to be like Mariam as observed during the Froebel Early learning project: 'Mariam adopted the role of a quiet, interested, listener who made pertinent but short comments and asked genuine questions' (Athey 1990: 72). I decided to 'go with the flow' and, rather than have set questions, to see what questions came up during each photo-sharing experience.

What questions did we ask?

Some children shared their photos with a key worker, which I videoed or tape recorded, and some children shared their photos with me. The questions asked during the photograph shares seemed to me to fall roughly into nine categories:

- Questions associated with belonging
- Questions associated with possessions

- Questions associated with naming
- Questions associated with acquiring further information
- Questions associated with place and orientation
- Questions associated with actions
- Questions associated with clarification
- Questions associated with preferences
- Questions associated with rules.

I say 'roughly' because I think that some of the questions could be placed in more than one category, for example 'Where do you sleep?' could be categorised as an orientation, rule, action or possession question. Also I have, for the present, separated out into two categories the information and clarification type questions, in spite of the fact that I think they perform a similar function in the photo share and therefore could be considered as one category.

When I listed the questions used for each child, it seemed to me that each set of questions reflected the interest of the child expressed sometimes through the content of the picture and sometimes through the content of the dialogue.

I think we used these questions with the children in this project in two ways: 1) questioning used to start a dialogue; 2) questioning prompted by and in response to what the child says.

Questions that were not born of genuine ignorance were spotted very quickly by the children and ruled out by me as a strategy. I asked three questions of that nature during Aidan's photo share. They were my attempt at a bit of playful, humorous interaction but they fell rather flat as Aidan chose not to connect with me. 'Is he real?' I enquired about the photo of the toy spider. There were obviously more genuine questions I could have asked.

Action, naming information, clarification and place/orientation questions were most numerously used by the adults during the photo shares.

This may be because these questions were:

- Effective at opening dialogue
- Effective at creating a connection
- Effective at maintaining a connection
- Effective at building shared understanding
- Reflecting the adult's interest
- Reflecting the child's interest
- Reflecting a co-construction of interest.

I think the frequency of these questions may reflect information not volunteered by the child but interests or concerns picked up from the dialogue and used to build bridges of shared understanding. If the child's photos and speech content were concerned with place and orientation then I tried to reflect those interests in the questions that I asked. For example, some of Aidan's pictures were of the different rooms in the house, and I felt that he was particularly

Table 3.1 Questions listed under categories

Preference questions	Information questions	Clarification questions
Which picture do you like most? Which car do you like? Why is that your favourite tree?	Why did you take that picture? What's in her mouth? Does she have claws in her feet? Sorry did that hurt? What does it say? How old are you now? Why are you happy? What made you smile? Who took this picture? Is he eating? Why have you got a police light on your telly? What will you grow there?	Is this car parked? He gave you one back for bedtime? That's whose house you're at isn't it? Is he real? Can you? Was it a happy meal? Are you sure it's a horse? Don't know . . . sun? (Zak's question) Is that a trampoline? Is it Mummy holding Solomon?

Rules questions	Possessions questions	Belonging questions
Who can sit in the car? Who can sit on the bean bags? Who can play the guitar? What do you do?	Is it yours? Are there any of your clothes in the basket? Who does Harry belong to? Whose tree is that? Whose bed is this one? Whose bed is this?	Who's Lily? Whose little tongue is that? Who's the carrot for? Whose knees are those?

Action questions	Place and orientation questions	Naming questions
What happened? x2 What happened to that car? What's happened here? What's your kitten doing? Who's having a ride on Thomas? Are they having a cuddle? What do you use that for? Can I do the writing? (Zak's question) Does Totty purr?	Where did you take this picture from? Where's the other one? Where do you sleep? Where did you take that photo? Is one of these windows your bedroom window? Which room are they in? Is that the little window at the front of the house? Where's his body? Where did you have your party?	Hey Clare! Do you know what this is? (Aidan's question) Hey Clare! Can you see who that is? (Aidan's question) No! Who is it? Who's that? x3 What sort of animal? What's this? x2 What is he? What's that? x4 Who's this? Who came to your party?

Table 3.1 Continued

Action questions	Place and orientation questions	Naming questions
Does Totty climb? Can Wallace climb? Is she eating a smelly sock? What's she doing? See him? (Elliot's question) What does he feel like? What's happening in this picture? How does it work? What are you doing? When you sing does he sing?	Which bit of the car is it?	What's this bit? What's this bit Clare? (Rhianna's question) What's that – my butterfly? (Rhianna's question) Don't know . . . what's this? (Zak's question)

interested in the bedrooms and where family members slept. My question therefore tried to reflect this interest: 'Where do you sleep?'

I think the questions also reflected our attempt to maintain a connection with the child and the photographs. I think the clarification questions were our attempt to respectfully acknowledge what the child was expressing. It was our way of saying 'I'm interested and place value in what you are telling me and I want to make sure that I understand you correctly'.

The 'naming' type questions of 'who?' and 'what?' seem to have been used frequently as a way of opening dialogue and creating a connection. It seemed to me that each time we looked at another photograph together we had to build small, new connections. I think the 'naming' questions were our way of saying 'this looks interesting and I want to know more'.

I was surprised at how few questions there were under each of the categories of rules, belonging and possessions, especially as my overall impression was that these interests had featured more predominantly in our shared conversations than the number of questions suggested. The smaller number of these questions may be because:

- The adult was not interested in these aspects
- The child was less responsive to these questions
- The child had already given the information voluntarily and therefore questions were not required
- My categories needed to be viewed flexibly.

If the child referred frequently to 'our' and 'my' when they were sharing their pictures then I tried to reflect that with belonging and possessions questions and also questions about rules over the latter. The amalgamation of these categories would give a larger number of questions asked and perhaps explain my impression that a greater proportion of our conversations had been around these interests. It could also be that the child had volunteered a lot of information about 'my' and 'our' and that the questions reflected the adult and child co-constructing meaning.

I was also surprised by how few preference questions were asked, three in total:

1   Which picture do you like most?
2   Which car do you like?
3   Why is that your favourite tree?

Questions 2 and 3 were in response to children volunteering the information. Aidan stated, 'My favourite tree', which prompted my question, 'Why is that your favourite tree?' I wished we had used this type of question slightly more frequently and I think the results would have been interesting.

Schema and language

I think the schematic content of the children's speech is reflected in the questioning (Athey 1990; Nutbrown 1994; Arnold 2003). When I listed the questions used during each photo share some individuals' lists were particularly dominated by one type of question; for example Zak's list had mostly 'what's happened?' questions reflecting his dynamic schema cluster of trajectory (horizontal and vertical), size, orientation and heaping. He talked about cars crashing and a mountain. Lily's list of questions had a lot of 'who?' questions reflecting her interest in people, faces, enclosure and horizontal and vertical coordinates. Other children had quite a spread of question types in their list; perhaps reflecting broader interests, larger schema clusters or a different pattern of social interaction.

During the analysis of the questions asked, only four questions asked 'why?' I think the 'why' questions are sometimes tricky for adults. In my experience they do not always elicit an immediate answer from the child. Usually it requires the child to give the question some thought. They may not at that moment have the knowledge or vocabulary to give an answer. Sometimes the question can be rephrased, for example I changed 'Why are you happy?' to 'What made you smile?' If it is a good 'why' question the child may come back with an answer days later. Perhaps the difficult questions are not appropriate when new connections are being formed.

The photographs were placed by the children into their profile. This enabled them to be re-shared and added to through the rest of the child's time at nursery. I think this provided time for both the adult and the child to digest the material and perhaps ask more searching questions.

Communication – not just verbal

Taking their own pictures and sharing them seemed to enable children and adults to communicate in different ways.

The act of sharing the photographs required close physical contact, sitting next to each other. Aidan wanted to sit on my knee to share the photographs. I felt that the physical proximity communicated interest, receptivity, acceptance, openness and companionship.

I think sitting next to each other compensated a little for the fact that slightly less eye contact was made during the sharing of the photographs. When looking at the photo shares captured on video most of the eye contact focussed on the pictures with glances at each other; either when a question was asked that required clarification and more information, or when the changeover of pictures occurred. Smiles and mirrored facial expressions were also exchanged at this time. I did not video all the photo shares for various reasons (Knight 2007: 24) but it is a method which provided interesting glimpses of how children and adults used non-verbal communication over the photographs.

Aidan wanted to hold the camera during the photo share, communicating his control. Some children used actions to demonstrate meaning when words were not enough. Joshua, who was videoed sharing his photographs, jumped about to demonstrate the different way his cat and dog moved.

The occasional joke and laughter I think showed evidence of the 'children's sensitivity to the interests and feelings of different people in their social world' (Dunn 1998: 111).

Humour

Discovering 'humour' about halfway through this research was a revelation for me. Despite it being part of our everyday social interactions with staff, parents and children I had never given it conscious consideration.

When I looked through the pencil notes of my photo shares with the children I noticed that occasionally I had written 'laugh' in brackets. The 'laugh' had clearly made an impression on me somewhere in my subconscious for me to note it down. Closer inspection of the notes showed that the children had instigated the 'laughter' and I had followed.

Their laughter seems to concur with Koestler's ideas about humour as an action of creation, occurring when something makes sense in one situation but not in another and to release any tension they felt about sharing their pictures (Koestler 1964; McGhee and Chapman 1980).

Some laughter was caused by comic situations; for example Elliot took a photo of a dancing snowman he has at home, and his brother Oliver, which caused much hilarity: 'He sings by himself (laughing). Look at Oliver! (more laughing)'. As Dunn says, 'Sharing a joke implies, at some level, an expectation that the other person will also find this distortion of the expected absurd or comic' (1998: 111).

Some laughter was caused by absurdity. Elliot took another picture of his police light on top of the telly. Joshua laughed at the incongruity of just his cat's head being in the picture – 'that's his head, just his head!' Some laughter was caused by a 'naughty' word. Lily said, 'Rudolf has the carrots and him poos in the toilet'.

I think humour helped to generate feelings of togetherness: 'the use of particular "naughty" or joking language was very effective in creating the group's common spirit' (Van Oers and Hännikäinen 2001: 107).

I think children also used humour to take control and to feel powerful as I believe my experience with Aidan showed.

Conversations, communication and connection

I think both adults and children used language and other forms of communication to create common ground where connections could be made (De Haan and Singer 2001). Aidan drew my attention to his guitar being like my guitar. Zak used 'we' to refer to himself and I, connecting us together. He said, 'Don't know . . . what's this?' I replied, 'I don't know either'. Zack: 'No . . . we don't know do we?' I shared with Elliot my experience of making a cave out of bunk beds and blankets. Elliot said enthusiastically, 'Yes! Yes! So do we', and I felt we connected.

I think the children used laughter and smiles to make connections – 'laughter is non-verbal behaviour reflecting in part the intimacy of an interaction' (Chapman *et al*. 1980: 158).

Reflections

Alan Prout's words of warning, 'Unfortunately children's participation is a subject high in rhetoric but sometimes low in practical application' (Prout 2003: 21), serve to remind us to be constantly reflective and pro-active in our practice with children and families and as professionals possess a 'revolutionary gaze' (Fleer 2006: 132).

Throughout this research I have referred to the photo share as a 'project' a word that can mean a one-off study or unit of work. However, I feel that the camera and photography as a medium has enabled a 'quantum leap' to happen in the connection between the home and nursery environments because mutually shared meanings are being established (Stern 1998: 168).

Aspects of togetherness

I think I encountered strong patterns of togetherness, connection and belonging throughout this project.

Belongingness seems to thread its way through in several ways:

•   The photographs of the possessions that children took and the labels they used such as 'my', 'his' and 'our'.

- The photographs and talk about the home and the surrounding environment.
- The photographs of family members and the use of their names which sometimes referred to their relationship with the child, for example 'Nan' 'uncle' or 'cousin'.
- Dialogue about rules, routines and communal living specific to each family.

Bringing this knowledge and family identity to nursery will, I hope, enable children to feel a sense of belonging in nursery; I want to foster again the understanding that nursery 'is an extension of the function of the home, not a substitute for it' (Isaacs 1954: 31).

Adult participation

I think all of those who contributed to this project – parents, children, colleagues and my tutors (particularly Colin Fletcher and Cath Arnold) – had a wish to connect, build bridges and co-construct a shared understanding. Van Oers and Hännikäinen define togetherness 'as a quality of an activity that describes the fact that an activity does not break down when problems have to be faced' (Van Oers and Hännikäinen 2001: 105). I found the adult support that helped to build this project essential and their honest feedback was useful in refining its development.

In terms of the balance of power between the contributing parties I think some children were good at negotiating the balance of help they needed. Some of the children appeared in their own photographs because they had asked for it to be so and this could be seen as self expression, just as if they were using the camera.

> Children collaborate with adults in arranging their own participation and level of responsibility . . . children are active in directing the support of adults and the adjustment of that support as their skills develop.
>
> (Rogoff 1990: 106)

From the start of the project we respected any child's right to turn down the opportunity to take the camera home when it was offered.

A child says no

A child and her mother wanted to make an album and joined the group in November. The child's grandma and grandpa attended the parent's group and fed back to her mum, because the family had work commitments that made it difficult for either parent to attend. Mum and child made an album together. The feedback was very positive. Both mother and child said they enjoyed making the album and the child and I spent a long time looking at the pictures.

I took pencil notes while the child talked as this was acceptable to her (videoing had been refused by the child). I decided to offer the camera to the child to take home. I was surprised at the very firm 'no' that came back from the child, a categorical refusal. The child's mother was obviously uncomfortable about her child's reaction and tried to persuade the child to change her mind, saying 'She always does this, she is going to miss out, ask her again she might say yes'. I tried to reassure the parent that her child saying 'no' was extremely positive and I was pleased she had felt able to say no. The parent said 'This is very typical. She has made a conscious decision and that's it.'

I met with both parents later in the same week and we discussed the positive aspects of their child's decision. I explained that their child's refusal opened up other avenues of discussion between their child and me and that I was looking forward to talking about contributing to the profile with their child. As Koestler puts it, 'Even an elastic strait-jacket is still a strait-jacket if the patient has no possibility of getting out of it' (Koestler 1964: 44).

Through this photo-share project and the Album Project I have built connections and shared understandings with parents. In our feedback sessions we exchanged personal information and shared our thoughts about each child. We have laughed and smiled but also have been quite serious at times especially when reflecting on traumatic events that have happened or discussing a point of view.

Projects can become nursery practice

This study has given me the opportunity to research and reflect on how to introduce, develop and support this project as part of our work with children and families.

The key aspects for professional practice, which I have taken from working with children and parents on this project, are:

- The parents and I meeting as a group at the beginning of the project and asking questions.
- The parents and I meeting as a group at the end of the project to share feelings, experiences and new knowledge.
- Having a parent facilitator who worked with the group as well as with me. The parents who took on a facilitating role within the group were able to share their own experience of participating in the project, answer questions from parents and pass on ideas and tips.
- Parents and children making the album first was important for setting the child's photographs within the family culture. It allowed me to develop a relationship with the parents and the children.
- The camera tag advice developed with Jo's help that supported the children and parents while they were using the camera at home.
- Provision for individual parents to feed back their experience.

- Time and space for the children to share their photographs, not just with me but with their peers and other adults.
- The approach and type of questions that practitioners asked the children about their pictures, especially the way questioning can be adapted to reflect and resonate with what the child was saying about the pictures they took.

Our personal responsibility as educators is that once we have genuinely invited children to give of themselves, to offer their thoughts and opinions and to contribute at a personal level then this process must be continued. As Prout says, 'The promise to be heard is taken seriously by children and the failure to see it through creates disappointment and even cynicism about democratic values' (Prout 2003: 21).

Reflections and questions

Clare and her colleagues made great progress in reducing the power differential between adults and children in their setting during this project.

- How aware are you of the difference in power between children and adults in your setting?
- How far would you go in following the agenda of individual children in order to support and extend their interests?
- How well do you know children and families using your setting?

Applying learning to practice

- This project very much illustrates the development of a 'research stance' as described in the introduction to this book. Clare continued to ask questions and to reflect on her pedagogy and on the children's meanings.
- The 'Album Project' provides a sound way of connecting with families and involving them in the life of the nursery while sharing important history from home.
- Digital cameras in the hands of children can give us real insights into their worlds and their concerns. The use of those photos to engage in dialogue with children offers us a great way of hearing children's voices.

References

Arnold, C. (2003) *Observing Harry. Child Development and Learning 0–5.* Open University Press: Buckingham.

Athey, C. (1990) *Extending Thought in Young Children: A Parent/Teacher Partnership.* Paul Chapman Publishing: London.

Chapman, A., Smith, J. and Foot, H. (1980) Humour, laughter and social interaction in McGhee, P. and Chapman, A. (eds) *Children's Humour.* John Wiley and Sons Ltd: New York.

Clark, A. and Moss, P. (2001) *Listening to Young Children, The Mosaic Approach*. National Children's Bureau: London.

Cohen, L., Lawrence, M. and Morrison K. (2000) *Research Methods in Education* 5th Edition. RoutledgeFalmer: London and New York.

De Haan, D. and Singer, E. (2001) Young children's language of togetherness. *International Journal of Early Years Education* Vol. 9 No. 2 pp.117–124.

Dunn, J. (1998) Young children's understanding of other people: evidence from observations within the family in Woodhead, M., Faulkner, D. and Littleton, K. (eds) *Cultural Worlds of Early Childhood*. Routledge: London.

Fleer, M. (2006) The cultural construction of child development: creating institutional and cultural intersubjectivity. *International Journal of Early Years Education* Vol. 14 No. 2 pp.127–140.

Flewitt, R. (2005) Is every child's voice heard? Researching the different ways 3-year-old children communicate and make meaning at home and in a pre-school playgroup. *Early Years* Vol. 25 No. 3 pp.207–222.

Gregory, E. (2005) Playful talk: the interspace between home and school discourse. *Early Years* Vol. 25 No. 3 pp.223–235.

Isaacs, S. (1954) *The Educational Value of the Nursery School*. The British Association of Early Childhood: London.

Knight, C. (2007) Calling the shots. Dissertation in partial fulfilment for Degree of Master of Arts in Integrated Provision for Children and Families. University of Leicester. (unpub.)

Koestler, A. (1964) *The Act of Creation*. Pan Piper Books Ltd: London.

McGhee, P. and Chapman, A. (eds) (1980) *Children's Humour*. John Wiley and Sons Ltd: New York.

Nutbrown, C. (1994) *Threads of Thinking: Young Children Learning and the Role of Early Education*. Paul Chapman Publishing: London.

Prout, A. (2003) Participation, policy and changing conditions of childhood in Hallet, C. and Prout, A. (eds) *Hearing the Voices of Children, Social Policy for a New Century*. RoutledgeFalmer: Abingdon and New York.

Rinaldi, C. (1998) History, ideas and basic philosophy in Edwards, C., Gandini, L. and Foreman, G. (eds) *The Hundred Languages of Children*, 2nd Edition. JAI Press Ltd: London.

Rogoff, B. (1990) *Apprenticeship in Thinking: Cognitive Development in Social Context*. Oxford University Press: Oxford.

Stern, D. (1998) *The Interpersonal World of the Infant*. Basic Books: London.

Van Oers, B. and Hännikäinen, M. (2001) Some thoughts about togetherness: an introduction. *International Journal of Early Years Education* Vol. 9 No. 2 pp.101–108.

Chapter 4

Is breaking a leg just another experience?

Using video to gain a bi-cultural perspective of risk-taking in the natural environment

Suzanne Taylor

In this chapter you will find:

- An account of a small bi-cultural study looking at risk and young children in the UK and Norway.
- The use of video of children from the UK and Norway to stimulate discussions about risk.
- The different attitudes expressed by small groups of early years workers from the two countries to children's risk-taking.

Introduction/context

Aged 4, I climbed a tree and sat on a branch looking at the ground below. I can still remember the satisfaction I felt from having got up so high and the different view it gave me of the world. This is my earliest memory involving risk-taking and the natural environment. Later, as a mum and nursery teacher, I enjoyed being outside with my children. Then, as part of a Teachers' International Professional Development, I visited Norway to look at the Norwegian forest kindergartens. I was amazed at the freedom children had in the natural environment – exploring woods and beaches, lying over the edges of unfenced concrete bridges looking at the water below or sliding down the hillside on branches. It appeared that staff allowed children to explore and had a relaxed and confident approach to managing risk.

I showed my Norway video to a range of audiences and always there were the same reactions from UK practitioners: the sharp intakes of breath as they saw children on unfenced bridges, children using sharp tools, and the nervous laughter as the child plunged over the edge of the mountain, riding on the tree like a toboggan.

Shortly afterwards, I became a Local Authority Adviser, supporting a range of settings. I found some practitioners protecting children so much from adult-perceived dangers that children were unable to function within the environment. For example, I observed 5-year-olds not allowed to access the outdoors by themselves because of three shallow steps. The practitioners wanted to make sure no-one fell, so insisted all children lined up before going outside so that they could walk down the steps safely.

Frost (2006) suggests that it is a common misconception that children must somehow be sheltered from all risk of injury. The European Child Safety Guidance for Inclusion in Standards (2005) shows us this is not the case: 'Minor injuries are part of every child's learning process and are a far more normal part of their lives than is the case for adults' (CEN, 2005: 7).

Do we as adults consider the situation or the personal competences of the child? Rinaldi comments that what we believe about children determines their rights and the educational contexts offered to them (2006: 83). Have adults stopped seeing children as competent beings, able to make choices and decisions relating to their own safety?

Furedi, in his book *Culture of Fear* (2002), suggests that when we talk about risk we have a perceived danger of an adverse outcome. 'Our litigious culture has helped foster a climate where adverse experience is readily blamed on someone else's negligence' (p.11).

When we watch television programmes or listen to stories other people tell us our brain relates to these experiences as if they were our own. We store the information, increasing the probability of harm in our minds. The 'discourses that surround us tend to focus us on the "darker" side of risk – seeing the uncertainty, the possibility of failure, of injury' not on the 'positive aspects of risk . . . adventurous, daring, brave, strong, confident and successful' (Stephenson, 2002: 42).

'Protection' from everything and anything has crept into our society: issues around safety; limitations to children's learning experiences; an attitude of 'no risk' rather than managed risks. Is it our personal experiences or the culture and society of which we are part that gives us a view of risk-taking? For example, is walking to school or riding around in a car more dangerous than going to play in the woods?

This research explores and attempts to discover what influences attitudes and perceptions to risks in the natural environment in Norway and the UK.

Methodology – the research

The aims of this enquiry were to:

* show video to observers to find out about attitudes to risk-taking in the natural environment;
* examine how those attitudes may have been formed;
* discover what influences and controls those attitudes.

Practitioners from the UK and Norway watched video films from both countries generating discussion and revealing attitudes, values and perspectives within the observers' own culture. The data were gathered in a social context:

developing 'ethnocentrism . . . a situation where members of one culture apply their own cultural values when evaluating another culture' (Olive, 2003: 53) and through default reveal their own. Each video was shown to staff in three settings in Norway and three in the UK.

The method builds on the work developed by Tobin *et al.* (1989), Jordan and Henderson (1995), Haggerty (1998), Rayna (2004) and Hansen and Jensen (2004) using video as a research tool. It worked on the premise, like SOPHOS (Second Order Phenomenological Observation Scheme) (Hansen and Jensen, 2004), that comments and observations by the observers would tell me something about their own attitudes and beliefs, particularly about their culturally based understanding. Alongside this, I used the personal reflections from UK practitioners' journals after they experienced Norwegian kindergartens first-hand.

Interpretation of video by observers

Interviews were taped to allow conversation to flow and to provide subsequent accurate, detailed transcription. My aim was to collect high quality data in a social context where the observers could reflect on their own views and attitudes responding both to the video and to the views and attitudes of others. The observers constructed their own meaning or constructed meaning with others, making their own interpretations of the video and using it to stimulate discussion. The data came from the observers as in Tobin *et al.* (1989), Haggerty (1998), Rayna (2004) and Hansen and Jensen (2004). I wanted to create a multi-vocal text. Transcribing the recordings was time-consuming but essential to the exploration of the similarities and differences between insider and outsider observers. As the researcher, I enabled the insider and outsider perspectives to meet in the analysis. An 'interpretive zone . . . a space where the knowledge, experiences and beliefs of outsiders and insiders interact to create new understandings' (Bresler, 2002: 1).

I used direct quotations throughout, enabling participant observers' voices to be heard – as do Tobin *et al.* (1989), Haggerty (1998) and Hansen and Jensen (2004). This would reveal their 'culturally-based understandings, attitudes and values' (Hansen and Jensen, 2004).

Tobin and Davidson (1990) point out that having a 'polyvocal' approach allows informants' voices to be heard in the final text, but questions whether we have a right as researchers to use practitioners' voices because they can be out of context. All words taken out of context can risk being misinterpreted by those that are recording or those that are reading them. We are powerless to prevent other interpretations, but this is only a possibility and therefore I do not believe this should stop use of a method that provides an effective vehicle for sharing cultural perspectives.

I also used personal reflections by first-hand observers of children using the natural environment in Norway as I led a group of eighteen UK practitioners to visit the Norwegian kindergartens whilst undertaking this research. By asking for personal reflections in this way, I was able to consider understandings and views from practitioners who had taken in information using all their senses rather than just the visual and auditory input experienced by the observers of the video. I also assumed they would be free from the influence of the facilitator.

Attitudes and beliefs about risk-taking from Norwegian and UK observers

Data were generated by practitioners on attitudes and beliefs and covered the following themes:

- culture and society;
- views about children and adults revealing underlying pedagogy;
- parents;
- risk-taking and safety.

Throughout, I have noted where the observers have responded to the stimulus of a particular video (i.e., Norway video, UK video) or where I quote journal comments. As with Hansen and Jensen's SOPHOS model (2004) there were themes that appeared directly and some that appeared indirectly from the comments.

Norwegian observers

Norwegian comments about their culture and society

The Norwegian observers commented about what people and families did or talked generally about children being allowed to get dirty or do the sorts of outdoor activities they saw on the video. They seemed to take for granted that most of the population would feel the same but that there would be exceptions:

> I think that some people would be different but most of the people in Norway would think it's a good thing that their children be dirty.
>
> (M) (Norway video)

The Norwegian observers felt it was important to understand that the experiences that the children were having were part of the cultural background. Not all parents would be able to take their children to the woods but they would appreciate other people doing it with their children. They would describe what some children would experience:

> And we are a walking people in Norway: on Sundays we go for walks in the woods, also it's part of that as well with the family.
>
> (SH) (Norway video)

One practitioner thought that the cultural heritage was important:

> We learn it to our children and our grandchildren, we want them to have
> this.
>
> (K) (Norway video)

The Norwegian observers also felt that there was public opinion supporting
the philosophy of taking the children into the natural environment because of
the benefits:

> There is an opinion, public opinion that I agree very much with – and that
> is the more the children are allowed to do, the more they can control their
> bodies better.
>
> (SH) (Norway video)

These types of statements appeared to indicate that the pedagogy was
influenced by what was going on outside the kindergarten.

Illustrating and highlighting why they do what they do

> Once we had a trainer for the woods and he said that the children are
> not cold, not too cold, not too hot, they never get wet, it's not strange that
> they sometimes try narcotics because they have never felt anything.
> Everything is just similar all their life. They have the very best tempers.
> They are always never too cold and never too hot, they are never hungry,
> they never get water into their shoes and you need to feel something
> sometimes, maybe to feel it hurts, it's bleeding or whatever and so what –
> you don't die of it.
>
> (R) (Laughs) (Norway video)

Norwegian perspectives on children and their learning

The Norwegian observers often reflected how they encouraged children's skills
and abilities:

> And I don't know whose idea it was with the tree – if it was the children
> or the adults – could have been the children, especially one of them who
> had the idea, and then we encourage them to use whatever they find.
>
> (SH) (Norway video)

> They have good self-esteem, they can do it, 'I believe in myself' and 'I can
> do it', 'I'm good and I have control'. And 'I can', and they have to try new

things too that maybe when they start to go to school – they start to have more 'I am not afraid', 'I can do that'.

(R) (Norway video)

All the Norwegian observers talked about responding to the children and what they were interested in; they allowed the children to lead the learning:

I think when the teachers are around the kids, the kids come to me and they want to show me something and I will tell them about the thing they are looking at and I will be there for them. I'm not so 'teachy', I'm not so 'Oh come here – look at this'.

(M) (Norway video)

Norwegian perspectives on the role of adults

The Norwegian observers commented on the adults having to know the children well because then they would know their capability, and that seemed key to what they would do in the natural environment:

If we know what they are capable of – that way we are sure that it is safe.

(H) (Norway video)

You saw the children down by the river – we saw only the children but every time the adults are standing back: we look at them, they are not alone.

(MR) (Norway video)

They reflected on the differences between the UK and the Norwegian videos in terms of the adult interaction and the controls imposed by the adult. They seemed to feel that children should be responsible for their own actions:

All the activities were more controlled by the adults and maybe it was the opposite in the other film: where the adults follow children and their ideas.

(H) (Comparing UK video and Norway video)

Observers talked about how they supported children in their risk-taking and built up their skill levels, describing their own practice. They felt it was important for the adults to respond to the children taking the initiative to do something:

The children decide more by themselves . . . Part of our ideology is freedom, (children) initiating, the children's fantasy is important, so we support that, we encourage that.

(SH) (Norway video)

We will ask them if they want to go up the tree and we will help them a bit. And some of them are tougher than the other ones and climb a little bit themselves and we will stand right under the tree and see when they are coming down and watch so they are learning.

(M) (Norway video)

The Norwegian observers showed empathy with the practitioners on the UK video, realising that they had not been taking the children out into the natural environment for very long and needed more experience. They described that they themselves were worried when they first took the children out and also how new staff can also be anxious:

It is experience, they get to know the children and trust them and see that they are capable and relax a bit more maybe.

(SH) (UK video)

Norwegian perceptions of parents' attitudes

The Norwegian observers seemed slightly puzzled when I asked them about how parents felt about children having this wide range of experiences in the outdoor environment and about the risks. They often responded by explaining that the parents thought it was a good idea and describing how the parents had chosen the kindergarten because it offered experiences in the natural environment:

They like that because they want this kindergarten because of that – that the parents say because when they are dirty they will know that they have been having fun.

(SH) (Norway video)

One Norwegian observer was also a parent of two children at one of the kindergartens and responded as a parent, reinforcing this view:

I feel because I have my two daughters here at the kindergarten and if I get a bag with wet and dirty clothes with me home, that I know that my daughter has been outdoors and had a great day. And I know also that the people in the kindergarten have changed her clothes and been there for her.

(M) (Norway video)

They also talked about parents having a lack of free time and therefore the parents would be grateful that the kindergarten had time to give children experiences that they could not:

Parents say 'We are so glad you have the time, we don't have the time to take the children outdoors.' Always they feel bad that they can't do that.

(R) (Norway video)

However, one Norwegian observer said that some parents would not agree and that they would have different tolerances and that there were some parents that would object to their children getting dirty:

They are different – some will do the same, some will stop them and some don't want them to get dirty, especially not the girls – the pink girls . . . and we try to tell the parents not to have the newest clothes on.

(R) (Norway video)

Norwegian views and attitudes towards risk-taking and safety

Norwegian observers seemed to show generally that they were very conscious of the safety of the children and that they had confidence in the children's ability:

Sometimes it maybe look dangerous. I think climbing perhaps. It depends on the kid doing the activity – which one. The kid has to make it on his own to climb, he has to do it on his own, he has to make his own decision. The climbing tree for example – if it is a big tree very high up – you won't help them along; you might stand at the side and tell them with words – support them with words.

(H) (Norway video)

They gave me the impression that this was an area they worked at all the time and was often talked about in staff meetings. Modification of their practice happened continually:

So we have been through a lot of discussions . . . security – yes, we had one last week about reflective vests (like we do in the traffic) but you would have them in the woods, you see them better and know where they are.

(SH) (Norway video)

The Norwegian observers showed their tolerance level in what they said but also in how they described how each adult had a different tolerance level:

All the grown-ups have different . . . (K)

It's what you feel. (SH)

Some are more worried when they are by the water. Some are more worried when they climb the tree. (SH)

(K and SH) (Norway video)

We are different too. We have different boundaries, for example, she allows things but maybe you don't allow the same; maybe I get afraid. We have to work on this, talk about it.

(R) (UK video)

So, you don't die from breaking a leg – it is also an experience.

(SH) (Norway video)

UK observers

UK comments on culture and society

The UK observers seemed to feel that the culture and society in which they existed prevented them from giving children the range of experiences in the natural environment. The practitioners often mentioned fear; such fears were driven by a variety of factors:

I think it's more the society because people sue each other. 'You do this to my child and I'll sue you', or 'You let that happen' and 'He was in your care and it happened'.

(A) (Norway video)

We seem to have developed a blame culture; if something happens then somebody has to be to blame; it's not an accident, somebody should have stopped it happening. Also, because people have got less freedom, therefore children are not building up the skills to keep themselves safe.

(F) (Norway video)

I think one of the most influential factors must be parents . . . I felt the parents were clearly supportive of their nurseries which enabled staff to take a more relaxed view to the children's risk-taking.

(J2) (Journal)

'Blame culture' – If it happens on your doorstop it is your fault, legislation – Who is going to sue you? Leadership – Are your leaders going to support your decision? Parental complaints – Do parents have unrealistic expectations? Education – Does everybody understand why we are doing this and what the benefits are to children's development?

(D) (Journal)

UK observers reflected that perhaps the Norwegian practitioners had done these types of activities themselves as children and that was why they were taking the children out. For example:

They perhaps have done it as children themselves, and know how important it is.

> (C) (Norway video)

And yet, when I explored whether they themselves climbed trees etc. when they were young, nearly all of them said that they had:

> I was brought up with brothers and cousins. I used to climb up trees because that's what they like to do. My mum was always a bit nervous about me doing it; she was alright with them doing it, but she was always, you know, 'Be careful', 'Watch her' and all that sort of stuff.
>
> (L) (Norway video)

UK perspectives on children and their learning

Some UK observers reflected that they believed that children did know their limitations and had some sort of self-preservation:

> Children will actually know their limitations if they have been out in the environment a long time.
>
> (B) (Norway video)

> I'm sure children do have a sense of fear because, if they climb to the top of the climbing frame and they won't jump off, they say 'It's too high' and they climb on the smaller one.
>
> (T) (UK video)

> I think I would worry, but it's better for them to realise and for them to know 'Well, if you are going to fall over, you are going to hurt yourself', so that you realise the next time you need to be a bit more careful.
>
> (T) (Norway video)

Journals revealed similar thoughts:

> I learnt how important it is for our children to take risks – and was reminded that we don't always give our children opportunities to take real 'risks' or to challenge themselves. I have re-defined 'risk and challenge' – children are actually very capable of judging 'risk' and challenging themselves.
>
> (K) (Journal)

Although some UK observers were not so sure:

Children can be fearless, they don't seem to have any sense of danger . . .
we think they ought to have.

(C) (Norway video)

UK perspectives on the role of adults

The UK observers reflected on what they saw the adults doing in both videos.
They seemed to observe that the adults were assessing risk and modelling
certain behaviours for the children in the Norway video:

She is modelling what would be safe options presumably, it's safer to peer
over the edge like this rather than lean.

(C) (Norway video)

They also observed differences in the adults' behaviour between the UK
and Norway, for example, adults leading the experiences rather than the
children:

Adults are making quite a lot of suggestions, rather than in Norway
[where] that lady was just laying down on the bridge just looking.

(C) (Comparing UK and Norway video)

In Norway the children found what they wanted to explore. In England
it was more led round and what you found on the way.

(E) (UK video)

I felt that there was a lot of independence in Norway because children were
allowed to take risks and it seemed the overall consensus was if they
couldn't do it, they weren't ready.

(H) (Journal)

More freedom to explore and learn through their experiences . . . This
enables them to meet new challenges with a high level of confidence and
to push the boundaries of what they are capable of doing. It also leads to
a high level of motivation and interest!

(S) (Journal)

The UK observers commented that the children in the UK were given a lot of
praise for physical tasks, something which did not appear in the Norwegian
video, but recognised that the children were doing things outside their normal
experience:

Yes, they are big steps and you've got to be encouraging – but is it such a mammoth task for them? And on the Norway video, it wouldn't be – they would just be going up there.

(V) (UK video)

They also pondered that, if adults did not give children these sorts of experiences, how were they going to learn; but said it would be dangerous to expose children to these experiences if they had never been in the environment:

I think if you took some of our children and you put them at the top of that rock, you could have problems because they wouldn't have had that grounding in how to behave in that sort of setting. So I think it's about learning from an early age.

(F) (Norway video)

Helping staff understand risk was important in the journals:

I am convinced that the level of risk-taking in English schools and nurseries should be increased – but it can only be effective if the staff are comfortable with and do not relate their own anxieties onto the children.

. . . learning to accept that accidents can happen and putting them in perspective, e.g., a broken arm is rarely going to change someone's life irredeemably.

(J2) (Journal)

UK perceptions of parents' attitudes

The UK observers were very concerned about parents' reactions to risk-taking and being out in the natural environment. There appeared to be a general level of fear:

Presumably the person has been brought up like that, they wouldn't worry about their child being allowed to do it. That would be my concern here, that I as an individual may feel it was okay for that child to be up that tree, but if a parent knew that's what we were doing then some parents might have a problem with that. The parents are then saying to teachers or whoever 'You should not have let my child climb the equipment because they have fallen off and broken their arm now, and it's your fault'.

(F) (Norway video)

I don't think the parents would be happy . . . Parents wouldn't like that . . . they are not even keen when children play outside of school – climbing trees.

(L) (Norway video)

They also seemed to feel that children were under some pressure, and that there is a different attitude from the parents in the UK:

> I think they are pressured, clothes and such like, or lack of experience too. I think there is a different attitude from the parents.
>
> (A2) (Norway video)

> I don't think parents would worry about it being dangerous; I can see some parents not understanding the value: 'All they are doing is mucking about in the woods. Why aren't they inside with a pencil and paper doing real things? If they are going to nursery, they ought to be doing real things.'
>
> (F) (UK video)

UK observers seemed to think it was to do with parents being generally over-protective of their children, and that this could be seen in the way that parents approached self-help skills with children:

> Well, it follows through to putting on a coat: if you don't feel it's necessary to encourage a child to even find their coat or take off their coat, let alone put it on, then it's a similar kind of thing – I am the mummy and I do everything and I protect my child and I don't subject them to anything that is potentially dangerous or outside of my cultural experience.
>
> (V) (Norway video)

Some UK observers thought that the experience would make UK parents uncomfortable and that parents needed to be educated:

> I would imagine that the Norway parents would expect their children to be out two or three days a week, whereas I expect the UK would need a bit of talking round as to what they are exactly going to do: 'What will they do if it rains? What will they do if they get wet?' They are just more protective because we are not used to our children being out in the environment.
>
> (E) (Norway video)

> Most of our worries are linked to parental perception of danger, risk and ultimately litigation – we therefore need to educate parents along with the children to manage risk sensibly without losing the excitement and challenges children automatically set themselves along the way.
>
> (J) (Journal)

UK views and attitudes towards risk-taking and safety

Reflection by some UK observers sounded like they thought activities were dangerous:

It's actually quite dangerous, isn't it? It really is quite dangerous because it's probably rock, I mean that must be so wobbly, uneven . . . It's a very uneven surface . . . I can see it; look at it . . . and woods are at the bottom, miles away aren't they?

(B) (Norway video)

There were conflicts between what the children were doing in Norway and what experiences they offered children:

We should not subject the child to any danger that the mother would not subject the child to. Which is really sad because we are here to be educating and offering a whole world of experience, but that is limiting. But that is sad if we can only match the expectations and experience of the parents.

(V) (Norway video)

I mean, who could predict that you would go out and get on a cut-down tree and slide down a hill? You can't predict that, can you?

(L) (Norway video)

Practitioners wanted to change practice and offer children opportunities:

I feel that, if we are not careful, we could be in danger of producing a generation of children afraid to take risks in the not too distant future!

(K) (Journal)

We need a balance – risk can always be managed, accidents will always happen, and if they do – we learn from them – not blame someone else for not keeping the child safe.

(J) (Journal)

Comments revealed how UK observers also had individual tolerance levels:

The further a child is from you in a risky situation the less control you have if they slip, they fall – and you wouldn't feel you could prevent it happening.

(E) (Norway video)

What is the danger that could happen to you potentially? It's not life-threatening: like, if you fell in the water, you would get wet; you would get wet, you'd have some dry clothes – and you'd be okay.

(V) (Norway video)

There were variations between countries and individuals in those countries. The chart on the next page compares and contrasts the views and attitudes from the UK and Norway.

Table 4.1 Comparing and contrasting UK and Norwegian observers' views and attitudes to risk-taking in the natural environment

	Culture and society	Pedagogy		Parents	Risk and safety
		Children	Adults		
Norway	• Families engage in walking • Parents and families like practitioners to give children these types of experiences	• Children know their own limitations • Children need to lead the learning	• Adults will help them • Adults will talk to children about new experiences • Video sections that caused interest or reactions: (Norway video) climbing a tree, child sliding down on the tree; (UK video) children round the ice	• Parents think that learning in the natural environment is a good experience • Being wet and dirty means the children have had a good time	• Consider the safety of children and have many discussions • Individuals have their own tolerance levels • 'Breaking a leg is just another experience'

UK				
• Culture of being safety conscious • Stories in the media • Not allowed to give children these types of experiences • Restrictions in place • Fear of litigation	• Anxiety about the competency of children • Children not thinking about their actions • Anxiety about being out of control • Children know their own limitations • Afraid children do not know their limitations • Children are afraid of getting dirty	• Adults make lots of suggestions • Adults lead children • Children need some directed time by adults • Video sections which caused interest or reactions: (Norway video) children on the hillside, climbing a tree, children standing on the bridge, child sliding down on the tree; (UK video) children round the ice, children scrabbling up the bank	• Fear of a reaction from parents – that they would not like this – either because it was too dangerous or because they would think children were not learning • Saw links to self-help skills – children's over-reliance on parents • Parents do not like children getting dirty	• Individuals have their own tolerance levels • Need to risk assess all the time and fill out forms • Potentially no more dangerous than the outdoor environment within a setting with climbing equipment • 'Breaking an arm is not life-changing'

Reflections and discussion

Considering questions and propositions about risk-taking in the natural environment

Do UK practitioners have a lower tolerance level towards risk-taking than Norwegian practitioners?

It would appear that each individual has their own tolerance level towards risk-taking in the natural environment: it is not culturally dependent. Norwegian observers talked about each having their own tolerance level for experiences within the natural environment. Some were prepared to let the children climb trees, others would find this more difficult. The Norwegian observers appeared to discuss their attitudes to risk regularly, to help practitioners come to terms with less familiar experiences. Their own tolerance levels had been built up from experiences over many years.

What practitioners can do is dependent on the support of parents

The UK and Norwegian observers held different perceptions of parental reaction. The perception was that parents had a positive effect in Norway and a negative effect in the UK. The UK observers were more fearful of parental reactions, either towards the care and safety of the children or towards the learning that was going on. For example, parental views differed over 'wet, dirty clothes'. The UK observers seemed to believe that UK parents would judge receiving a bag of wet, dirty clothes negatively, suggesting that the child had not been cared for. Conversely, the Norwegian observers considered their parents would receive such a bag as affirmation that the child had been cared for, because the practitioners had changed them and they had obviously had a good time. There was a general consensus over this, although one Norwegian observer did say that some parents did not like their children getting their clothes dirty: she referred to them as 'the pink girls' and 'the Spiderman boys'.

In the UK, reactions about parents also suggested a perceived fear of what parents might say if they knew, for example, that their children were climbing trees, whereas the Norwegian observers felt parents would be pleased their children were outside doing such activities, because parents themselves had no time to take children into the natural environment. The UK observers discussed how they did not think parents would see value in the activities and the inherent learning, and that justifying to parents was hard. This suggests that observers' perceived views of parents affect the opportunities and activities provided for children around risk-taking in the natural environment.

Each society influences the experiences that can be shared with children

We are all embedded within a social and cultural context. It appeared that the Norwegians shared 'mutually consistent values' (Schwarz and Thompson, 1990) in attitudes towards risk-taking and learning. The Norwegian observers thought that their culture and society supported and encouraged the experiences they were offering their children and would indeed want them perpetuated. They described themselves as being 'a walking people' and that parents did not have time to give these experiences to their children, so were very appreciative. Were the Norwegian observers acting out in their pedagogical practice the 'dominant voice' in their society, or was this more limited? As these observers worked in kindergartens that offered children experiences in the natural environment their attitudes towards risk-taking may be localised.

The UK observers gave diverse views: some were very unsettled by the episodes on the video, others were very comfortable and quite excited. Many seemed to relate their feelings to the sensitivity of what they thought parental reaction might be. Some believed that parents would be fearful for their children; some that they would be 'sued' by parents. Others thought they would be unable to carry out such activities because of 'restrictions'. However, when probed, they were usually unable to articulate these 'restrictions'. According to one observer, the reason why they were unable to give children these experiences came from 'up above'! Ball (2002a: 35) describes risk behaviours being 'in part at least a function of how human beings, individually and in groups, perceive the world and that risk choices, whether by experts or non-experts, are driven by values and beliefs as much as by facts.' The UK observers' beliefs seemed to reinforce this: in their comments and reactions they used a wide range of words such as 'scared', 'protect', 'control', 'panic', 'danger', etc. UK observers appeared to see a protective society that influenced and governed pedagogical practice.

Anthropologist Mary Douglas (1978) and her co-workers looked at two key questions of human existence – 'Who am I?' and 'How should I behave?' – and developed 'cultural theory'. She argues that personal identity is determined by the individual's relationships to groups and that behaviour is shaped by the extent of the social prescriptors that an individual is subject to: a spectrum that runs from the free spirit to the tightly constrained. (This account of cultural theory is cited in Schwarz and Thompson, 1990.) Using the two dimensions of sociality and the four rationalities developed by Mary Douglas – hierarchists, egalitarians, individualists and fatalists – I have mapped the comments from the Norwegian and UK observers and their journals to show their contrasting views and how they are influenced by society.

Figure 4.1 shows that predominantly the UK observers sit above the line with externally imposed restrictions on choice and the Norwegians sit below with no externally imposed restriction on choice. I think there is another

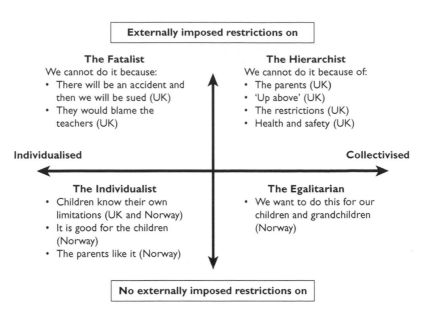

Figure 4.1 Attitudes to risk-taking

Source: Based on Douglas (1978)

dimension to this: although many UK practitioners had experienced the natural environment when they were younger, for some reason this had become subsidiary to other influences in their current pedagogical practice, whereas for the Norwegian observers such experiences appeared to continue to exert strong influence.

Do practitioners in the UK and Norway have different views of the child? Do practitioners believe that children are aware of their own limitations?

The Norwegian observers seemed to share common ideology regarding children and their learning: they saw children as capable, independent and responsible beings with whom they shared experiences. This 'socially constructed' view of learning seemed to be reflected in how they viewed the experiences that children were offered. They promoted a view that children should be encouraged to lead, take initiative and be supported in their choices. They felt children were quite capable of deciding their own limitations but, if they thought a child might go beyond its capability, they would discuss with the child to alert them to the possible consequences.

The UK observers were divided: some appeared to see children as autonomous and capable; some talked about being out of control in the natural environment and children needing some directed time. Sometimes it was unclear through which lens they were looking at the child – was it in reference to the child itself, or to themselves as adults with responsibility for the child? Some thought children were conscious of their own limitations, others that children had no awareness – but that it did depend on the situation.

For both groups of observers the assumptions about the learner were not always the overriding prescriber of pedagogical practice. There appeared to be other factors at work, such as their perceptions of native culture and society.

The opportunities children are given may be dependent on whether practitioners view the environment as friend or foe

UK observers commented about children needing to be safe in the environment and that it was important to have experiences in it from a young age. UK observers felt that children would be in more danger if they just went out and had those experiences now: to have grown up in the environment having graduated experiences would enable children to be safer.

Risk implies an element of choice, but, in order for this choice to happen, children need to have access to a variety of environments so that they can have a breadth of different experiences and contexts to challenge them. Some UK observers seemed to feel the perceived risk precluded children having these opportunities, rather than trying to guide or help children manage the risk. The Norwegian observers seemed to believe they had a duty to help children manage risks, modelling how to be safe in the environment and teaching the children the necessary skills. A Norwegian practitioner illustrated this: one child at a time could climb 2 metres high onto the roof of the shelter outside the kindergarten. The practitioner explained that a child had fallen and cut his head. After this accident, the Health and Safety officer had visited. I was expecting the practitioner to say that as a result the children were now not allowed on the roof; however, the Health and Safety officer had asked why the child was not wearing a helmet if he wanted to climb on the roof. The philosophy behind this seems to be that the risks are not taken away, they are managed.

Summary and future directions

What did I learn about attitudes to risk-taking in Norway and UK?

This was a limited study and must be seen through that lens. It gathered data from observer practitioners in six settings in two countries. However, by using the journals, I sought a wider check on attitudes to risk-taking in the UK – the views of UK practitioners, headteachers, teachers and unqualified staff who had experienced Norwegian kindergartens first-hand. These views were not influenced by the researcher and did tend to reinforce the perceptions found in the interviews. The data could have been widened to include parents in Norway and the UK to see if the observers' perceived beliefs about parents are founded on fact or conjecture. With more time, I think that the work could have also been extended better to balance the genders (there was one man) and also to have children's voices. I would like to extend this research to show the videos to a wider group of observers, for example, those who participate in Forest School in the UK.

Although this small sample is not necessarily representative, it does highlight cultural differences and draw out cultural norms. Unlike the Norwegians, the UK observers appear to have cultural perceptions which are fearful of risk-taking in the natural environment as a result of their perceptions of parents and litigation. The stress that some UK practitioners seem to feel about risk makes me question whether they are able to assess risk accurately. UK practitioners may lack confidence in giving children experiences within the natural environment because of perceived societal and cultural pressure. Contemporary stories about accidents and danger appeared to supersede their recollections of climbing trees as children. Bruner (2006: 231) argues that 'one of the principal ways in which our minds are shaped to daily life is through the stories we tell and listen to – whether truth or fiction. We learn our culture principally through the stories that circulate within its bounds'. For the UK observers, these new stories had become current reality and seemed to influence their pedagogical practice – and thereby the learning experiences provided for children and their attitudes to risk.

These attitudes appear to be a tension between forces, such as observers' fears about the children's ability within that environment and their perceptions of support from their society and culture. Risk-taking was not seen positively by UK observers, owing to perceived societal pressure and fear of what might happen. This appeared to dominate UK journals and UK observers' responses. As Rogoff (1990: 190) found, 'Neither the individual nor the social environment can be analyzed without regard to the other as the actions of one have meaning only with respect to those of the other'.

Each of us appears to have individual levels of tolerance around risk-taking; there was not a culturally based norm. Each perception will affect us on an individual basis, both positively and negatively. Both UK and Norwegian observers appeared to comment positively that offering children opportunities to take risks, make choices and initiate learning for themselves would be beneficial.

Recommendations for risk-taking in the natural environment

Whilst this sample is not representative, some tentative recommendations can be made to broaden pedagogical practice within the UK:

- We should respect that each of us has our own tolerance level with regard to risk-taking within the natural environment.
- Some are more comfortable than others in the natural environment. To help one another grow in confidence we should perhaps discuss risk and safety and try to understand what risk-taking means and how risk can be managed.
- We need to encourage dialogue with parents because through our con-straining perceptions we may be limiting the experiences that all children are offered.
- Fear seemed to dominate the UK observers – perhaps we need to explore what we are frightened of? This fear does not appear to be of children hurting themselves but generally of practitioners being held to blame for any potential accident. We are perhaps in danger of perpetuating our prejudices and thereby confining our curriculum.
- Perhaps we should think about the opportunities and experiences we give children and the environments we share with them. What does outdoor learning look like for most children?
- Perhaps we should consider a view of interdependence in risk-taking in the natural environment – rather than independence (freedom) or depen-dence (control) – and not be frightened of helping children manage risk within the natural environment.

Reflections and questions

In this chapter Suzanne has strongly challenged our current attitudes in the UK to risk-taking and the outdoor natural environment.

- How are you supporting children in accessing the outdoor environment and in taking risks in your setting?
- How do you perceive parents using your services?
- Have we become a risk-averse society?

Applying learning to practice

- A sound first step would be to have a discussion about risk in your staff team.
- You could adopt Suzanne's technique of using video as a stimulus to discussion.
- When you have established what different staff members consider to be acceptable risk, you might want to share your discussion with parents and invite their views.

Bibliography

Note: the interviews in this chapter were taken from the author's video film from her 2004 presentation entitled 'Riding a tree in Norway'.

Ball, David J. (2002a), Understanding and Responding to Societal Concerns, *Health and Safety Executive Research Report 034/2002*, Norwich: HMSO.

Ball, David J. (2002b), Playgrounds – Risks, Benefits and Choices, *Health and Safety Executive Research Report 426/2002*, Norwich: HMSO.

Bresler, Liora (2002), Introduction, in Bresler, Liora, and Ardichivili, A. (Eds), *Research in International Education: Experience, Theory and Practice*, New York: Peter Lang.

Bruner, Jerome (2006), *In Search of Pedagogy, Vol II, The Selected Works of Jerome Bruner*, London: Routledge.

CEN (European Committee for Standardization) (2005), Guide 12, *Child Safety – Guidance for its Inclusion in Standards*, March, retrieved 11.01.07, http://www.cenorm.be.

Davis, Bernie and Waite, Sue (2005), *Forest Schools: An Evaluation of the Opportunities and Challenge in Early Years*, Plymouth: Faculty of Education, University of Plymouth.

Douglas, Mary (1978), *Cultural Bias*, Occasional Paper 35, London: Royal Anthropological Institute of Great Britain and Ireland.

Fjørtoft, Ingunn (2004), Landscape as Playscape: The Effects of Natural Environments on Children's Play and Motor Development, *Children, Youth and Environments*, 14(2), 21–44, retrieved 10.10.06, http://www.colorado.edu/journals/cye.

Frost, Joe L. (2006), The Dissolution of Children's Outdoor Play: Causes and Consequences, paper presented at The Common Good Conference 2006, retrieved 11.11.06, http://www.ipema.org.

Furedi, Frank (2002), *Culture of Fear: Risk-taking and the Morality of Low Expectation*, New York: Continuum.

Gill, Tim (2005), If You Go Down to the Woods Today, *The Ecologist*, October, 3–9.

Haggerty, Margaret Ann (1998), *Sighting, Citing and Siting Te Whaariki: Exploring the Use of Video Feedback as a Tool for Critical Pedagogy*, MA thesis, Victoria: University of Wellington.

Hansen, Helle Krogh and Jensen, Jytte Juul (2004), *A Study of Understandings in Care and Pedagogical Practice: Experiences Using the Sophos Model in Cross-National Studies* (Consolidated Report), available at www.ioe.ac.uk/tcru/carework/htm.

Jensen, Jytte Juul (2004), *Understandings of Pedagogical Practice in Centre Based Services for Young Children: Experiences Using the Sophos Model in Cross National Studies in Denmark, England and Hungary*, available at www.ioe.ac.uk/tcru/carework/htm.

Jordan, Brigitte and Henderson, Austin (1995), Interaction Analysis: Foundation and Practice, *Journal of the Learning Sciences*, 4(1), 39–103.

Murray, Richard and O'Brien, Liz (2005), *An Evaluation of Forest School in England*, Forest Research Nef, available at http://www.forestry.gov.uk/pdf/ForestSchool EnglandReport.pdf.

Olive, Paul (2003), *The Student's Guide to Research Ethics*, Maidenhead: Open University Press.

Rayna, Sylvie (2004), Professional Practices with Under-ones in French and Japanese Day Care Centres, *Early Years*, 24(1), 35–47.

Rinaldi, Carla (2006), *In Dialogue with Reggio Emilia, Listening, Researching and Learning*, London: Routledge.

Rogoff, Barbara (1990), *Apprenticeship in Thinking: Cognitive Development in a Social Context*, New York: Oxford University Press.

Schwarz, Michael and Thompson, Michael (1990), *Divided We Stand*, Philadelphia: University of Pennsylvania Press.

Smith, S.J. (1998), *Risk and our Pedagogical Relation to Children: On the Playground and Beyond*, Albany, NY: State University of New York Press.

Stephenson, Alison (2002), Opening up the Outdoors: Exploring the Relationship Between the Indoor and Outdoor Environments of a Centre, *European Early Childhood Educational Research Journal*, 10(1), 35–43.

Taylor, Suzanne (2005), How can Norwegian Forest Kindergartens Influence Learning in a Setting? (Unpublished assignment towards MA – undertaken at Pen Green Research Base, Corby, Northamptonshire).

Tobin, Joseph (1999), Method and Meaning in Comparative Classroom Ethnography, in Broadfoot, Patricia, Alexander, Robin and Phillips, David (Eds), *Comparative Education*, Oxford: Symposium Books.

Tobin, Joseph and Davidson, Dana (1990), The Ethics of Polyvocal Ethnography: Empowering vs Textualizing Children and Teachers, *Qualitative Studies in Education*, 3(3), 271–283.

Tobin, Joseph T., Wu, David and Davidson, Dana H. (1989), *Preschool in Three Cultures*, London: Yale University Press.

Chapter 5

How can we provide an optimal learning environment for young children's imaginative play?

David Westmore

In this chapter you will find:

*   An account of a small action research project designed to encourage imaginative play in a nursery setting.
*   Staff making observations and reflecting on their own actions as well as the children's actions.
*   The development of a framework to use when reflecting on observations of children.

Context

This action research was undertaken at a children's centre in the London Borough of Lewisham, which developed through the integration of a nursery school and early years centre in 2001. We became an Early Excellence Centre, and a children's centre in 2004. We employ a multi-professional team of around 40 people, and offer a range of family support services. Our action research project took place between September 2005 and September 2006, and was facilitated by me in my role as Deputy Head of Centre. Most of the actual work with children took place between January 2006 and July 2006. I am currently Head of Centre.

Introduction

The crucial role of imaginative play in young children's development has been widely discussed and debated over many years. For Piaget, 'symbolic play is the apogee of children's play' (Piaget, 1977, p.492); it is a symbolic language that can be modified and developed by the child according to need (p.493). Vygotsky identified the role of play in the development of abstract thought (Vygotsky, 1978, p.99): the child begins to use symbols to represent reality and explore ideas. And because play is pleasurable, the child is motivated to renounce immediate gratification and subordinate herself to the rules of the play, an important facilitator in building social relationships. Contemporary news coverage has highlighted the fact that children no longer have the freedom to play, particularly outside, as they once did. Our concern for the safety of young children has had implications for their longer-term development and mental health. This is expressed clearly by Vivian Gussin Paley when she talks of the pressure to begin formal learning at an earlier and earlier stage, pushing down expectations from class to class, down to the early years. Her belief is that it is time that is the issue:

> Having not listened carefully enough to their play, we did not realise how much time was needed by children in order to re-create the scenery and develop the skills for their ever-changing dramas. We removed the element – time – that enabled play to be effective, then blamed the children when their play skills did not meet our expectations.
>
> (Paley, 2004, p.46)

The concept of play as a means of expression, or language, through which children explore their growing understanding of the world is complex, and involves the negotiation of meaning and development of relationships. It contributes significantly to the whole process of development and has deep implications for the practitioner. It implies a need for careful understanding of the context of children's play. This relates to the learning environment and resources that are available. Are they flexible and interesting enough to allow for creative responses from all children in the setting? Do they represent children's lives and experience? Do children have free access and choice about how and where they are used? How is the time organised? Does it give children time and space – perhaps over a period of days – to develop imaginative play scenarios that fulfil their interests? How do practitioners relate to the children and consult with them? Is their role-play acknowledged as important? Is it supported appropriately, with subtle interventions as opposed to taking control in the interests of adult-initiated learning intentions? If we accept the paramount role of imaginative/symbolic play in the early years, what is it that we are doing to make it happen in the most positive and fulfilling way for children? What is our role, as practitioners, in helping to develop and extend children's ideas?

Research methodology

The investigation into young children's imaginative play was set up as a small, action research group enquiry, involving a multi-professional group of six staff members, including teachers and nursery nurses with varying levels of experience. The group was involved in a participative process to define the field of enquiry, and in the agreement and construction of the methodology, in order to build motivation, and a strong sense of agency. The investigation offered the opportunity to introduce innovations that could enhance learning opportunities for young children, and drive professional development.

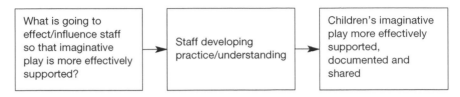

Figure 5.1 Project rationale

The testing of theory and its relation to practice uses an action research model originally defined by Kurt Lewin (1997 [1948], p.146) as proceeding 'in a spiral of steps each of which is composed of a circle of planning, action, and fact-finding about the result of the action'. At the beginning is a fact-finding and planning stage, which results in decisions about the initial course of action. This is carried out and subjected to a process of evaluation. A further cycle of planning, action, fact-finding and evaluation follows. Our cycle of planning began with an initial meeting, which defined the focus for the action research and developed a methodological framework through group discussion. Involving all participants at the outset was crucial. Lather talks about the empowering of 'those involved to change as well as understand the world' (Lather, 1991, p.52). Our aim was to challenge accepted custom and practice, and our own understanding of imaginative play within the context of our setting.

Elliot cites the importance of nurturing reflexive practice by involving teachers in the research process. This is more effective than supplying specialist expertise, which has the function of 'externally regulating their activities' (Elliot, 1991, p.54). The practitioner/leader needs to be the expert in her own practice, understanding her own pedagogical approach through a process of self-analysis and critical dialogue with peers. In this way the research is owned and real for the participants. This is vital if we want to carry out research work that empowers practitioners/leaders, has resonance and meaning for our centre, and makes an impact on practice.

It was decided that four research group members would each target two children in their key group. This was a negotiated agreement deemed manageable by practitioners. My role would be to facilitate release-time for participants, keeping an informal overview of how participants were feeling about the progress of the research, and supporting with ongoing difficulties as they arose. As practitioners, all participants had timetabled opportunities within their teams when they organised focused activities for children. These activities are negotiated within teams, and build on knowledge about individual children's interests and learning needs gained through observation and discussion. There is flexibility with targeting children, and it was felt that it would be a straightforward process to develop opportunities for imaginative play based on observations. This gave participants the time and opportunity to develop the research work without significantly adding to workload. A fifth group member (not a key worker) would focus on looking at groups of children as they engaged in imaginative play. This participant worked throughout the centre and had developed a particular interest in incorporating resources reflecting popular culture into the centre to test children's responses. She would carry out her interventions as a part of her usual round of team visits. The commitment to use resources from popular culture was made by all participants. These resources included:

- superheroes (Batman, Superman, Spiderman, Power Rangers);
- figures from children's TV (Tweenies, Teletubbies, Bob the Builder);
- Barbie (and Ken);
- Action Man;
- comics and annuals (representing the above).

Participants made a commitment to resource this, mainly through car boot sales and charity shops. An early response to this area of interest, instigated and organised by the research group, was an INSET day looking at the important contribution these resources could make, emphasising the link between home and setting.

Participants would also focus on traditional contexts that supported imaginative role-play. We wanted to look at the home corner, dressing-up, small world play (doll's house, animals, duplo, etc.) and role-play in the outdoor environment.

Woven into the research process was the centre policy on children's self-assessment (Gura and Hall, 2000). This would provide a means of capturing children's responses to the work carried out. It related well to the use of journals by all participants (including myself), involving all groups in a reflexive dialogue. Photographs would be taken in order to reflect the experience back to the child, giving an opportunity to listen to the individual voices of children involved in the project.

We agreed to collect detailed observations, a well-established methodology used by Susan Isaacs in her exploration of young children's social and intellectual development (Isaacs, 1930). This is already an embedded aspect of centre practice. Information obtained during these initial observations would be used as a basis for planning interventions. We adapted involvement and well-being scales (Laevers, 1994) in order to provide evidence of the effectiveness of the learning experience for individual children, and to help us to identify strategies for further interventions. The involvement and well-being scales acknowledge the link between deep learning and involvement, providing a framework by which we can assess the match between the learning environment and the child's needs. When high levels of involvement are visible, the practitioner knows that there is a match between the two.

We wanted to focus on the skills and qualities that we, as adults, brought to the process of supporting imaginative play. We wanted to know what it was we did, and the ways in which it made a difference in our interactions. The process of discussion generated a wide range of strategies that attempted to capture the subtlety of the way in which practitioners worked. Because the list of qualities and skills was generated through group discussion, there was a high level of commitment to the process of investigation. The qualities and skills identified were:

- observation
- questioning
- adaptability
- reciprocity
- learning environment
- spontaneity
- commitment.

In particular, the concept of the 'learning environment' is seen as inclusive not only of equipment and resources available to children, but of the way time is organised, and the prevailing ethos encountered by the child. The centre is a 'dispositional milieu' (Carr, 2001, p.36), which encourages (or discourages) attitudes and behaviours. Carr locates dispositions not only in the child, but also in the environments that the child inhabits. Interaction between these (including adult responses to behaviour) can change the character of this dispositional milieu.

We had to find a way of analysing our practice with reference to these skills and qualities. A framework that provided space for comment, which could be used after an intervention, was widely accepted as a useful format (see Figure 5.2).

This would enable me to examine how our initial ideas related to our practice – the interaction of qualities and skills is clearly a dynamic process. I took responsibility for analysing ongoing results to monitor the success of the framework, summarising this for the research group. This enabled an informed discussion during a final research group meeting on how the qualities/skills framework worked in practice.

Key to the process is critical self-reflection. We employed the use of learning journals to enable participants to consider experience reflexively, and provide valuable information about the learning process. Some release time for group members was provided in order to support the collation and analysis of evidence, and giving time for reflection.

A final research group meeting was planned to discuss results, draw conclusions, enabling us to celebrate the work and to examine our findings in relation to our initial list of qualities and skills.

We sought parental permission through personal consultation by key workers with all parents of children involved in the project. All families were

Name:	Date:
Observations *What have my observations told me?*	
Questioning *What has been the result of my questioning?* *What have I learnt about effective questioning?*	
Adaptability *How have I adapted my planning to support this child's interests?*	
Reciprocity *How have I been responsive to this child?*	
Learning environment *What have I learnt about the learning environment in terms of supporting this child?*	
Spontaneity *In what way have I been able to be spontaneous in my responses to this child?*	
Commitment *What has supported my commitment to fully engaging with this child?*	

Figure 5.2 A framework for analysing interventions

given a letter explaining the purpose of the project, and asking for signed permission.

Figure 5.3 summarises the methodologies used.

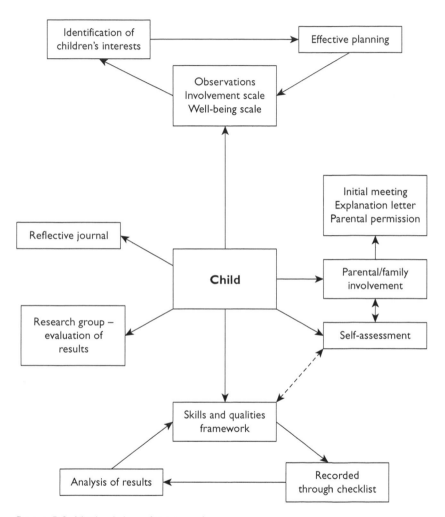

Figure 5.3 Methodology framework

Research findings

Observations/involvement/well-being scales

The involvement and well-being scales were new to participants, and yielded interesting results, suggesting a slight but consistent increase in involvement/

well-being levels as staff worked with children over a period of time. I suggest that as participants focused on children's activity, and were able to identify interests, confirming the success of activities with reference to involvement scales, they were able to better support children and to engage them. Supported by reflections from participants' journals and self-analysis, the evidence is compelling. Their introduction proved to be an important development, and the use of involvement and well-being scales are now being introduced throughout the centre. Use of involvement and well-being scales proved to be a significant tool in identifying the needs of young children as they interact with the learning environment, helping participants to really focus on how far that environment was meeting children's needs, and to make appropriate adjustments.

Name	Date	Involvement level	Well-being level
Child C	25/5/06	4	5
Child S	14/3/06	4	4
	21/4/06	4	4
	8/5/06	4	5
	23/5/06	4	4
Child O	21/4/06	?	1
	2/5/06	2	2
	8/5/06	4	3
Child P	2/5/06	4	4
Child A	14/3/06	2–3	4
	15/3/06	3–4	4
Child T	14/3/06	3–4	3–4
	15/3/06	4	4
Child B	26/5/06	1	2
	22/6/06	2–3	2
Child R	26/5/06	4	2–3
	22/6/06	4–5	3–4
Group Observation	5/5/06 (am)	2–3	3
	5/5/06 (pm)	4	4
	18/5/06 (am)	4	4
	18/5/06 (pm)	5	5
	6/6/06 (am)	4	4
	6/6/06 (pm)	4	4

Figure 5.4 Involvement/well-being levels

Most interesting were the children identified with low levels of well being at the outset, and the careful analysis staff brought to this information. Whilst lower levels of involvement required an analysis of the curriculum available, and how this met the current needs of the children involved, identifying the causes for low levels of well being was more complex, and for some participants led to a deeper understanding of the nature of motivation and involvement. After an analysis of the qualities/skills framework, I include a case study, which shows how the framework helped one participant in the analysis of one child's needs, and how she could best support these.

Qualities/skills framework

The qualities/skills analysis form provided a framework for participants to evaluate each observation session. This proved to be a good reflective tool, giving participants an effective means of structuring their thinking after each targeted intervention. The categories provided good information about our understanding of how we effectively support young children's learning. Participants' use of the framework also identified problems with some of the categories themselves, with participants quickly identifying where they felt the framework needed changing. This provided valuable information during the final evaluative meeting, leading to a revision of the framework (see 'Group meetings/project evaluation' below).

A summary and analysis of the categories (below) reveals participants' detailed thinking around the strategies they employ to facilitate successful learning experiences. Two participants tended to focus on what they had learnt about the individual child in each intervention. Two (more experienced) participants generalised their comments, drawing wider conclusions about their interventions.

Observations

This produced a lot of information about how we support children. Making regular observations is integral to our practice. One participant shared the difficulty of observing/getting involved at the same time. All identified the key role of the adult, and how this differed from child to child. Some children, who depended on an adult presence, needed the support more than others. Different children required different types of intervention when it came to facilitating involvement. Three participants identified the importance of knowing when to intervene and when to watch – intervention is not always appropriate, and there is a danger that children can be swamped by attention that doesn't allow them to develop their own ideas (and motivation, independence). They revealed the sensitivity they brought to their role. Those participants who were able to generalise their observations generated particularly valuable information; gradually developing a curriculum area, for example, so that an anxious child is able to access the area, build confidence and remain engaged over a period of days. This enabled children to build on their previous day's experience. Facilitating play to enable children to work together without dominating, as an adult partner, emerged as another key observation. We learned to look past the mess and to observe the quality of the play and the importance of challenging ourselves as practitioners to focus on the content of the play, and not to be sidetracked by inconvenience. One participant noted that a 'loud, vigorous screaming game can mean a child is operating at a high level'. This was play that was 'complex, imaginative and it excited, scared and fulfilled this child and her friends'. The desire for friendship was a key motivator, and can play as important a role in engaging children as the activity itself. For some children (see 'Case study – Child O' below) this was the prime motivator. Finally, one participant focused on group play, exploring the introduction of figures from popular culture. She observed that these figures were used as a way into imaginative play. Although the play was initially superficial, as the initial excitement wore off children became more involved.

Questioning

This category immediately came under close scrutiny. Participant A noted that she was 'fed up with this box!' For her, the key was conversation. She stressed listening and responsiveness. Participant B talked of the subtlety of knowing when to question, observing that it can put children off. Participant C asked how effective her questions were in helping her intervention with a child craving adult attention. How could she find the most appropriate way of supporting him through her interactions? All participants noted that questioning was not always an appropriate response, stressing the importance of listening and gathering information first. Verbal responses needed to clearly relate to and support children's interests. Participant A noted that 'conversation is the key' describing how she supported and extended imaginative role-play with a hospital theme. Sometimes short enquiry-type questions were required to help the practitioner to access the play. And for some children lacking confidence, simple questions, requiring one-word answer/gesture responses, enabled a child to indicate her wishes without requiring extended talk.

Adaptability

Participants referred to the need to 'tune in' to the child, and 'taking a lead' from the child. For one participant it was about being responsive to a child and helping to facilitate. Participants found that this category and 'reciprocity' overlapped, and used them flexibly when recording responses.

Reciprocity

One participant talked about helping by discussing plans and facilitating skills – working alongside children and encouraging support from more experienced children to those less experienced. Another participant related this category to her introduction of figures from popular culture – providing resources identified as of interest to individual children, and having an open mind, attempting to link home/centre experiences. Two participants who team-worked demonstrated reciprocity in their organisation and approach, bouncing ideas off each other and providing practical, organisational support. The sharing of ideas and of interest and enthusiasm generated momentum for the work, and proved an important part of the relationship between participants and myself.

Learning environment

This category provided a rich source of information – participants identified practical priorities, which led to effective support for imaginative play, in particular the importance of encouraging free-flow play. Where children were able to move resources around the learning environment spontaneously in order for play to develop, the play was identified as being richer. A picnic, for example, could enable children to gather resources/dress up in the home corner area, then move to the block area for the picnic to take place. The movement around the room itself lent momentum and purpose to the game, leading to long periods of pleasure and involvement. Similarly, with popular culture figures, it was noticed that when children were able to move the focus of play from one space to another, play was extended and involvement deepened. For example, superhero figures were moved from a small world scenario to the water tray, which led to extended play and experimentation. Dinosaurs had already been set up in this space, and readily represented the villains. The water provided opportunities for the superheroes to swim in order to escape the dinosaurs. The turbulence caused in the water caused great delight and exploration. The children were 'laughing in delight'. This participant concludes that 'the children who are regularly using action heroes are using them to explore a wide variety of learning experiences. Rather than stultifying play, as I thought might be the case, they are enriching it'.

Spontaneity

One participant identified the importance of involving themselves in children's play based on understanding (through observations), and on knowing when to stand back. When successful, this supported the development of play. For example, when children engaged in a hospital role-play scenario (set up as a result of an observation) she noted that boys were initially reluctant to engage in the play, which took place in the home corner. She decided that the home corner environment was seen as the domain of girls, and was therefore not a space where they felt ownership or purpose. By referring to children by name and consulting on the condition of individual patients, using appropriate role-play titles (e.g. 'doctor') she facilitated their involvement. She was then able to introduce and model a wider, relevant vocabulary.

Commitment

For all participants the key points were first, a fascination with seeing how play develops and what direction it takes. Second, great pleasure in seeing the satisfaction that the play brought to children. One participant referred to the high levels of involvement and well being evident during the role-play. Finally, two participants identified the pleasure of supporting individual children to access group play and to develop relationships.

Use of the framework in conjunction with the involvement and well-being scales clearly demonstrated successful intervention for individual children. Three participants had used the project to target children in their key groups who they felt needed support. In two cases, the children targeted showed low levels of well being, and were of particular concern. A case study of Child O follows, giving an overview of how Participant A used the framework over a number of interventions in order to evaluate her support and raise levels of well being and involvement.

Case study – Child O

An analysis of Child O demonstrates how the qualities/skills framework provided information about one child who showed low levels of well being. This had in fact informed the decision of the participant to focus on this child for the purposes of the project. The participant demonstrates clear pedagogical leadership in her planning and interactions, tailoring her interventions to the child's current needs. At the outset of the project, Child O is identified with a level of well being measuring 1. The participant has difficulty determining her level of involvement. In the self-analysis, the participant identifies in her observation the child's lack of confidence, and desire for friendship, something she is currently unable to fulfil. She understands that the child needs simple questions at this time – particularly those requiring one-word answers or gestures. This enabled her to indicate her wishes without requiring extended talk, something she found difficult with her low level of confidence. Looking at the learning environment, the participant reflected that she needed to use what the child liked using in her self-directed play in order to work with her, and develop her confidence (and the relationship). Her commitment was strengthened by the child's obvious pleasure at the end of the session, as she plays successfully with another child – someone that she identifies as a potential (and desirable) friend. A following session sees the practitioner again recognising the importance of standing back ('not worrying that I should be interacting all the time') and giving the child space. She appreciates just how hard this child is working at making friends, and on being included in the play. By the third observation, the child is identified as less anxious and more comfortable. She now values an adult presence that is 'quiet and companionable' – her body language demonstrates less tension. She sees how to work with the learning environment for this child, developing an area gradually so that the child feels comfortable, and gradually extending her areas of interest. During this final observation, the child's levels of well being have risen to 3 (from 1 in the first observation). Involvement levels have risen to 4. The participant's commitment has been strengthened by the child's decreasing anxiety and apprehensiveness when invited to play.

Figure 5.5 shows a summary of the reflections made by Participant A in relation to this child, using the qualities/skills framework.

Observations *What have my observations told me?*	1 2 3	Child wants to have friends – needs time to gain in confidence PSE all-important. Short observations gave me lots of information to consider and evaluate (increased understanding about the complexity of children making friends) Less anxious – more comfortable
Questioning *What has been the result of my questioning?* *What have I learnt about effective questioning?*	1 2 3	Simple questions needed – particularly those requiring one-word answer/gesture (enables her to indicate wishes without requiring extended talk that she currently finds difficult – confidence issue None – watching and listening (able often to learn more by watching and listening – then able to plan for further needs) Values adult company that is quiet and companionable (body language demonstrates less tension)
Adaptability *How have I adapted my planning to support this child's interests?*	1 2 3	Initial observations show child interested in water play – doll activity designed to include bathing As above Developing an area gradually to enable child to feel comfortable in an area and then extend the area of interest
Reciprocity *How have I been responsive to this child?*	1 2 3	As above As above – helps me to plan effectively for *this* child As above

Figure 5.5 Qualities/skills analysis – Participant A (Child O)

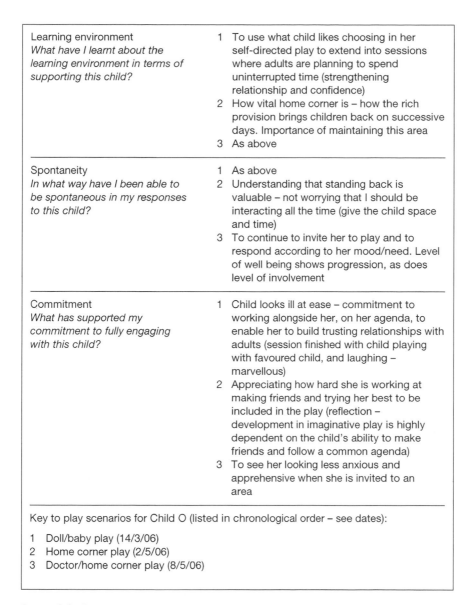

Learning environment *What have I learnt about the learning environment in terms of supporting this child?*	1 To use what child likes choosing in her self-directed play to extend into sessions where adults are planning to spend uninterrupted time (strengthening relationship and confidence) 2 How vital home corner is – how the rich provision brings children back on successive days. Importance of maintaining this area 3 As above
Spontaneity *In what way have I been able to be spontaneous in my responses to this child?*	1 As above 2 Understanding that standing back is valuable – not worrying that I should be interacting all the time (give the child space and time) 3 To continue to invite her to play and to respond according to her mood/need. Level of well being shows progression, as does level of involvement
Commitment *What has supported my commitment to fully engaging with this child?*	1 Child looks ill at ease – commitment to working alongside her, on her agenda, to enable her to build trusting relationships with adults (session finished with child playing with favoured child, and laughing – marvellous) 2 Appreciating how hard she is working at making friends and trying her best to be included in the play (reflection – development in imaginative play is highly dependent on the child's ability to make friends and follow a common agenda) 3 To see her looking less anxious and apprehensive when she is invited to an area

Key to play scenarios for Child O (listed in chronological order – see dates):

1 Doll/baby play (14/3/06)
2 Home corner play (2/5/06)
3 Doctor/home corner play (8/5/06)

Figure 5.5 Continued

Participant A reflects in her journal that Child O's levels of involvement and well being are rising. She is 'definitely more responsive to me – will this continue, or will level fluctuate according to adult/peers responses to her? I need to give her regular input'.

In summary, the qualities/skills framework helped participants to identify a number of strategies that supported the learning and development of young children, and to relate these to the principles established at the outset of the project. The final evaluative group meeting led to a re-evaluation of these, which is discussed below (see p. 100).

Research journals

The reflective research journal proved to be a valuable tool for participants when it came to generalising learning from observations recorded using the qualities/skills analysis framework. It gave space for lengthier reflections: for articulating thoughts and feelings that were tentative and exploratory. Participants used the journals to explore feelings about how they were working and interacting, to reflections on the curriculum and how it could be adapted to successfully support children in different circumstances. And importantly, it caused participants to question practice – if children benefit from taking resources from one area of the curriculum to another, why do we discourage it? Practice was found to vary in subtle ways from room to room. The journal provided a focus for explicitly questioning practice. The workload, in terms of writing and record keeping, was referred to by a number of participants. Participant A felt that 'this project is lots of hard work, however, informative and exciting!' She also felt that 'if I don't do a lot of writing that aids reflection, how will I do a good job?' There is journal evidence that providing an opportunity to focus on children's play gave space to participants to become absorbed and learn from what they observed.

Participant A was able to 'link my new learning gained from this research with the play I observe every day'. She also linked her learning to planning further interventions through small key group sessions. The journals revealed participants' fascination with the play they observed. Participant A was 'astonished at the complexity of this play and the sophisticated restructuring of the play'. Experienced practitioners were revitalised, expressing exhilaration. Participant B said that she felt she wanted to write about other children because so many children were deeply focused. There were struggles. Participants grappled with the difficulty of observing/interacting/recording – Participant D speculated about using video to capture and analyse. But the overall feeling was one of enthusiasm – Participant A again: 'What is interesting as I look at this work is its breadth and the impressive levels of involvement and well-being that are achieved during imaginative play'.

The introduction of popular culture figures (also supported by comics) provided a lot of debate and reflection. Concerns did seem to quickly evaporate, despite initial reservations. Participant D noted that whilst initial feelings were that the play seemed superficial, as the play developed in different curriculum areas, using different resources, play became more collaborative, and children more involved. Participant A felt that 'the boys have had their interest in action heroes recognised at last.They are able to incorporate these into their play and the violence I feared has been minimal. Rather, they play out morals around good/evil – generally the figure considered good always triumphs'. Initial concerns about the potential violence, and the consumerist aspect of these toys were reconciled to the perceived wider benefits. Play quickly moved on, with the new resources providing a means of exploring children's deeper concerns. This echoes the observations of Vivian Gussin Paley, in a rich description of children's imaginative role play:

> The children were actors on a moving stage, carrying out philosophical debates while borrowing fragments of floating dialogue. Themes from fairy tales and television cartoons combined with social commentary and private fantasy to form a tangible script that was not random and erratic.
>
> (Paley, 1988, p. 12)

The process of reflection and discussion, as well as generating high levels of enthusiasm, generated new understandings. As a model for staff development, it seemed that involving practitioners closely in pedagogical development produced richer results, and a high level of commitment.

Self-assessment – the child's voice

Here, F tells the story of his superhero play:

> I was doing those superheroes. Me and C was the giants. The superheroes were stuck in the mud [represented by paper wrapped around them and sellotaped]. C had Spiderman, I had Batman. I bring the fighting Red Ranger and he took the sellotape off. Then they got out but they stay still 'cos they were ice. That was the invisible baddy.

Using the superheroes in the graphics area allowed for a novel use of resources and skills, and an aid to storytelling. Allowing for a more flexible choice of resources enabled F to go in a different direction with his story. What came first, the desire to wrap the figures, or the need to represent mud? Importantly, allowing this play to flow from one area to another supported boys to access an area often dominated by girls.

In another scenario, action heroes were taken to the water tray. This scenario has been described above in the analysis of the learning environment. One child subsequently told his story of the action to Participant A, who acted as scribe:

> I was getting ready to play a boat game and Batman fell in the crocodiles. All the crocodiles eat him for dinner. I helped him. I was Spiderman. I helped him, I crawled on the floor and I got the crocodile. He didn't get me 'cos I'm good. I got Batman and now he's safe. At the end Spiderman

went on crocodile's leg and he didn't get eaten. That's 'cos the crocodile was under the water and he never knew. Crocodile was very sad 'cos he can't eat Spiderman and Batman.

This again affirms the ongoing exploration of morality that is played out is these scenarios. These stories were told some time after the event: elaborate descriptions of the action recalled in retrospect.

This flow of play led to deep involvement, which could continue over a period of days. Children's descriptions also focused on personal relationships, and the significance of being with their friends, evidenced by the reflections of three girls. Participant A organised a self-assessment session, to review an ongoing game, sharing photos with three friends. S said: 'I was just playing with my baby. He was playing. I put her shorts on and this is my friend O and C. We play in the park – me and C put the cover down for picnic in the park. We put it on the ground.' She then takes the photo away to share it with O and C and they chat together about the picnic play. Lots of discussions and laughter are heard about the game. O reflected (looking at the pictures), 'I made food for the baby to eat. I be the best friend with S and C. They doing playing like me and we start singing Bob the Builder. And J come and put food in the basket for the baby.' This is a bilingual child speaking, who spoke only French on her arrival at the centre. A learning environment, which offers meaningful opportunities for children to engage with each other in imaginative role play, provides an effective support for language development. All of the children refer to their peers as 'friends' or 'best friends' during these discussions. Participant A notes that 'imaginative play and ownership of the joint scenarios is evidently a significant factor of role play to these children'.

Group meetings/project evaluation

The final project evaluation meeting allowed for a full discussion of the framework, and consequent revision of the categories. The 'questioning' category, viewed negatively by participants as they began using the framework, was the first to be discussed. It was decided that 'dialogue' provided a more accurate description of the process. This better characterised a positive engagement with, and response to children's interests. Participants had also found the distinction between 'adaptability' and 'reciprocity' blurred. It was felt that 'empathy' better expressed the original intention of 'reciprocity'. The emphasis here is clearly on 'tuning in' to the child. 'Adaptability' then referred clearly to the adult's ability to respond to the child's interests, and modify planning and expectations accordingly. The importance of reflection was discussed at length. Why did this not feature in our original list? It had been implicit in our thinking throughout (we were using reflective research journals) and clearly needed to be included. The process of working with children is subtle, and demands sensitivity and responsiveness – it could be a small

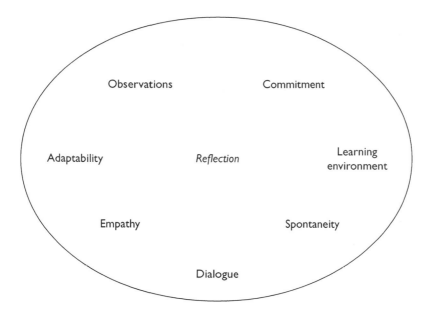

Figure 5.6 Supporting young children's learning

thing that starts/extends play. The static list of qualities and skills was re-conceptualised, with 'reflection' underpinning the whole process (see Figure 5.6). We wanted to portray the qualities and skills as dynamic and inter-related – not as a static list. Further discussion also highlighted the importance of experience – all practitioners involved in the project were experienced and knowledgeable. Training would clearly be needed for less experienced practitioners.

Conclusion

Undertaking the research into imaginative play provided an opportunity to look into how effective learning takes place. During the research we found that our beliefs about the importance of play were well founded, and discovered ways of supporting its ongoing development within the centre. Beginning a research project is a commitment that needs careful consideration and planning. It must be balanced against other commitments, and allow time for all parti-cipants to plan, reflect and discuss, and get the balance right between oppor-tunities for discussion, individual support, research and reflection. Involving participants at the outset of the research project in identifying the focus for research proved critical for commitment. The ongoing group discussions also proved effective and supportive. Where I believe action could have been more effective was in individual support. Developing planned, supportive responses to individual participants could have further enhanced confidence, and raised contributions across the research group.

I was impressed by the potential of the group, as things came together by the end of the research process. Without carefully planned time and support participants will feel a sense of frustration, stress and ultimately, failure. It should be a positive process; even if results are unpromising or unreliable, it is a learning experience. The initial period of uncertainty, as we struggled to find a focus was difficult. It demanded responsiveness and flexibility – for some participants it proved stressful. Living with the uncertainty was a necessary process.

A commitment to team working did lead to a far stronger research focus and structure – I learnt to let go of ideas and to work with the momentum of the research group. The benefits were a carefully explored and documented investigation, which also resulted in the establishment of an effective team. I learnt the effectiveness of small, task-based teams in the exploration of ideas and development of practice.

The research verified for me the universal commonalities between adult and child learning, and the importance of paying attention to the learning process for adults, as well as children. It has highlighted the importance of development being rooted in individual and group practice, in intrapersonal reflection, and the integration of new learning, and interpersonal learning, sharing and discussing ideas and developing new understandings. Fundamental to our work are relationships. Wenger emphasises the importance of 'active participation in social communities'. We must develop

> inventive ways of engaging students in meaningful practices, of providing access to resources that enhance their participation, of opening their horizons so they can put themselves on learning trajectories they can identify with, and of involving them in actions, discussions, and reflections that make a difference to the communities that they value.
>
> (Wenger, 1998, p.10)

The process itself, as a means of professional development, has implications for the ways in which we develop practice. Finding ways of facilitating ongoing development through practitioner research, involving practitioners in diverse and meaningful groups to drive change from a shared basis in vision and principles is a future challenge. Well-organised and planned practitioner research can release creativity and enthusiasm, leading to the development of practice in early years settings.

In our own setting, the research has contributed to our understanding of how young children learn, and the subtle strategies we use to ensure we make the most of opportunities to engage and inspire. It has led to an understanding of how using popular culture can not only motivate and enthuse, but also provide comfort and familiarity, helping children to make links with home life. Using involvement and well-being scales made an impact on all parti-cipants, focusing attention on the processes of learning. Giving involvement and well being a high profile ensures that children's interests and needs remained paramount, and inspired confidence with participants. Their effec-tiveness as a tool has led to adoption as a centre policy.

My involvement in the action research project has given me a greater appreciation of the way in which knowledge is constructed – action research provided an ideal opportunity to test and explore understanding. Fullan's assertion that 'turning information into knowledge is a social process' (Fullan, 2001, p.6) held true. Through dialogue and co-construction we were able to develop a model of adult–child interaction, which allowed us to examine our own practice. Lather's observation that research should empower individuals to change, as well as understand, underlines the human dimension to edu-cational research (Lather, 1991, p.52). It is not only a process for generating new knowledge, but also a tool for individual and collective human develop-ment. Knowledge is not something that is 'out there', but within us, and between us, in our interactions with the world.

Reflections and questions

David has argued for the important role of play in children's development. In this project, this meant tolerating children moving resources around, more noise and mess.

* How do you respond to children moving resources around in your setting?
* How do different workers in your setting perceive increased noise and mess?
* Are these the sorts of issue you discuss: among yourselves and/or with the children?

Applying learning to practice

* You might begin by thinking about 'play' and what constitutes play.
* Making observations of children's play gives you data on which to operate. You could try out using the framework developed by this team to reflect on your observations.
* You might then want to experiment with allowing children to take the lead more, including moving resources around more often and see how the play develops.

References

Carr, M. (2001) *Assessment in Early Childhood Settings: Learning Stories*, London: Paul Chapman Publishing.
Elliott, J. (1991) *Action Research for Educational Change*, Milton Keynes: Open University Press.

Fullan, M. (2001) *Leading in a Culture of Change*, San Francisco: Jossey-Bass.

Gura, P. and Hall, L. (2000) Self Assessment – Listening to Children as They Learn, in *EYE – Early Years Educator*, June, London.

Isaacs, S. (1930) *Intellectual Growth in Young Children*, London: Routledge.

Laevers, F. (ed.) (1994) *The Leuven Involvement Scale for Young Children*, Leuven, Belgium: Centre for Experiential Education.

Lather, P. (1991) *Getting Smart: Feminist Research and Pedagogy with/in the Postmodern*, London: Routledge.

Lewin, K. (1997) [1948] *Resolving Social Conflicts and Field Theory in Social Science*, Washington: American Psychological Association.

Paley, V. (1988) *Bad Guys Don't Have Birthdays – Fantasy Play at Four*. Chicago: The University of Chicago Press.

Paley, V. (2004) *A Child's Work: The Importance of Fantasy Play*, London: University of Chicago Press.

Piaget, J. (1977) *The Essential Piaget: An Interpretive Reference and Guide*, ed. Gruber, H.E. and Voneche, J.J., London: Routledge and Kegan Paul.

Vygotsky, L.S. (1978) *Mind in Society: The Development of Higher Psychological Processes*, London: Harvard University Press.

Wenger, E. (1998) *Communities of Practice: Learning, Meaning and Identity*, Cambridge: Cambridge University Press.

Chapter 6

Knowing individual children through involving their parents

Janette Harcus

In this chapter you will find:

- An account of a small practitioner-led action research project designed to help staff get to know children better in a nursery setting.
- Some discussion of 'self-concept' and 'othering'.
- Questioning of the power imbalance that exists between professionals and parents.

Introduction/context

This chapter presents my own interactionist thinking and practice about supporting and developing young children's learning. It draws on my own experience of trying to help children make links between new and existing ideas, skills, experiences and feelings.

The concept of making links stems from the work of Piaget (1940), who theorized that learning is an active process in which children either *assimilate* new experiences into thought structures they have already developed or *accommodate* new information by adjusting previous thought structures to accommodate new patterns. In this theory the child needs to work out the link between the existing and new experience so that their thinking can adapt through either accommodation or assimilation. It is through this adaptation to the world that learning is advanced. Piaget described this continuous re-adjustment as a process of *equilibrium*. Piaget explained that

> each new behaviour consists not only in re-establishing equilibrium but also in moving towards a more stable equilibrium than that which preceded the disturbance.

> (Piaget 1940 p.7)

Knowing a child well is an important prerequisite to helping them learn. It is my experience and belief that a practitioner cannot support learning effectively if they do not know enough about a child, their family's context and ideas, the experiences they have had and the family values that underpin them. A practitioner cannot help a child make links in their experiences if they are unsure to what they are linking new learning.

The project presented in the following pages details a period of practitioner action research that I undertook at the nursery where I am Teacher/Manager, supported by the nursery staff team and a group of twelve children and their parents, during the last months of 2006 and early 2007. Part of an Early Years Centre on the south east coast of England, the nursery offered twenty-six funded places, for children aged 3 and 4.

The staff views, involvement and participation that influenced my investigations are drawn mainly from the two established core team members working within the nursery at the time. Time constraints meant I was unable to involve the temporary workers. This was unfortunate as undoubtedly their views and opinions would have added much to the study.

The locality where the centre is sited scores highly on the indices of deprivation used by the Office of National Statistics to identify those communities who are in need of the greatest range of services. There is a rich diversity of cultures, parenting styles and life experiences within the families that access the nursery for their children.

The centre is managed by a large, national childcare charity which is highly committed to inclusion and the celebration of diversity. The charity's policies and ethos have a strong influence on the approach and practice within the nursery. The staff are influenced by the work of Whalley (2001 p.97), who argues that it is the responsibility of the practitioner to continue to offer wider and more diverse ways for parents to be involved rather than to simply assume lack of interest on the part of the parent if they do not get involved.

Approach to the research

I approached the study using Elliott's (2001) framework for practitioner action research. The cyclical series of steps he suggests seemed clear and straightforward and fitted with my own thoughts about discussing with staff to find the area of action we wished to impact on, finding out about the current situation, making some changes and then evaluating the impact of the changes. I have summarized his action steps as follows:

- identifying the idea
- reconnaissance
- describing the facts
- explaining the facts
- constructing the plan
- implementing and monitoring the action steps.

I was mindful that to act alone could create resentment and inequality in terms of staff perception of power and control and I wanted to make the whole reflective process of practitioner research part of the work of the nursery. The timeline for the project was as follows:

Table 6.1 Timeline for a project

October 06	– discuss general idea with staff
	– develop and undertake reconnaissance activities
	– collect data
November 06	– discuss and analyse data
	– develop actions
December 06	– undertake action activities
	– collect data
January 07	– undertake action activities
	– collect data
February 07	– analyse data
	– develop changes to practice

The general idea for the project

I used one of our weekly pedagogical staff meetings to discuss the general idea for the project. We generated a long list of questions and also began to think about how we might explore them. The general idea seemed to be; how well do we know children already? Are our current ways of knowing them effective and what do we do with the information we have?

Through the reconnaissance stage of the cycle I wanted to explore as widely as possible what exactly we meant by this general idea. We began at another team meeting to list some questions about it that we could investigate to clarify the idea. They included:

- What do we mean by knowing individuals?
- What use do we make of children's individuality?
- What do we do at the moment to get to know children and their families?
- Do we know what is important to individual parents?
- Do we know the significant people in children's lives?
- Do we know what experiences children have at home?
- Which children do we know well, which not so well?
- Do we know those children and families who are most like ourselves best?
- Which parents do we speak to most and least?
- What do we speak about?

Developing the reconnaissance activities

Through discussions with my tutor and within the team I identified some methods to gather evidence that would help us answer these reconnaissance questions.

Table 6.2 Reconnaissance activities

Technique	Participant	Focus	Purpose
Activity 1 Questionnaire	staff	to find out staff's views about which children they knew well and what they interpreted 'knowing an individual well' to mean	to identify some common threads of definition and analyse why staff know particular children
Activity 2 Diary sheet	parents	to identify the everyday activities that children were involved in outside nursery	to illuminate some aspects of children's lives that staff were unaware of and stimulate debate about the usefulness of this information to discover how difficult parents found the exercise and consider whether we might regularly build such a request into our ongoing practice
Activity 3 Questionnaire	parents	to identify the significant people in their child's life	to reveal what we knew and didn't know about children and stimulate debate about how useful such information could be for staff in developing relationships
Activity 4 Record sheet	staff	to record interactions with parents over the course of a week	to reveal evidence of which parents we actually spoke to and what about
Activity 5 Short interviews	parents	to identify when they had last spoken to a member of staff and what it had been about	to offer a parents' perspective on staff/parent interactions

The project

As I researched the literature I found it led me time and time again to thinking more about the child's context and identity which is namely their home and family environment. Harter (1999) points out how children often describe themselves in terms of their behaviour, possessions and preferences. Children's own views of themselves are usually positive and do not distinguish between the real and the ideal. They do not typically allow contradictions of traits or see their attributes in comparison with others as is typical of adult evaluations of self.

It would have been useful to talk to the children about their views about themselves as part of my initial exercise of finding out how much staff felt they knew about children. Identity is about our own views of ourself and how this impacts on how others see us. The staff's views of the children typically included more references to social and psychological aspects than to physical or active traits. On reflection, I should have placed more emphasis on asking parents about their views on the child's individuality. I think this would have revealed a lot about the family's values and aspirations and possibly given an insight into how these contribute to the development of the child's self concept.

Harter also makes the point that young children tend to try and match their behaviours to those of important care givers and often evaluate their behaviour in terms of adult standards. Knowing something of what Harter calls a child's socialization history, can help staff to know and understand a child better. She talks about the need for children to receive acceptance and approval in order to develop a positive sense of self. She describes how conditionality can be very damaging to a child's sense of self worth. I am mindful here of how we, albeit unintentionally, treat children whose families are not perceived by us to meet the conditions we value at nursery. I think this could have implications for us as a staff team in terms of our ability to accept children and their families unconditionally and to respond positively to the diversity of parenting styles especially those that are different from our own.

I read with interest some work by Vandenbroeck (1999), which explores this issue. He writes about the way we tend to see people from cultures different to our own as *other*, forgetting that we too are an *other*. He discusses extensively the way that people in a dominant culture tend to try and make others conform to their way of behaving or being, wanting to make *the other, the same*. He discusses the premise that positive self image is fundamental to a child's self concept. Vandenbroeck writes about the multiple identities we have as individuals concerning the way we see our culture, nationality, family heritage and personality. He examines this hierarchy of identities and how this hierarchy is established according to the way the society we live in responds to us. The identities we develop form according to the different roles we have and groups we belong to, and combine to establish who we are and the kind of self image we develop. He then explores the power implicit within these multiple identities and deals with the lack of reciprocity that children from minority cultures often experience. The term *other cultures* applies to all of us, as all individuals have a complex mix of identities which define their individuality. The education system can be seen as a dominant culture and those with alternative viewpoints about what is good and best for young children and how they should be raised can be viewed as minority cultures. This is something we have discussed at nursery but it needs to be the subject of further dialogue.

The five reconnaissance activities formed a major part of the data we generated and played a major part in developing our learning. The data collected provided the scaffolding on which we developed our actions.

Reconnaissance Data Collection Activity 1: A staff questionnaire to find out staff's views about which children they knew well and what they interpreted 'knowing an individual well' to mean

Of the twenty-one children that staff discussed, just under a third were felt to be known well, about a third not so well and the remainder not well at all.

I grouped staff's references about what made a child individual to reveal an indication of the types of definitions about individuality that staff were using. The four most frequently referred to areas were: emotional needs/well being; activities child enjoys at nursery; family size/position of child in family; and disruption or challenging circumstances in family life.

Reconnaissance Data Collection Activity 2: diaries of what children do when not at nursery

I grouped the responses of the five returned diary sheets to provide a summary of the eleven main types of activities mentioned by parents. Most frequent of these was watching TV, playing at home alone, visiting friends and relatives and being involved with everyday family routines.

After looking at this information staff immediately began to say things like, 'now I see why she . . .', 'hey, you know what we could set up for . . .'.

Reconnaissance Data Collection Activity 3: a questionnaire for parents about the significant people in their child's life

I grouped the responses of the five returned sheets to try and identify any common patterns or threads. I hoped that this would help us to see the sorts of regular contacts children attending the nursery had. The responses were individual and varied especially in terms of family size. There were some commonalities which included regular personal contacts with close family members, contacts with family and friends through phone and email and the significance of family pets.

For some of the individual children the staff team were surprised to learn of the relationships with extended family and had not previously been aware of their significance in the child's life. For three children it seemed that nursery was the only time they interacted with children other than their siblings.

Reconnaissance Data Collection Activity 4: record of interactions with parents/staff over the course of a week

The number of parental interactions recorded was thirty-nine. The number of individual parents was twenty-four. Eleven of the interactions were parent-initiated and twenty-eight staff-initiated. The lengths of interactions varied from under two minutes, and this was by far the most frequent, to over five minutes.

From the notes made of the subject of conversations, I was able to summarize the topics of conversation. These most frequently referred to issues of health, activities enjoyed at nursery, family circumstances and children's behaviour. Only about a quarter were directly linked to children's learning activities. This surprised staff and provoked a lot of discussion.

Reconnaissance Data Collection Activity 5: short interviews with seven parents about their most recent conversation with a member of staff

The responses from the seven parents I spoke to indicated clearly the parents' concern about their child's well being and happiness at nursery, their keenness that their child was noticed and cared for as an individual. They pointed to four main areas of concern:

1   Helping their child to settle in.
2   Awareness of basic physical needs (e.g. sleep) and how these might affect the child at nursery.
3   Concerns about emotional needs and difficulties, especially events at home that might affect the child's well being.
4   Sharing their child's interest to help them make connections with nursery experience.

It became clear that the more contact staff had with a child's family the greater they felt they knew them. This underpins our belief that parents know and understand their own child better than anyone else and our need to engage with parents in order to capitalize on this expertise. If the practitioner knows the experiences and relationships a child engages with at home they can adapt and present new experiences in a way the child can readily access. My central role as an educator is working out how to do this for each individual. Given our knowledge-based curriculum framework, it is even more important.

Bennet (2005) draws precisely this conclusion in his critique of different European approaches to Early Years education. He contrasts our prescriptive pre-primary curriculum with the Nordic countries' emphasis on social pedagogy, well being and broad curriculum aims and notes the range of dilemmas that result. In particular, he points to the difficulty of reconciling the pre-primary approach with the broad traditions of early childhood education that are influenced by the social pedagogic approach, including the need for educators to mediate between the curriculum and the child.

Vygotsky (1978) has the concept of mediation as a central theme in his theories about how children think. He describes the way that higher order thinking is characterized by children and adults mediating their response to an experience rather than simply responding to a stimulus. Helping children in this mediation would seem a worthwhile role for early educators. Vygotsky identified the *zone of proximal development* as the area of learning where a child requires help, the learning that is just outside the child's current capabilities.

> It is the distance between the actual developmental level as determined by independent problem solving and the level of potential development as determined through problem solving under adult guidance or in collaboration with more capable peers.
>
> (Vygotsky 1978 p.86)

Feuerstein (1979) used Vygotsky's work to develop mediated learning experience theory. Research and development by the Israeli writer Klein (1992), which built on this theory, proposed that in order for children to fully access their zone of proximal development, there were four prerequisites that adults need to offer or ensure are present for the child. These are: *intentional focus*, *positive affect*, *competence* and *extension*. Paying attention to these, she argued, would have a profound effect on the child's learning experience.

> Mediated learning as distinct from direct learning through the senses occurs when the environment is interpreted for the child by another person who understands the child's needs, interests, and capacities and who takes an active role in making components of that environment, as well as of the past and future experiences, compatible with the child's current level of understanding.
>
> (Klein 1992 p.108)

Learning opportunities children encounter at home are embedded in significant and important personal events for the child, events that make personal sense. Donaldson (1978) makes this point strongly and argues it is when an experience makes real life human sense to an individual that learning is effective.

By the time they come to school, all normal children can show skill as thinkers and language users to a degree which must compel our respect, so long as they are dealing with real-life meaningful situations in which they have purposes and intentions and in which they can recognise and respond to similar purposes and intentions in others . . . these human intentions are the matrix in which the child's thinking is embedded.

(Donaldson 1978 p.121)

Many researchers point to the fact that it is in these contexts that leaps in learning are made since wanting to know and understand one's own social context is a powerful motivator.

The thought that struck the whole staff team was the amount of knowledge and expertise children have about their own lives and that of their families. When written it seems a very obvious statement but it was not something which we had thought deeply about. We began to question our practice in terms of the opportunities we allowed children to demonstrate this knowledge and how we could better use children's expertise to explore diversity within the group. We also talked about the significance of helping children develop imaginative play scenarios around these home experiences. It was interesting to note that playing at home was not a frequent event in some of the children's lives. At first I was saddened by this lack of play opportunities. On thinking about the work of Dahlberg and Moss (2005), however, I was able to reflect that play as a mechanism for learning is a particular educational approach influenced by, amongst others, Piaget's work. Other perspectives allow for other approaches including watching and talking with adults. Whilst I believe that play is important for young children, I would agree that it is not the only way young children learn. Assuming that play is a universal concept for development may be misleading, since it is based on only one way of thinking about children. The importance and definition of play is clearly different in different cultures.

The data revealed that staff initiate twice as many conversations about children as parents. It seemed likely to us that because we are keen to develop and maintain relationships we were more likely to initiate conversations with parents. Staff noted that as time is limited, it is often not practical to wait for parents to initiate an interaction.

However, whilst this may be so, we needed to consider the possibility of power imbalance. It could be that parents do not perceive it as appropriate for them to question what has been happening at nursery, deferring to staff's perceived professionalism. If our aim is to work closely with parents to better support a child's education, then we need to develop an approach that values what parents think and feel about their child's learning. If we create a situation where parents feel that their views are not important or valued then this will be difficult to achieve. Freire (1970) argues that this imbalance is inevitable in situations like our current system of education where knowledge is viewed as *a gift* that can be given to the less knowledgeable i.e. the parent and child, by the more knowledgeable i.e. the professional. Such a relationship, he argues, is inevitably oppressive and does not allow the oppressed partner to recognize and value their own contribution and knowledge of a situation or experience. He argues that true education is concerned with control over one's own life and only comes as a result of equal dialogue.

> It is not our role to speak to people about our own view of the world, nor to attempt to impose that view on them, but rather to dialogue with the people about their view and ours. We must realize that their view of the world, manifested variously in their action, reflects their situation in the world. Education . . . which is not critically aware of this situation runs the risk . . . of preaching in the desert.
>
> (Freire 1970 p.77)

The most significant data for me personally was that from the interviews with parents because it so clearly gathered the views of what is important to individual parents about their child.

In terms of identifying trends, all the responses focused on the emotional well being of children and on wanting the children to be able to make links between home and nursery experiences both in terms of the content of activities and in terms of the way nursery staff would respond to their needs. The responses seemed to indicate that parents wanted to make sure there was some continuity between the experiences their child had at nursery and at home. This is significant because it illustrates a need to pursue in earnest a shared understanding between parents and staff. The responses also indicated the concerns that parents had about leaving their child in the care of somebody else.

All the parents in the sample seemed interested to talk with staff about their children. This does not always mean that staff and parents are interested in the same things and this returns to Freire's argument about dialogue outlined earlier.

We discussed the data from the reconnaissance at length within the team and identified three actions we wanted to try out as ways of improving how we get to know children that would support them in making connections in their learning.

Action activity 1: second home visit to discuss their child's learning and development

I summarized the responses from the three staff about the four visits carried out as follows:

1   Information about the child's current family life and history – 'I learnt he was an IVF baby, very, very precious'.

Table 6.3 Actions planned following reconnaissance

Technique	Participant	Focus	Purpose
Action activity 1 Second home visit	staff and parents	to discuss children's learning and development	to develop better relationships with parents and encourage a better balance in information sharing
Action activity 2 Photo books	parents	to make photo books of things at home that are important to children	to help widen staff's knowledge of things that are important to individual children
Action activity 3 Videoing	staff and parents	to make a video recording of individual children playing at nursery	to share and discuss with parents what children are doing at nursery and why they are engaging in these ways

2   Relationship with the child and the parent – 'Mum was very welcoming and said she was pleased I'd come as she didn't often have visitors'.
3   Parents' concerns and what they think is important that their child knows – 'She was very keen to show me all he could do, counting and letters and the clock'.
4   Information sharing about home and nursery learning – 'He sang several songs to me, but he never sings at all at nursery'.

The main aspect of the visits that parents reflected on was the contribution to relationships. 'I'd been going through some stuff and things have been hard for him, so I just like talked about it so you can just sort of understand.'

Action activity 2: parents taking photos at home for a photo book about things that are important to their child

I spoke to the two parents who took part in this activity and to the staff team as a whole and summarized the responses.

1   The process: 'I didn't know what to take photos of.' 'It was a long time to develop the photos and get the parents to put comments on and make them up.'
2   Parent's/child's response to the activity: 'He was so pleased and showed his Nan and all.' 'He brings it to me to look at and I've seen him looking at it himself. He's very possessive of it.' 'I think his dad was really pleased that we did it, you know showed we were interested in him and what he likes.'

Action activity 3: sharing video film of children at play in the nursery

I spoke to the two parents whose children had taken part in this activity and to the staff team as a whole. Both were very supportive of the video filming in general.

The parents' responses whilst watching the films with me included: 'See her concentrating face she does that with her mouth at home too'. Some of these comments reflected an awareness in parents of the concept of involvement that as practitioners we could celebrate and develop. The staff responses included: 'It wasn't as long winded as I had expected. You just filmed her over one session.' 'Mum couldn't wait to see her on the film, she was really chuffed.'

I undertook the analysis of the data from the three action activities in relation to two straightforward questions: Does this idea work in practice? Is it useful?

The most obvious difficulty that arose with the home visiting action was the time demands of releasing staff to carry out the visits. The staffing ratio was favourable at the time of the study, so I had hoped that this would make release straightforward. However, the fact that we had two new members of staff and a high level of staff absence through illness during that time made it rather difficult. The mostly positive responses from both staff and children indicated it was worthwhile, so it will be a matter of finding a way to do it. It was clear that most parents were more comfortable in their own homes. I suspect this feeling relates to power relationships and the way parents feel more control and confidence in their own environment. I think I sometimes underestimate how difficult it is for some parents to come in to nursery. This is a recurrent theme in Freire's work (1970) on community education in the terms of his discussion of the *oppressed* and *oppressor* relationship that can be present in professional and non-professional interactions.

The responses from staff clearly indicated that the visits had raised their awareness of children's family circumstances. Having more knowledge about the make up of the family, the child's social networks and about the child's physical home situation enabled staff to make better sense of their own observations and judgements.

Several parent responses referred to the emotional support gained from a good relationship with staff. There was a lot of discussion around children's well being from staff as well. Duncan *et al*. (2004) describe the importance of emotional support for children as a factor for mothers choosing childcare in their study and I think this was echoed in the families involved in my study.

During the visits the conversation about learning interests and cognitive development was limited. It may be that staff lacked the confidence to move beyond the social and emotional aspects of the child's development in their discussions with parents. This was our first experience of follow-up visits and staff may have been over-concentrating on developing relationships.

Staff may have lacked confidence in articulating cognitive development in children and have been unsure of how to share this with parents. Parents may have been unsure what to share with staff and what staff would see as important and significant. I was at first greatly disappointed that staff had not felt able or skilled enough to talk about children's cognitive development. I was heartened to note that practitioners at the Pen Green Centre in Corby, now widely recognized for its successes in working in partnership with parents, found precisely this pattern when they first began.

Initial strategies developed at Pen Green helped

> parents to maintain a creative dialogue with nursery staff and gave us useful information about children's rich social lives, they did not help us to consistently support and extend the child's learning in the nursery . . . It seemed that if parents were to be able to enter into a dialogue about their children's learning, then nursery staff and parents needed to have a shared conceptual framework.
>
> (Whalley 2001 pp.13–14)

Our next action must be to develop this framework.

Children and their families were pleased with the photo books and both reported that they had been well received by the child's wider family. Staff felt the books had emphasized to parents that we were willing to take time and make an effort to get to know their child.

For both children who were involved in this activity, there was a contribution to their self esteem that showed in their pride and excitement about the books. Clark and Moss (2001) talk about the use of photographs and how young children quickly recognize their value and significance in the adult world. In addition they gave staff 'a way to listen to young children about their own lives' (Clark and Moss 2001 p.11), especially where the parent had involved the child in deciding what to photograph. The books did go some way to help staff understand about children's lives but more importantly they gave children a reference to talk about their own lives and a focus for staff to discuss with them.

It was clear from some parents' comments that they had been unsure what to photograph. I think that sharing with parents Laever's concept of 'Involvement' (1994) would have been helpful. It would have helped parents think about the things that interest their child and are therefore likely to be significant to them.

The sharing of video footage with parents was the most successful activity in helping us think about children as individual learners. Many comments offered by parents were linked to learning. The other two action activities gave us more information about a child's social and emotional development rather than their learning. I do not suggest that either are more important since both concepts are interwoven, but I think that, as a team, we are better at thinking and discussing with parents about children's emotional well being and their social relationships. It is in finding out about and sharing children's learning interests that we lack strategies beyond our own nursery observations and internal staff discussions.

An obvious omission was not including video recording of children at home. The time and organizational constraints made it too ambitious to attempt at this time. Being able to draw on children's experiences at home and to draw out with parents the activities in which children become deeply involved would have really helped us to understand children as individuals. It would have made a child's 'cognitive constants' (Whalley 2001 p.146) more accessible to us. Watching their own child on film at nursery and having the opportunity to look closely and think why they might be behaving in particular ways was a source of fascination and delight for both parents.

The responses from parents challenged the assumptions we had made about why children behaved in particular ways and offered an explanation for behaviours we did not understand.

Reflections and discussions

Different strategies work for different families so we need not abandon too quickly those that seemed less effective in this brief study. I need to talk with parents about the strategies we could try as well as presenting others like diaries of learning and video film, photo books and questionnaires and data collection forms similar to those I used in the reconnaissance part of the study.

What I have also learned is that it is important to make a small start with strategies that are possible and then grow and develop from this. I think that perhaps I have been wary of initiating changes because it never seemed the right time. The study has helped me recognize that sweeping changes to our approach are not always needed but rather a series of tentative adjustments that may develop into a change. Trying some small actions with a small group of parents and children can reveal ways to make changes that will have a positive impact.

There were some problems that arose during the process of the study. Notably these were: time constraints, difficulties caused by staff instability and lack of technological expertise. Whilst they had an impact, none of them caused major disruption to the planned methodology.

The study has helped me to adjust my view of my own professional self-importance. When I think about myself as a parent of a 4-year-old at nursery, I am well aware of the learning and development that my daughter receives from our family. I know what knowledge, attitudes and behaviours are important within our family culture and we try to ensure that she develops these. Whilst I acknowledge the contribution her nursery experience makes to this, I certainly do not overestimate the impact it has on her development. Her family is clearly the more powerful educator.

When I go to work, however, and work with other people's children, there is a tendency for me to forget all of this and to overestimate my significance. The study has helped me to challenge this assumption and be more humble about my professional knowledge. I still think that as a nursery team we can offer a lot to support and encourage a child's development but this belief is balanced by the greater role played by the family. Easen *et al.* (1992) talk about the sharing of views about a child in this way:

> The roles of professional experience and parent's every day experience are seen as complementary but equally important. The former constitutes a 'public' (and generalized) form of theory about child development, whilst the latter represents a 'personal theory' about the development of a particular child. An interaction between the two theories or ways of explaining a child's actions may produce an enriched understanding as a basis for both to act in relation to the child.
>
> (Easen *et al.* 1992 p.285)

For all the team there has been an improvement in our understanding of parents as individuals rather than one group and a greater awareness of the need to use a variety of strategies to engage with different parents.

The study has built on the reflective practice we have started to establish within the team. It has emphasized the need for me to be sure I understand what is already going on before I attempt to instigate changes. I think that I am prone to want to make improvements to the way we do things at nursery without really being sure what needs improving. Finding out how a situation is viewed from multiple perspectives before developing actions to improve it will now feature more heavily in my work approach. I learnt that changes to the way we think about children and families take time to embed and be established within the team. This needs to take place through debate and discussion. The team are clearly interested in this process as was demonstrated by the large amount of discussion about the implications and possible causes of trends we identified during the data collection.

Several of the parents involved in the study talked about their increased awareness of their children in terms of seeing things from a different point of view and paying attention to areas that they had not previously thought very much about. Almost all of the parents expressed pleasure at their child being the focus of staff interest and attention. Several expressed the contribution the study had made to their feelings of being valued and listened to. This came across most powerfully in the home visits and the video recording of children playing at nursery. Both of these strategies involved staff taking time to focus with parents on their individual child. The very act of doing this emphasized a commitment and interest to the development of their child that the parents clearly valued.

For the parents of the children involved in the video filming there was an opportunity for us to share the behaviours and attitudes that we as practitioners valued in children and to explain why. This helped in conversations about what children were learning as they played at nursery.

Some parents who agreed to take part did not in the end do so. I was disappointed initially, but came to realize that I needed to respect their decision. For some parents daily difficulties made it too difficult to take on even a small extra thing to do. I could have found a different way to involve them. Others perhaps needed more explanation of why and what I was exploring than I gave them. Ultimately it was a case of accepting that our agendas did not always coincide. It is, however, important not to make assumptions as to why parents do not engage well with staff.

The information we gained surprised us at times. The social isolation of one particular family and the lack of contact with birth fathers for several children were two particular examples. Staff have already begun to discuss possible ways of trying to talk with families about these issues.

The children involved in the study all seemed to enjoy the attention and focus from staff in the range of actions that we explored. The key workers reported an improvement in their relationships with the child, especially in terms of interactions and communications. This was shown in three ways: in increased depth of interactions, in children seeking out more interactions and in parents encouraging a closer relationship between the child and the key worker. I think the latter is particularly important as children who see that their parents value interaction with nursery staff are more likely to engage in it themselves.

Implications for practice

I have always found working with children's families of great interest and I think the study has helped develop both my confidence and my awareness of being respectful of parents' views even when I do not agree with them. It has also raised my awareness of gaining accurate information about children rather than making assumptions based on my limited view of the child at nursery.

In a small study Riddick and Hall (2000) looked at the way both parents and staff described children. They found that staff often made negative assumptions about children and their families, particularly when children were perceived by the staff not to be doing well. Such negativism was more apparent in those situations where parents and staff felt that they did not know each other well.

It has raised my awareness too of my tendency to focus on eliciting the information from parents that I think will be useful or that I think it is important for the staff team to know. I hope that as a result of the study I will be more mindful of enabling parents to focus on what is important to them during discussions with staff. Finding a way to link the two perspectives will better enable us to work together in supporting the child's learning and development, because our focus of attention is more likely to be shared. I think that one way to do this is sharing video of children learning in action.

There have been three main outcomes of the study in terms of what I intend to implement next. These are to continue with second and third home visits for all those parents who want them, to video children and share this with parents for a larger pilot group and to offer some training sessions to parents to share with them some of the frameworks we use to think about children as learners. I think it is important for the team to take forward these actions over the remainder of this academic year, before other changes are undertaken.

We need to look as a team at how the information parents give us can be built in to children's records and plans for learning and how we can be sure we are using the information parents share with us effectively. We may need to make some adjustments to our systems to do this. We also need to look at the information we ask parents to share with us and decide how to include more information about who the significant people are for that child and what children spend their time doing when they are not in nursery.

The final outcome of the study is that action research is now becoming part of the continuing practice in the nursery and will significantly contribute to our development over the coming months and years.

Reflections and questions

Janette was able to express her view, both as a professional worker in the early years and as the parent of a 4-year-old.

*   How often do you try to 'stand in the shoes' of parents using your services?
*   In what ways do you try to reduce the power differential between you and families using your service?
*   How important is it to you to get to know children and families well?

Applying learning to practice

*   You could try out any of the ideas Janette and her team used in order to connect more effectively with children and families.
*   Finding a few minutes to ask parents about the last conversation they had with a member of staff, seems a worthwhile starting point.
*   Bringing children *and* families up for discussion among staff is another way of valuing knowledge of home and home learning.

References

Bennet, J. (2005) Curriculum issues in national policy making OECD, in *European Early Childhood Education Research Journal*, Vol. 13 No. 2 pp.5–23.

Clark, A. and Moss, P. (2001) *Listening to Young Children, The Mosaic Approach*, National Children's Bureau, London.

Dahlberg, G. and Moss, P. (2005) *Ethics and Politics in Early Childhood Education*, RoutledgeFalmer, London.

Donaldson, M. (1978) *Children's Minds*, Fontana, Glasgow.

Duncan, S., Edwards, R., Reynolds, T. and Alldred, P. (2004) Mothers and child care: Policies, values and theories, in *Children and Society*, Vol. 18 No. 4 pp.254–265.

Easen, P., Kendall, P. and Shaw, J. (1992) Parents and educators: Dialogue and developing through partnership, in *Children and Society*, Vol. 6 No. 4 pp.282–296.

Elliott, J. (2001) *Action Research for Educational Change*, Open University Press, Milton Keynes.

Feuerstein, R. (1979) *The Dynamic Assessment of Retarded Performers*, University Park Press, New York.

Freire, P. (1970) *The Pedagogy of the Oppressed*, Penguin Books, London.

Harter, S. (1999) *The Construction of Self*, The Guilford Press, London.

Klein, P.S. (1992) More Intelligent and Sensitive Child (MISC): A new look at an old question, in *International Journal of Cognitive and Mediated Learning*, Vol. 2 No. 2 pp.105–115.

Laevers, F. (1994) *The Leuven Involvement Scale for Young Children, LIS-YC Manual*, Centre for Experiential Learning, Leuven University, Belgium.

Piaget, J. (1940) The mental development of the child, in *Six Psychological Studies* edited by Elkind, D. (1980) Harvester Press, Brighton [originally published in *Juventus Helvetica*].

Riddick, B. and Hall, E. (2000) Match or mismatch: The perceptions of parents of nursery age children related to those of the child's main nursery workers, in *Early Years Education*, Vol. 8 No. 2 pp.113–128.

Vandenbroeck, M. (1999) *The View of the Yeti*, Bernard van Leer Foundation, The Hague.

Vygotsky, L.S. (1978) *Mind in Society: The Development of Higher Psychological Processes*, Harvard University Press, London.

Whalley, M. and the Pen Green Centre Team (2001) *Involving Parents in their Children's Learning*, Paul Chapman Publishing, London.

Chapter 7

Acorns to oaks

Growing leadership in community nurseries

Ana Sevilla

In this chapter you will find:

- An investigation of leadership among five female leaders of community nurseries.
- Discussion of what a female construct of leadership might look like.
- Some discussion of 'emotional intelligence', 'Founder's Syndrome' and Maslow's 'Hierarchy of Needs'.

Context of the study

The need for effective dynamic leadership in all early years settings is recognised as a vital component in improving outcomes for young children. This study aims to build a picture of leadership from the perspective of the lives of nursery managers working in the voluntary sector. It is based in a relatively small inner city borough with a wide-ranging population in terms of cultural and economic diversity. The Local Authority (LA) recognises the important role that the voluntary sector has to play in shaping and delivering public services, and building strong communities. The government has also made it clear that the voluntary and community sector has a vital role to play in the *Every Child Matters: Change for Children* programme, and that voluntary sector organisations are key partners for local authorities in the development of children's trusts (DFES 2003). However, with the expansion of childcare through the children's centre and extended schools agendas, relationships are now under pressure and concern is being raised about the sustainability of the community nursery concept.

Historical perspective

Community nurseries evolved out of the playgroup movement of the late 1970s and early 1980s in response to the demand for affordable childcare for working mothers. They were an attempt by (usually middle-class) mothers to fulfil a community need. They were frequently housed in community halls and were originally funded through the Greater London Council (GLC). Limited funding and the need for parents (mothers) to help through a volunteer rota and on fundraising committees provided the opportunity for many women to gain experience, and then qualifications, through their involvement in their child's setting.

The ethos and culture of the community nursery is based on feminist principles in that they were set up by women for women as 'not for profit' organisations. Most are now registered charities. Since the demise of the GLC, funding for the surviving community nurseries has been transferred to local authorities.

A unique feature of the community nursery is the management structure. All community nurseries featured in this paper are managed by a management committee made up of parents whose children currently or have recently attended the setting. The majority of the committee members are not childcare professionals and have limited business skills or management training.

Constructs of leadership

I believe that leaders are people we remember, people who have made a difference, left their mark on their field, on their local community. A study by Hatherley and Lee based on the 'Educational Leadership Project' in New Zealand, defines leadership as

> having a vision, being able to articulate this vision in practice, strengthening links between the early years centre and the community, developing a community of learners, community advocacy and giving children leadership.
>
> (2003, p.15)

I would contend that effective transformational leadership is organic in nature, fluid like a river; it is not something held by an individual, rather something that is shared with others. I particularly like Whitaker's definition of leadership, which incorporates the complexity of the role:

> Leadership is concerned with creating the conditions in which all members of the organisation can give their best in a climate of commitment and challenge. Leadership helps an organisation work well.
>
> (1993, p.74)

Over the last few years there has been considerable interest in the concept of leadership in the early childhood field. Effective leadership is widely accepted as being a key constituent in achieving organisational improvement (OFSTED 2000). The Effective Provision of Pre-school Education (EPPE) project (1999) presents findings that show a strong correlation between the childcare and education qualifications of the centre manager and the quality of provision in the setting.

Theories of leadership

Much of the literature on leadership is androcentric, based on a worldview from a male perspective. Schein's (1995) critique of androgyny theories suggests that there are innate or ingrained socialised differences between males and females. The overwhelming majority of the research has been conducted by men, on men in positions of leadership with organisations that employ predominantly men. I would therefore suggest that the majority of the research on leadership is inappropriate for this study. As theories of leadership are derived principally from a masculine construct, leadership behaviour is often characterised by masculine traits of 'aggressiveness, forcefulness, competitiveness and independence' (Blackmore 1989, p.100).

Recently researchers have argued that traditional theories of leadership are no longer valid in the current changing and complex society (Fullan 1998, Sergiovanni 1998). Theorists are now calling for a new perspective on leadership, one that involves delegation and a shared approach to leadership (Lambert 1989, Day *et al*. 2000). Southworth (1998) discusses 'situational leadership', which involves consideration for the situation or context in which the leader operates. Leithwood *et al*. identify 'cognitive flexibility' – 'controlling one's negative moods and approaching problem situations with an air of calm confidence' (1996, p.92) – as a characteristic of effective leadership. Thus, effective leadership encompasses far more than cognitive skills and behaviour. Early years settings are dynamic organisms, continually evolving and therefore require a flexible leader who is able to adapt.

Women, power and ambition

The career paths of men and women are usually very different. Men tend to follow a clear planned career trajectory, from schooling to employment. Women's career journeys do not necessarily follow such a neat linear path. They tend to have 'stop and start' career pathways as the majority of women have additional family responsibilities and roles that require a constant juggling act. As women, we have many roles as mothers, partners/wives, carers, daughters. Adler *et al*.'s study (1993) found that men viewed their career paths as having clearly defined steps leading to an end goal. Women viewed their career paths more holistically allowing for the reality of their lives. Their study, like others (Grant, 1989, Hart, 1989), found that the career paths of the women studied were described as 'luck' or 'fate' rather than a clearly planned career trajectory.

Emotional intelligence

There is a growing body of research on emotional intelligence and the individual's potential for leadership (Goleman 1998, Dulewicz and Higgs 2000). Emotional intelligence is in essence the capacity to recognise and use your feelings in ways that help get the results you want.

Emotional intelligence connects with women's leadership style. The ability to manage feelings and handle stress is an aspect of emotional intelligence that has been found to be important to success and women naturally tune in to emotions and non-verbal language better than their male counterparts. Emotional intelligence has as much to do with knowing when and how to express emotion as it is with controlling it. For instance, the ability to recognise accurately what another person is feeling enables one to develop a specific competency such as influence. Handling the fear of loss of control can be a significant part of the emotional experience of the leader. Empathy is a particularly important aspect of emotional intelligence.

Methodology

My methodological approach was based on an open interview that allowed for narrative and rich discussion. I wanted to study leadership within a particular organisational and policy context and to find out what leadership is like for the women in my study. I carried out a short pilot study with two participants and this process gave me the opportunity to fine-tune my interview style. From this pilot I learnt not to ask questions but rather to sit back and listen to the stories the women had to tell.

I wanted to understand what leadership means for the women in this study. My methodology was underpinned by the belief that the place to begin studying resilient leaders was by hearing their perspective on their lives and career journeys. I explored what sustained them or kept them where they are. My emphasis was on understanding their constructions of what has enabled them to thrive within the context and constraints of the community nursery.

The participants were all female, aged 35–58, three were white British in origin, and two were first generation immigrants. All were employed as managers/co-ordinators of community nurseries that provided a range of services including full day care and family support. Two of the settings were designated children's centres. Four of the five women have spent all of their careers – between fifteen and twenty-five years – in early years, working within the voluntary sector, mostly in the same centre working their way up the promotional ladder. I wanted to explore whether they stayed out of loyalty or fear of change or whether they had really found their utopia.

The parallel between the participants' personal and professional experiences and my own were an important component of the rapport that developed. I wanted a researcher–researched relationship that eliminated any power hierarchy. I knew this would be difficult to achieve. Feminist researchers are particularly concerned with developing empowering and non-hierarchical research methodology. My intention throughout this project was to create a context that would empower these women to reflect on their leadership.

In contrast to mainstream research, which generally seeks to attain value neutrality, feminist researchers often integrate their own personal experiences into their research. I used a method of collecting data that incorporated 'narrative', a method that would allow for deep reflection, dialogue and an appreciation of the journey each individual had experienced in becoming a leader.

After each interview I returned my transcripts to the participants for them to verify that I had recorded their thoughts and feelings accurately and give them the opportunity to add further comments. I then examined the transcripts for evidence of common concepts and characteristics of effective leadership such as adversity, resilience professional growth, etc., and, as Spradley (1980) suggests, analysed the transcripts for cultural themes or domains.

Findings

Once I had collated the data generated through individual in-depth interviews and learning journeys, I began looking for similarities, themes and common threads and comparing my interpretation of the findings with the literature. I expected to find certain skills and behaviours in these women's style of leadership. I also expected to see some of the indicators of effective, trans-formative leadership that I had read about in the literature.

Themes and common threads

Sharing power

The women in this study describe their organisations as having a minimal hierarchical structure with a strong focus on developing relationships with staff members, parents, children and the local community. The nature of the community nursery, managed by a committee of trustees, usually parents, lends itself to a flattened, distributed management structure that is based on a collaborative working relationship and distribution of power. Hall (1996) reported that the women leaders in her study, though committed to sharing power, were aware that ultimately they were the leaders. The women in this study are also highly committed to a collaborative leadership style but at the same time are aware that the burden of responsibility rests on their shoulders:

> I think my leadership style is collaborative. We all carry out a leadership role. I don't like it when I have to assert my authority. Sometimes it can't be helped; I'm the head so if there is an issue I have to get it resolved. But

I try to work in a way that encourages the team to find a solution to the problem together.

(Charley)

Despite their commitment to a collaborative style of leadership, there were difficulties in enacting their leadership style in the way they wanted. These difficulties included:

- Balancing their personal and professional selves.
- The need for accountability.
- The constraints of working and being managed by a management committee made up predominantly of parents with little if any professional experience.

However, they have developed the ability to continue to find deep and sustaining personal and professional satisfaction in their work despite the presence of multiple adverse factors that have impacted on the voluntary sector.

Change and moral purpose

Effective, sensitive leaders are able to manage the change process in such a way that ensures everyone involved in the process feels included, consulted and a valued part of the process. Fullan argues that the ability to manage the change process requires the leader to understand and have sensitivity for the 'implementation dip' that occurs within the change process. He argues that the 'affiliative leader pays attention to people, focuses on building emotional bonds, builds relationships, and heals rifts' (2001, p.41).

Nancy described the responsibility she feels for the setting as it goes through the transition phase of developing into a children's centre.

When the building work is finished and we move back home we'll be a children's centre. We already provide a lot of the key services but I know things will change. What's important is that we don't lose our identity, that we remain a truly community based centre, that we don't get too big too soon and lose people on the journey. That's what I see as my job – holding it all together so that we come out the other side stronger and closer than before.

(Nancy)

Nancy clearly understood that an 'implementation dip' was likely to happen as a result of the change process and she saw her role as leader as one of containing the anxiety and 'reculturing' (Fullan 2001) the organisation. She also appreciated how vital communication is in the process.

A further contributing influence for all participants was the moral purpose underpinning their work. All were committed to making a positive difference to the children and families, their individual nurseries and their local communities with whom they work. The community nurseries in this study have all provided an environment that fosters a rich community spirit and personal growth. Fullan argues that 'moral purpose' and relationships and organisational success are closely interrelated (2001, p.51).

Freedom and flexibility

All the participants perceived that they had freedom to construct their work in ways they valued and saw this freedom as key to their resilience and survival. The rewards offered by other sectors, which include higher salaries and better working conditions, were not appealing because of the anticipated constraints.

> Things have changed so much here over the years but I'd never work in the private or maintained sector. I remember when we used to complain about all the legislation, inspections and stuff. We thought that as it was only a playgroup there wasn't really a need to make things so formal. I now understand how important it is. We provide high quality learning experiences and we need to be able to provide evidence that we do. What we do is important, it always has been but before we didn't value it ourselves now we do and we are able to tell people why it's so important.
>
> (Charley)

Sense of belonging

An overarching factor for four of the five women studied is that they have all grown in, and been nurtured by, the organisations they are now leading. Like my own learning journey they became involved in the childcare field through their own children. Charley, Kelly, Nancy and Nelly started their journeys as volunteers and were nurtured and supported to gain qualifications and build a career for themselves by the very same organisations that provided services for their children. This has resulted in their having a deep-seated sense of belonging and responsibility for the organisation and the people within it.

> I feel responsible for it (the centre). It is my baby, an extension of myself I suppose. I cannot leave because there is no one to take it on; the community needs the very best care I can give them.
>
> (Nancy)

This sense of belonging was evident but I could not determine if these women stayed because they felt it unsafe to move on or if they felt so safe, secure and supported that they do not need or want to move on.

Founder's Syndrome

'Founder's Syndrome' (McNamara 2000) appears to manifest itself in 'not for profit' organisations or charities. It occurs when a single individual or a small group of individuals bring an organisation through tough times (a start-up, a growth spurt, a financial collapse, etc.). Often these sorts of situations require a strong passionate personality – someone who can make fast decisions and motivate people to action. Initially I was excited to discover this syndrome; perhaps this was the reason these women have never pursued a change in employment when opportunities for qualified early years practitioners of their calibre are greater than ever.

Founder's Syndrome becomes an issue if the organisation is managed according to the needs of the leader rather than the needs of the customers or group. I found no evidence that these women had Founder's Syndrome. They embraced change and prioritised the needs of children, parents and the local community. Their careers have followed an ecological approach, which can be conceptualised as concentric circles radiating from the central core, their setting. They have become custodians of their communities, holding it all together. Their community's respect for them as individuals is important to them and they have a real commitment to their settings and passion for what they do.

To some extent there is a sense of co-dependency in their relationships with their organisations. The 'need' felt by the leader for the setting and the community's dependence on the leader can create a dependency culture.

> I haven't ever thought about moving on, this is where I'm meant to be. The community needs this provision and so do I.
>
> (Kelly)

I can relate to this sense of attachment. I, too, felt a great sense of responsibility to the first setting that supported me in my career journey and I had difficulty letting go. It had become part of me; my identity, my very being was tied in with the nursery. To this day I remain a very active member of the management committee and meet with the staff team regularly to nurture and support their development.

An interesting observation is that Jenny does not appear to have this sense of belonging. She does feel committed to the organisation but not at the same level as the other women.

> I don't know about the future, you know . . . I'd like to leave when the reputation of this place was a bit better, we do a good job but it needs to be a lot better. I don't know any more, I'm tired of it all.
>
> (Jenny)

Jenny entered the childcare field from college as a young woman, rather than through her own experience as a mother. It may be that she has not developed the same level of secure attachment with her organisation that the others have. On the other hand it may be that she did not have the same emotional needs as the other women in this study who joined their organisations as parents and the organisations supported them in their parenting role. She has also been exposed to other childcare sectors and therefore has broader experience. Additionally, she may not feel as secure in her sense of 'self' as the other women in this study.

Empowering environments

Their settings have provided an 'empowering environment' – a context in which these women feel able to achieve. I would argue that passionate early years leaders hold a social and moral responsibility for the children and families they work with. These women were responsible for providing quality services that promote the welfare of the child and provide access to a quality early years curriculum. They work with the most vulnerable and powerless members of our community and are advocates for children's rights. This is central to the ethos and cultural values underpinning community nurseries.

Cultural expectations

Another characteristic of these women's stories is the oppression and lack of expectations they experienced as a result of cultural and gender expectations as they were growing up. For Nelly and Nancy, education was available but parental expectations were that daughters did not need the same level of education as sons or a career and that, once married, they would devote their time to raising a family and being a good wife.

For Kelly and Charley, both from white working-class backgrounds, family aspirations were low. Kelly describes how being the middle child made her feel insignificant. Charley also describes low expectations and how she felt invisible as a child in the school system.

> When I went to secondary school, all I can remember is daydreaming in nearly every class. The teachers all ignored me, as if I was no one. I felt invisible. I didn't do very well and, in the end left without taking any exams but my parents didn't mind I don't think they thought I was very bright.
>
> (Charley)

Both these women left school with few if any qualifications, which was the norm for women for their generation and social class at the time. To a certain extent this remains the case for white working-class inner-city women. As early years professionals we are all aware of the damage that can occur when stereotypical assumptions are made and when adults have low expectations of children. These women clearly remember the feelings associated with these experiences and are aware of the impact they have had on them as women and as leaders.

For Freire (1970), oppression is conceived in class terms and education is viewed as the vehicle in which to overcome it. Each interviewee shared with me their memories of their mothers as role models:

> My mother always wanted to please everyone not upset them. In my culture women shouldn't be assertive. They are submissive. They look after everyone else's needs.
>
> (Nelly)

Skeggs (1997) describes how we are positioned by macro structures such as nation, class and sexuality, and these macro structures affect our access to education and employment, and what we understand as possible in our lives. Education has given the women in this study the opportunity to break down cultural and class boundaries and they are now nurturing other women along the same path.

> I want to be a role model for other women of my culture. In my culture, there isn't really any expectation for girls. I didn't want to stay home and keep house.
>
> (Nancy)

The findings from this study are comparable to Beham's (1997) study of minority ethnic women school leaders. She found that the journey the women had taken to leadership had strengthened their sense of identity and social justice.

Relationships – children and others

The relationships the women had with staff, parents and the management committees were complicated and multifaceted. The leaders were often part employer, part employee, part role model and part friend, partly to be admired and partly to be resented. Coping and managing the dynamics of these relationships is the mark of an effective leader.

The interviewees talked about the importance of planning daily to spend time with children and to be available to talk to parents. Working directly with young children provides intrinsic motivation for these women – a vital ingredient in their daily work that reinforced their commitment to the nurseries. In reality this meant covering staffing levels over lunch periods or at the beginning or end of the day. The women describe how rewarding they found this special time:

> Even when I'm really busy I make time everyday to have lunch with the children. It's a really important part of the day for me we get to talk. You can get great pleasure just from sharing a meal or putting a little one down to sleep peacefully. I find out what they've been doing and how they are feeling. It's those little things that make all the difference.
>
> (Kelly)

For the women in this study, close, personal and supportive relationships beyond the organisation are vital to their emotional well being.

> My husband and family have always supported me. I'm often still here until late into the night and it's okay with them. They know how important this place is to the community, they know why I have to do it. I see this nursery as my child, part of my family.
>
> (Nelly)

Communication

For the women in the study, communication and relationship building are key concepts for developing their practice as leaders and childcare professionals. Effective leaders are people centred (Rogers 1983) and their practice is underpinned by a set of personal and professional values that place human needs before organisational needs. The women in this study prioritised time and space, physically and emotionally, for relationship building:

> Having empathy is very important and talking to people about my experience. I always put myself in their shoes and think about how I would feel if someone treated me like that.
>
> (Charley)

Leadership

Leadership for these women is not simply what the leader does; it is more to do with what occurs within relationships. Clark and Clark (1996) state that taking a leadership role has to be an active choice for the individual for the leadership to be effective but the women in this study took a leadership role in most cases because they were in the right place at the right time.

They were confident in and accepted their leadership but also distributed power and responsibility to others. They viewed leadership as a reciprocal relationship rather than a position within a group. Leadership was about inspiring, empowering and nurturing children, staff members and parents and a collection of practices and behaviours that create a climate of trust and collaboration. Muijs *et al.* (2004) found that no single style of leadership was suitable for all types of early years provision but the most successful early childhood leaders create a 'participative culture': one based on a philosophy of sharing knowledge and a flattened hierarchy that encourages individuals to share power and responsibility. Collaboration and creating an environment that fosters shared responsibility was important for all the women in this study:

> I never really thought as myself as a leader, not until you rang and asked me if I'd consider doing this . . . I think I lead by example, I never expect anyone to do something I wouldn't do myself. I'm passionate about my work with children and families and expect my team to be the same. You have to be really committed to do this job otherwise there's no point. I think my leadership style is collaborative, you know what it's like here we all carry out a leadership role. I don't like it when I have to assert my authority, sometimes it can't be helped, I'm the head so if there is an issue I have to get it resolved. But I try to work in a way that encourages the team to find a solution to the problem together.
>
> (Charley)

The development of the individual – child, staff member or parent – plays a key role in the kinds of culture the women are trying to engender. Using Sergiovanni's (1998) analysis the participants developed social capital by encouraging collaboration amongst their communities. Building a strong sense of community is an important aspect of the leadership role. A key theme throughout this study has been how these women perceive their work as being connected to and responsive to the needs of their communities.

Life long learning

Continuous professional development is an inherent part of the culture and philosophy of community nurseries and of the women in this study. Sergiovanni (1998) refers to 'pedagogical leadership' as a role that involves developing 'human capital' by helping settings become 'inquiring communities'. Three of the five women in this study are currently in the final year of a degree course in Early Childhood Studies. All expressed the difference that studying at degree level had made to their pedagogical practice and to their self-esteem and general well being.

> In 2003 I started the degree course. When I applied to the university I felt scared, I worried about [the] interview and my English. In the end it wasn't as bad as I thought. At the interview [the interviewer] told me I had a lot to give to the other students, I couldn't believe she felt that I had experience that would help others, I was very nervous at the interview. But she was right, the best thing about the course is that we are encouraged to learn from each other, to share experiences and really think deeply about our practice. Every week in our staff meetings I share with the team what

I've learnt, this course hasn't just made a difference to my practice it's had an effect on the whole staff team.

(Nelly)

Claxton refers to the link between life long learning and leadership. He regards the development of 'dispositions for "lifelong learning" as fundamental for leaders who are responsible for enabling, encouraging and evaluating other people' (2000, p. 78).

I try to make sure the staff team accesses as much training as possible. It's funny, isn't it, I hated school and now I can't get enough of education. If only you could turn the clock back.

(Charley)

Four of the women in this study stressed how important it was for them to share their learning journeys with parents and staff teams. For them, returning to education has fostered their self-esteem and well being and they feel the need to share their stories with everyone:

It's important for them (parents) to know how we got here, it gives them confidence to try and achieve what they want out of life. I always say to them if I can get a degree anyone can, you just have to want it enough.

(Kelly)

Pressures and problems

Dissatisfaction with the increase in bureaucratic tasks resulted in increased pressure. Whilst the need for accountability was accepted as a necessary evil, the constant requests to complete various reports and audits for funders increased participants' workload tenfold.

I spend hours each week completing monitoring requirements for one funder only to be asked for the same information again in another format by another department, why can't they just talk to each other? And as for the current changing childcare agenda, my staff team have just got to grips with Birth to Three, and now I have to prepare them for the Early Years Foundation Stage. They (DFES) never give enough time to see how stuff works.

(Jenny)

The nature of the governance of the community nursery added additional constraints. Management committees are made up of volunteers, often busy working parents whose children attend the setting. These relationships needed to be nurtured carefully as they can create a conflict of interest, for both parties.

There was very little flexibility or time for many parents to take on a more active role in the setting. Roles and responsibilities between the manager and management committee were often unclear, resulting in the leader feeling unsupported. Consequently, the women described their working relationships with their management committees as problematic.

> The one thing I've found is that it can be very isolating in the voluntary sector. I don't have a line manager as such and there's often no one to talk to. The committee say they do something but then they don't and it gets left for me to pick up, it can be very frustrating sometimes.
>
> (Charley)

High turnover of committee members resulted in the women being reluctant to spend time inducting and educating new members. Consequently, there was an illusion of the committee being in control when in reality many had little understanding of their roles and responsibilities.

> The MC doesn't take responsibility for anything. I want to make them understand that they are supposed to be running the nursery, they are legally responsible but at the end of the day they leave everything to me. You see they don't get proper training like school governors do and if I try to explain their responsibilities they get scared and don't want to be involved.
>
> (Kelly)

The two settings in this study that had embraced change had active committee members who had been involved with the groups for many years. Both Nelly and Nancy nurtured their relationships with the key committee members and recognised the importance of keeping them on board. Kelly and Charley also recognised the support they received from a few key members of their committees and saw the committees as important assets to their settings. The women in this study held the power within their nurseries and controlled how much information they shared with their management committees. In some cases it appeared the management committees were reactive rather than proactive with information being shared only when the leader felt it appropriate.

Another problem these leaders had in common was managing their time and balancing their workload. Funding constraints meant that staffing levels in their nurseries were usually at the bare minimum. Managers often had to cover staff ratios at short notice leaving general managerial duties to be completed outside their normal working hours.

Reaching the stage of 'self actualisation'

In 2005 the Primary National Strategy (DFES) carried out a pilot project to support developments in leadership with private, voluntary and independent

(PVI) early years settings. Six LAs took part in the initiative to explore how they could support the development of quality leadership in the early years. One, Nottingham, adapted Maslow's 'Hierarchy of Needs' (1968) and developed a new framework 'Aspects of motivation' (DFES 2004) (Figure 7.1). Both frameworks build on factors needed in an individual and/or organisation before the person can reach the stage of 'self actualisation' – the point at which higher level learning can take place.

Despite my reservations, I thought it might be a useful exercise to share the framework with the women in the study. I asked them to study both frameworks and decide where they felt they were placed in relation to their leadership skills. I also used the information I had gathered through my interviews and their learning journeys and then compared the results.

Nelly and Nancy both felt they were operating at the level of 'self actualisation', which was where I had plotted them on the framework. They have both embraced change and used opportunities to maximise the services they provide for children and families as well as their own professional development. They were both confident in their position as leaders. Kelly also positioned herself in a similar position as I had. This suggests that she is confident and has high self-esteem and is aware of her sense of 'self'.

Charley placed herself slightly lower than I had on the framework. The difference could be perceived as insignificant or alternatively, could indicate that she is not as confident in herself as she appears to others. Jenny placed herself significantly lower than I had anticipated on the framework, which highlighted for me her low self-esteem. She presented as a confident professional manager but throughout our interviews expressed lack of confidence in her abilities. Her understanding of herself as a professional early years leader appeared to be underdeveloped.

In my view aspects of both frameworks must be interwoven like a spider's web for the leader to be effective and the organisation to flourish.

A vertical framework gives the perception that the individual moves up in steps through each level until the stage where they can operate effectively. I would contend that the threads of the web need to be entwined and when breaks occur they need to be repaired immediately. The threads, like emotional pathways, connect individuals and allow for a flow of energy that is invisible but powerful.

I met with each participant again after this exercise and shared with them my rationale for positioning them on the framework. The meeting with Jenny evoked difficult feelings for both of us. I was concerned that she might feel I undervalued her as a leader and the last thing I wanted was for this study to contribute to her low self-esteem. An open and honest discussion followed and I shared with Jenny my hypothesis that individuals move up and down this framework depending on external factors at any given time.

Hodgkinson talks of the need for the leader to 'know thy self' (1991, p.139) and I would conjecture that Jenny does not have the same developed sense of

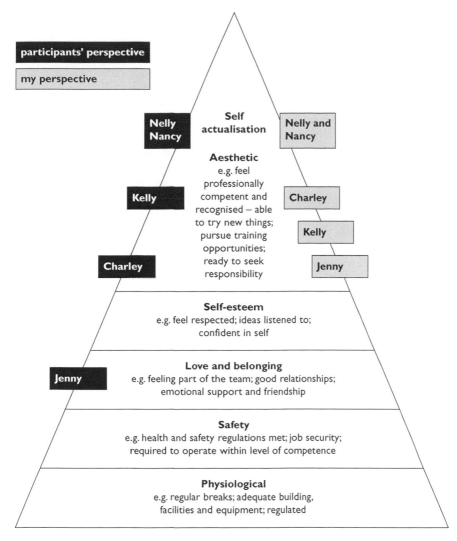

Figure 7.1 Aspects of motivation. Based on 'Hierarchy of Needs'
Source: Based on Maslow (1968)

'self' as the other participants in this study. The women in this study are not a homogenous group and therefore can hold different culturally conceived ideas about their role as leaders.

So what? Implications for practice

This study has explored the personal theories of leadership from the perspective of five early years' managers working in the voluntary sector.

I began this study expecting to find women who had taken on a leadership role simply because they were in the right place at the right time. I had a feeling that many of the practitioners remained loyal to their individual organisations out of fear of the unknown.

I was expecting to find women with low self-esteem and little confidence – women who avoided change and liked playing safe. What I discovered were strong powerful women, community activists who are passionate and truly committed to making a positive difference to their local communities. I found women who have overcome adversity, and have bags of resilience; women with empathy and compassion,

The 'Aspects of motivation' framework developed by Nottingham could be a useful self evaluation tool if used with caution to encourage reflective dialogue. Both Nottingham's and Maslow's frameworks imply that the individual moves vertically in stages and I would argue that any hierarchical theory is based on a male perspective. Hall argues that Maslow's theory is 'problematic for women, particularly in emphasising achievement, adequacy and becoming competent' (1996, p.123). Surprisingly Nottingham's model follows this hierarchical theory even though it was developed to support leadership training within the female-dominated early years field. It makes no allowance for feminine dispositions to learning or for intrinsic motivation and I would argue that effective leadership does not operate vertically but weaves and winds like a spider on a web.

Data gathering was limited to interviews and the collection of supplementary material. While these are valid methods of collecting information they did not give the complete picture of the way in which these women work which might have been gained from shadowing these women in their settings, watching them at work and talking with them over a period of time. I have tried to ensure throughout my study a realistic portrayal of life in the community nursery. I did not want my study to romanticise leadership in the voluntary sector, rather to celebrate the strengths and accomplishments of these remarkable women.

It remains indisputable that the decision to follow a specific career path presents greater dilemmas for women than for men. The flexibility offered by the voluntary sector was a major contributing factor for the women in this study. In many respects they have all become leaders by 'default'; none of the women in this study had any type of career plan. They just seemed to be in the right place at the right time.

This study has also led me to question how we promote and support Adult Education. Research clearly highlights that increased economic well being and improving outcomes for children can only be achieved by raising the aspiration of parents and getting more to return to work and/or study. The experiences of the women in this study have highlighted the important role the early years setting has in supporting that learning.

My research has demonstrated the high levels of responsibility of these leaders for children, parents, staff and their local communities. They also have the additional responsibility of supporting their management committees and the only effective support structure they have access to is through informal peer support.

Based on the information from this study I would argue that local government policy needs to be reviewed. Consideration needs to be given to funding early years services at full cost recovery and given the limited resources available this may require difficult decisions to be made. All LAs have a duty to ensure sufficiency of childcare; however, ensuring sufficiency should not compromise quality, and quality services need adequate funding.

The question of whether community nurseries should or can be managed effectively by a management committee made up of lay people needs to be debated. I would suggest that even the most effective leaders in this study need to do more to forge active collaborative working relationships with their management committees. Management committees have high expectation of leaders and readily hand over all control, perhaps out of ignorance or fear of responsibility. Many are not fully aware of their roles and responsibilities. Sharing 'power' in most cases only happens when the leader decides to divulge information, and therefore I question whether the rhetoric of working in partnership with parents is happening in reality at a more strategic level in the community nursery. This needs to be addressed if the traditional community nursery is to survive along with training and support to increase the level of participation of the management committees.

These leaders want to improve life chances in their communities and their knowledge and skills helped them to make alliances with other groups and organisations to achieve their goal. Their skills and knowledge have enabled good, ethical management in the day-to-day operations of their organisations. Relationships are a crucial element of the leader's role and these women leaders work well with people inside and outside their organisations. They do this by building relationships and environments that promote a culture of empowering others and supporting people to work together. They are creating community leadership

In my opinion, the main contribution of this study lies in helping to conceptualise the role that the traditional community nursery plays in developing strong, resilient, resourceful, reciprocal leaders. A 'culture of learning' is alive and well in the voluntary sector.

> Here we are seen as acorns, and if we receive the right nourishment, and are supported and helped we shall grow into giant oak trees, standing tall, confident and competent. But for acorns, truth and knowledge come from within. We just need the right environment in which to grow.
>
> (Eales-White 1994, p.x).

Reflections and questions

In this chapter, Ana reveals some of the complexity of leadership among women leaders and also within the voluntary sector.

• How are you managed and supported within your current work role?
• How would you perceive this idea of co-dependency between identity and career, i.e. 'I need my job and my job needs me'.
• How can you see power and responsibility being shared within your organisation?

Applying learning to practice

• Sharing learning journeys might be a good starting point for thinking about leadership in your organisation.
• There are obvious implications for management committees e.g. more training is needed, and also more contact with practice.
• There is a great deal to be gained in 'growing your own' future leaders but it may require some sort of 'scout' or person who can spot potential and foster growth.

References

Adler, S., Laney, J. and Packer, M. (1993) *Managing Women: Feminism and power in educational management*. Buckingham: Open University Press.
Beham, M. (1997) Silences and serenades: The journey of 3 ethnic minority women school leaders, *Anthropology and Education Quarterly*, 28(2), 280–307.
Blackmore, J. (1989) Educational leadership: A feminist critique and reconstruction. In J. Smyth (ed.) *Critical Perspectives in Educational Leadership*. London: The Falmer Press.
Clark, K. and Clark, M. (1996) *Choosing to Lead*, 2nd edn. Greensboro, NC: Center for Creative Leadership.
Claxton, G. (2000) *Building Learning Power*. Bristol: Henleaze House.
Day, C., Harris, A., Hadfield, M., Tolley, H. and Bersford, J. (2000) *Leading Schools in Times of Change*. Buckingham: Open University Press.
DFES (2003) *Every Child Matters*. Nottingham: HM Government/DFES.
DFES (2004) *Ten Year Strategy for Child Care*. Nottingham: HM Government/ DFES.
Dulewicz, V. and Higgs, M. (2000) Emotional intelligence: A review and evaluation study, *Journal of Managerial Psychology*, 15(4), 341–372.
Eales-White, R. (1994) *Creating Growth from Change*. Maidenhead: McGraw-Hill.
Effective Provision of Pre-School Education (EPPE) project (1999). London: DFES and Institute of Education, University of London.
Freire, P. (1970) *Pedagogy of the Oppressed*. New York: Continuum.
Fullan, M. (1998) Leadership for the twenty-first century: Breaking the bonds of dependency, *Educational Leadership*, 55, 6–10.
Fullan, M. (2001) *Leading in a Culture of Change*. San Francisco: Jossey-Bass.

Goleman, D. (1998) *Working with Emotional Intelligence*. London: Bloomsbury Publishing.

Grant, R. (1989) Women teachers' career pathways: towards an alternative model of 'career'. In S. Acker (ed.) *Teachers, Gender and Careers*. Lewes: Falmer.

Hall, V. (1996) *Dancing on the Ceiling: A study of women managers in education*. London: Paul Chapman.

Hart, L. (1989) Women in primary management. In C. Skelton (ed.) *Whatever Happens to Little Women? Gender and primary schooling*. Milton Keynes: Open University Press.

Hatherley, A. and Lee, W. (2003) Voices of early childhood leadership, *New Zealand Journal of Educational Leadership*, 18, 91–100.

Hodgkinson, C. (1991) *Educational Leadership: The moral art*. Albany, NY: State University of New York Press.

Lambert, P. (1989) Women into educational management, *Adults Learning*, 1(4), 106.

Leithwood, K., Tomlinson, D. and Genge, M. (1996) Transformational school leadership. In K. Leithwood, J. Chapman, D. Corson, P. Hallinger and A. Hart (eds) *International Handbook of Educational Leadership and Administration*, Part 2. Dordrecht: Kluwer Academic.

Maslow, A. (1968) *Toward a Psychology of Being*. New York: Van Nostrand Reinhold.

McNamara, C. (2000) *What is 'Founder's Syndrome'? Do we have it? How do we recover?* Santa Barbara, CA: Prisma Leadership Group, http://come.to/plg (accessed 27/01/07).

Muijs, D., Aubrey, C., Harris, A. and Briggs, M. (2004) How do they manage? A review of the research on leadership in early childhood, *Journal of Early Childhood Research*, 2(2), 157–169.

OFSTED (2000) *Improving City Schools*, London: Office for Standards in Education.

Rogers, C.R. (1983) *Freedom to Learn for the 80's*. London: Charles Merrill.

Schein, V.E. (1995) Would women lead differently? In J. Thomas Wren (ed.) *The Leader's Companion: Insights on leadership through the ages*. New York: The Free Press.

Sergiovanni, T.J. (1998) 'Leadership as pedagogy: Capital development and social effectiveness, *International Journal of Leadership in Education*, 1(1), 37–46.

Skeggs, B. (1997) *Formations of Class and Gender: Becoming responsible*. London: Sage Publications.

Southworth, G. (1998) *Leading Improving Primary Schools*. London: The Falmer Press.

Spradley, J.P. (1980) *Participant Observation*. Fort Worth, TX: Harcourt Brace Jovanovich College Publishers.

Whitaker P. (1993) *Managing Change in Schools*. Buckingham: Open University Press.

Chapter 8

Effective leadership, effective learning

It's all about relationships

Gill Allen

In this chapter you will find:

- A brave study of leadership in which a leader invites honest comments from her team about her leadership.
- The use of a 'critical incident' to unpick what was happening in an organisation.
- The application of Bion's 'Basic Assumption' theory to understand group processes.

Introduction

I have been the head of an organisation that has been on a significant transforming learning journey for seven years. During that time it has changed from a traditional maintained nursery school with six staff, offering part-time funded education, to an Early Excellence Centre and now a children's centre with over forty staff offering integrated provision for children, families and practitioners. I wanted to examine how we worked together as a group to achieve this transformation in order that we could do more, develop it further and share our insights with others.

I relish the opportunity leadership offers to initiate things that make a real difference to more and more people, believing that I have the skills and knowledge to do so. I need to guard against my desire to forge ahead, leading from the front and sweeping others along with me. The best way to do that would be to '. . . ask the natives, they usually know' (Handy, 1990, p.24). I know that collaborative learning is more effective because it gives the opportunity for all to give and to gain. I know that what we communicate is not always what we intend.

I believe that learning is a reciprocal social activity, making the relationship between learners crucial. As practitioners we are always striving to 'tune in' to children in order to find out what connections are being made in their brains, so that our interactions are relevant and supportive. As the team of adults working together are a crucial part of the learning community, I wanted to enable a deeper 'tuning in' to happen between me and team members and between the members themselves. Lambert and Walker said that 'leadership is the reciprocal learning processes that enable participants . . . to construct meaning' (2002, p.152). My hope was that this openness would result in closer connections amongst team members. If they could reflect and comment on their relationship with me with positive results, then they would surely be able to do so with each other. A greater understanding of our needs, feelings and opinions would increase our support for each other, which in turn would raise self- and group esteem, a prerequisite for successful learning and development.

Much of our understanding about the subject of leadership was as a result of old paradigm research, which, like old paradigm learning, was based on the right ways to do things, taught by those who know to those who do not. Tests were then devised in order to measure if they were right. That kind of research might help me to learn someone else's theory but not necessarily how it could work for me.

A constructivist view of learning is one of a unique, continuous interpersonal group experience in which people of all ages can work together to make meaning of the world as they encounter it. The leadership relationship is one aspect of that learning experience and it needs to be equally reciprocal. Action research, 'a process of trying to understand how values are lived out in practice' (McNiff and Whitehead, 2002, p.40), is an apt methodology for the constructivist.

It is suggested that action research should begin with a problem, an issue to be resolved. This smacks of the old regime that works from the deficit model. I wanted to find out what was working well in the leadership relationship so that I can do more of it and encourage others to try it. Success is the best motivator. Working from the positive, one can then move on to discover what more could be done to help the team develop further.

This openness, self-reflection and communication about personal feelings by team members, has the potential for leaving people feeling very vulnerable. Deep reflection about one's feelings and views can be traumatic and for some, unexpected, if they have avoided looking inwards before. The reason for not acknowledging the inner person may be that there is a lot to come to terms with. For people who joined the organisation to work with little children, this may seem rather heavy and unnecessary. There is a tension between the right to privacy and the right to know (Elliott, 1999). It is therefore important to give participants control over their contribution.

The Johari window concept is applicable to all participants in this kind of investigation. I especially relate to Charles Handy's exposition of it (1990, pp.65–66). He likens the facets of a person to a four-roomed house (see Figure 8.1).

Room 1 is the public space that we and others see. Room 2 is how others see us, of which we are unaware. Between rooms 1 and 3 is the gap between our view of ourselves and how we would like to be (ibid., p.93). Room 3 is the hidden room – the subconscious or potential, of which no one is aware at the present. Room 4 is our private room, the part of each person that they know about but do not share with others. Each person controls the size of the rooms

	Known to others	Not known to others
Not known to self	2 blindspot	3 unknown
Known to self	1 public	4 private

Figure 8.1 The facets of a person
Source: Based on Handy (1990)

and holds the key to each. The size of the rooms and openness of the doors differs for each person with whom we have a relationship.

My quest is to make room 1 in my house the biggest. I opened the door to room 2 and invited members of the team, colleagues and family to share their perceptions of my leadership with me. That involved their opening room 4 in their own house to reveal some of their hitherto private thoughts about me. In fact, opening my room 2 probably resulted in just as much opening of their room 4. It is also important to remember that what they make of me is influenced by their view of themselves, but is altogether valid because that is the present reality between us. I needed to remember that there may be a tendency to project negative views onto others as we try to bridge the gap between what we think we are and what we would like to be (ibid., p.93).

Methods

First, I took a long hard look at my own experiences from childhood, using available literature to gain insight into the way I do things. A colleague and personal friend was invaluable in supporting me through this process, acting as a critical friend. Second, I involved a group of four people who had worked in the organisation long before me and who worked with me to change the organisation. Rather like the elders of an ancient community, we seem to hold the history that remains a significant core of the organisation as it is today. I involved this core group in a focussed group dialogue that sought to understand the traumatic events that occurred when I first joined the organisation, followed by one-to-one dialogue, as needed.

I chose the word 'dialogue' because of its Greek root meaning 'flowing through'. I hoped that as we examined the traumatic early days of our journey together we could share our individual perspective, but come to a collective understanding of our experience. The purpose of revisiting the past is not to blame others or to justify ourselves, but to acknowledge what each of us experienced during that time. I hoped to achieve what Senge described as 'the free and creative exploration of complex and subtle issues, deep listening to one another . . . and the suspending of one's views' (1992, p.237). This was my hope, that together we would find meaning in the story of the beginning of our journey together. This group dialogue reinforced the importance of shared experiences and group story. The resulting story is anecdotal, which is a relevant expression of learning as it is authentic for participants, and connects with readers' human experience.

Third, I engaged with the group of nine people who have been developing integrated care and education for 3- to 5-year-old children, based on the original education provision, for three years. It included the core team. I gave them the following questionnaire:

1 What skills have you acquired in your role and as a member of the team in the last few years?
2 What do you think has helped you to achieve them?
3 What else would help you?
4 Do you express your feelings, views and ideas to me and/or the team as much as you could or would like?
5 How could it be made easier for you?
6 What would you like help/support with?
7 What is it like to be a member of this team?
8 What kind of leader am I?
9 What would you like me to do more of?
10 What would you like me to do less of?
11 What would you like me to do differently?
12 What else would you like me to do?
13 How would you describe your relationship with me?
14 How would you like it to be?

I collated their responses, recording the most used phrases and the number of times those phrases were used and quoted some significant whole sentences. I shared the collated responses with the team and then we engaged in a dialogue about the findings.

There were many developments from this work, which were difficult to capture in a single method. After four months I wrote a piece of reflective prose, using journal entries, written and spoken comments by team members, as well as reflection on my part.

Findings

What did I discover about myself?

I concluded that leadership was an inevitable mantle that fell on me at an early age. It is not a job I do; it is something I must be. It has continued to occupy my energy throughout my life, creating much pain and pleasure. From a very young age I had a sense of moral purpose, a driving passion for the common good. I had strong views about many aspects of family life, which I expressed. My paternal grandmother thought I was 'too big for my boots'.

My father encouraged me to be a perfectionist and to work extremely hard. However, he suffered prolonged ill health and was extremely sensitive, perceiving any 'misbehaviour' on my part as a personal attack on his success as a father. This, along with my mother's lack of self-confidence, led to my having the 'emotional responsibility' for our family. I argued a lot with my mother and became strong-willed and opinionated. My childhood experience makes it difficult for me to be cared for professionally, but it is something I crave at home.

I was a successful product of what Carl Rogers (Kirschenbaum and Henderson, 1989) graphically calls 'the jug and mug style of education'. Despite a working-class background with no academics in my family, I thrived on my grammar school experience, delighted that my mug could retain information poured in to me. When I was 10 I determined to offer similar experiences to children by becoming a teacher when I grew up. During my teacher training I was shocked to discover that there are better ways to learn than by instruction.

I no longer have any specifically religious beliefs, but I remain committed to the spirituality of mankind, with a belief in a higher order of things than the day-to-day comings and goings of people.

Something happened in our small council house with hardly any facilities, which made me believe that I could be who I wanted to be. My parents loved and believed in me, my father had very high expectations of me, but made no threats nor offered material rewards. I was able to work things out for myself. These attributes and experiences led me to leadership, and my need to care drew me to early years. But I also longed to be cared for and traumatic events within my immediate family finally led me to access skilled counselling. This enabled me to throw away blame and learn that we cannot change the things that happen in our lives but we do have control over its effect on us. I gained the courage to be imperfect (John, 2007), to ask for help, to step back and allow others to care for me, trusting that they could. I gained the inner peace that comes with self-knowledge. By acknowledging the past we can be freed from its encumbrance. I no longer felt the need to be a big, loud and charismatic leader. I discovered the joy of flying together in a team like geese in a 'V' formation, relying on each other, taking turns to lead and to honk encouragement from the rear. It is a powerful way of travelling.

When I became the headteacher of what was then a traditional nursery school I needed a way to connect with the team; but entering a new group is, for me, de-skilling and unnerving. We all need to feel accepted and valued in order to function in a group and that goes for the leader as well as the team members:

> Leader successors are newcomers who must be integrated into existing groups, validated by social processes and granted legitimacy before they can have significant impact on the actions of others.
>
> (Hall, 1996, p.64)

On closer examination and after discussion with my critical friend, I believe it goes much deeper than that. My need to be invited in to any group or relationship stems from my feeling of class inferiority. I lived on a council estate as a child; my father, although very bright, worked in a factory. My mother reminded me that she had missed vital time at school through ill health and was therefore 'not very clever'. I did very well at grammar school, but it was not recognised; my family name was not carved on the boards celebrating past successful students. I went to teacher training college, not university, gained a diploma not a degree, taught early years not statutory school age, married a non-graduate. I am not wealthy.

What did the core team and I discover?

The five of us met together for a focussed dialogue, prompted by a paper which I wrote, inviting them to reflect on the things that had happened during our early time together. They had been together for many years and at the point when I joined them had retreated to their classrooms and did what they believed to be the best for children. I wrongly assumed that they were connected to each other as a team. To the non-discerning eye the practice was good, supported by an OFSTED inspection report. The majority of children were articulate and entered the nursery with wide experiences. There was no strongly defined pedagogy, but parents appeared to be very appreciative of the practice. All six practitioners had been at the school for more than ten years, two of them attended as students on placement and stayed. The majority of staff were clearly committed to the job and had high self-expectations.

Unfortunately, there had been no clear leadership for a long time. Pollard recognised that 'there is an existing culture, set of relationships and way of doing things in any organisation. This institutional bias is disturbed by the appointment of a new headteacher' (Pollard in Woods, 2003, p.5). I longed to connect with them so that we could begin our journey of learning and discovery together. However, the first term ended with the team and me staring suspiciously across the table at each other. I will never forget persuading my new team to tell me what I was doing that prevented our relationship from developing positively. They said it was my criticism of them and I felt gutted.

I had not uttered one word of criticism; I was going very gently, learning how they did things and why. But my lack of praise and my silences were interpreted by them as criticism and that is what mattered. Peter Senge observed that, 'In any new experience, most people are drawn to take in and remember only the information that reinforces their existing mental models' (Senge *et al.*, 2000, p.67). I was surprised and asked the team for examples. They realised that it was in fact my lack of praise that they interpreted as criticism.

We discovered that there had been a critical incident that was the turning point in our relationship and in the journey of the centre. This was when the governing body told me to revert back to original teaching methods immediately, as the health and safety of the children was at serious risk. Children had been working in separate classrooms with a teacher and nursery nurse offering some choice of activities. Our move to an open environment where children could move freely and access resources for themselves was seen as dangerous. I told staff that I could not revert to working in the original way and that I was not about to leave, as some had thought I would. I was discouraged by the intervention by the governing body, but my past experience of learning through adversity meant that I did not pass on that discouragement to the team. That commitment, together with the power of the learning that we had begun to see occurring, led to their stating their allegiance, saying 'we will give it our full commitment'. This was probably a good example of Goleman's view that 'Leaders who can stay optimistic . . . even under intense pressure radiate the positive feelings that create resonance' (2002, p.47).

I believe that there were many unconscious processes at work in the team when I arrived; the shiny wooden ceilings and flat roof were holding everyone down. The Tavistock Clinic's work with clients (Obholzer and Roberts, 1994) resulted in theorising that fits with my perceptions of the team. People experience conflicting emotions based on their earliest childhood memories and, in order to deal with them, split them and project one feeling on to one person and another on to someone else. Hierarchies and separate teams support this 'paranoid-schizoid behaviour' (Halton, 1994, p.14). The team operated as three independent pairs in separate classrooms. Like players in a drama, each was ascribed a role, with some subterfuge between pairs and a false hierarchy completing the plot. This kind of stuck team may be ambivalent about breaking the mould. I certainly experienced that: I was told that the team were waiting for a new headteacher to lead change and development, but then found that they blocked my attempts to make connections with them as they sensed that I would be making big changes.

The team exhibited all three aspects of Bion's basic assumption group theory: basic assumption dependency, basic assumption fight/flight and basic assumption pairing (Stokes, 1994). If any change was to be contemplated I would have to tell them exactly what to do, and how to do it, holding responsibility for everyone's safety and children's learning (basic assumption dependency). There was always a reason to wait – until we could knock some walls down, until everyone had learned how to do it, until the next group of children had left (basic assumption fight/flight). Maybe the new curriculum due to be published would provide all the answers (basic assumption pairing). The hope and faith in a new leader to bring about great development remains until a real leader materialises. Basic assumption groups subvert the primary task, in this case the development of a pedagogy, becoming instead absorbed with group relationships. However, a future event did in fact bring about the beginning of the solution. The external enemy, against whom the team could unite, appeared in the form of the directive by the governing body to 'put it all back'. Local authority support and my determination to continue led to a commitment by the team to break the pattern.

What did I discover with the nursery team?

Members of the nursery team said they found the questionnaires difficult to complete, although they helped them to voice things they had not realised before. The freedom to be heard is matched by the responsibility to take the consequences of doing so. One member said 'Thanks for asking. It can be so much easier to be open and honest if you don't have to make the first move'. They all said that they had never been asked to express their views in this way in any other job role. Valerie Hall suggests that 'Self-knowledge involves blindspots, for example, in terms of knowing their impact on others' (1996, p.203). I regularly suggest that what we think we are saying or doing will be perceived very differently by others. It is important to acknowledge the validity of their perception, explain our own, then move forward together with a greater mutual understanding. Answers to the questionnaires and the ensuing dialogue certainly reiterated this point.

I learned that one thing that I do that worries and even scares some people is be silent in particular situations, in contrast to my usual interactive style. They said that it feels like disapproval and that matters to them. With the help of my critical friend I was able to offer some possible explanations:

- 'I did not have the perfection I imagined was necessary to speak up' (John, 2000, p.8). I am heartened by the fact that 'within Individual Psychology, inferiority feelings are regarded as innate to all humans' (ibid., p.6). It may be difficult for others to see this as I appear very confident and capable. Sometimes I feel very sure about my thinking but fear that I may not articulate it with enough clarity for people to understand it. That matters, not just for me personally, but for the sake of the children, families and practitioners that it may affect.
- I may be listening hard and thinking deeply about what is being said, suspending my view in order to hear that of others. Then I need time to let the thoughts mingle and transform into new group ideas. I use the analogy of a cake here; we each come as separate ingredients, which need

careful mixing of the correct amount then slow baking to produce a cake. The separate ingredients become transformed, along with others, and become a new and greater product.

- I am used to solving my own problems, making my own decisions and not used to taking up group time on my personal issues.

Staff members are now able to assure others that my silences are not to be feared, explaining what they may mean. Some have also begun to talk about their own issues and ways of dealing with things.

A really big dilemma that I have as a leader surfaced as a result of the dialogue; should I express my view and influence decisions or should I take a back seat in order to let others lead? Words used in the questionnaire to describe my leadership included 'strong, challenging, powerful', but also 'coaching and involving'. Examples of the effects of this can be seen in the following comments:

> I sometimes feel nervous about talking to you about personal issues, I don't know why. It could possibly be that you are the boss and I do respect and look up to you . . . after recent chats I feel more at ease talking to you. You listened to me and made me feel my issues were important.

> My initial impression was that you were a forceful person, very much in command. I felt in awe of you. As our relationship has developed I now see you as a friendly, caring person with whom I can share some of my past experiences and that you have a good understanding of me as a person and how the past affects me in the present.

Huffington suggested that leadership in the twenty-first century needed to be 'people centred personal influence . . . collaborative relationships, not control' (2004, p.54). My colleagues agreed that I often articulate the next aspect of the vision, but then engage closely with colleagues to agree the method, timeline and actualisation of it. I shared my dilemma with them. I want our organisation to practise social constructivism, where we all bring our knowledge, experience, feelings and opinions to the group table. Then we need to suspend all of that whilst we engage in deep listening to our colleagues. The resulting dialogue will then be 'greater than the sum of the individual parts'. The role of the leader/facilitator is to coach members to do this. I need to be able to share my expertise, whilst facilitating others to do the same, validating their expertise so that they do not withdraw, feeling that they have to comply with my ideas. Group members made suggestions about how we could deal with my dilemma. We agreed that, as the next step, when a subject is raised for consideration I should make it clear whether I have a clear vision of where we should go, but the means of getting there is up for discussion, or that I really do not know what we should do and an equal dialogue is required.

Another aspect of my influence that was highlighted was that frequently it was I who introduced ideas that challenged their thinking, leading to disequilibration (Piaget, 1997). By my 'skilful interaction' (their words) they somehow find themselves undertaking something new 'as if by magic'. Although empowering, it can sometimes feel unnerving and slightly manipulative. Peter Gronn offers a meaning of the word 'leadership' as 'influencing others to do what they might not have otherwise have done' (2008, p.4). The important consideration is whether or not the recipients are being influenced willingly or not. If they are, then it is effective leadership. The team concluded that any problems they may have had with the power of my influence had been minimised by my sharing my aims and dilemmas with them. They know me better and understand what I am trying to do, which makes them feel more comfortable. This in turn helps them to offer their contribution.

The questionnaires and dialogue revealed practical problems that we went on to solve together. It afforded people a wonderful opportunity to discover the strength and support of the whole team, which led to a huge celebration party, but also provided an ongoing reserve of comfort and strength. This was exemplified in comments like:

> I have been on a real personal learning journey . . . knowing and trusting others has been invaluable. Being part of the team has been vital.

> You always have someone to celebrate with, laugh with, cry with or just scream with. If you trip or fall there is always someone, if not everyone to help pick you up.

> After being one of two stuck behind closed doors it's great being a member of a big team who share and celebrate together.

It was acknowledged that finding the appropriate word that expressed exactly how they felt, without hurting anyone's feelings was hard. Initially 'efforts to get people to trust one another . . . produced the opposite effect by drawing attention to the lack of trust that currently exists' (Senge et al., 2005, p.33). Taking the risk of sharing concerns about different ways of working was painful, but necessary if the relationships are to develop. Free discussions about differences have ironically brought members closer as there is now no need to compare and compete. Instead people share and learn from each other.

Reflections after four months

I believe that the crucial question about my leadership relationship with members of the team is whether I appear too powerful and charismatic to achieve collaboration. The staff that raised the issue confirmed that highlighting this from their responses to questionnaires and initial tentative discussions and bringing it into open discussion was a turning point in our relationship. The fact that I shared my dilemma about leading from the front or 'honking from behind', to use the geese formation analogy, was in itself enough to remove any power inequalities. We agreed that they wanted the benefit of my expertise, but understood that they have current practice wisdom that they should share. I will continue to be bold in offering a huge nudge to people to take their next steps. If we waited for people to be ready or completely confident they would never take the risk, especially people who have been a product of a system that expects them to be compliant and judges them against some artificially imposed criteria. If someone believes in the person so much and has the skill to support them, they can surpass their own doubts and anxieties and find themselves actually taking their next steps. If they then reflect and acknowledge their success, they have truly learned by doing.

Colleagues in leadership roles challenged my conviction about the value of close relationships between a leader and team members. Does it compromise management assertiveness? I strongly believe that it does not. Working together within a shared vision avoids confrontational situations and difficult conversations can be held in a caring manner. Actions may be challenged, but not the person. I feel less isolated and out of step with humanity. Through my own research and reading that of others, I feel more connected with my team and with a wider group of respected professionals who share my optimism.

Implications for practice

I exposed myself to a mirror that I may not have been comfortable with. Working in a high profile leadership role and choosing to research its personal manifestation, then submitting the findings towards an academic award was very challenging. It was a sure test of personal mastery, needing enough openness and resilience to face the mirror, enough humility to learn from others' perceptions and enough self-belief to hold on to my own perceptions. However, the risk continues to reap rewards. I am so much more comfortable with myself and with team members than ever before. Many members report that they also feel more at ease with themselves, with me and with each other. The opportunity to tell our story 'encompasses a capacity for reinterpretation and change. Stories can be retold, reframed, reinterpreted. Because they are fluid, open for retelling and ultimately reliving, they are the repositories of hope' (Cooper, 2002, p.113). The trust between us has grown, our relationship has deepened and with it the capacity for more risk taking together. Since completing the research our organisation has faced traumatic events and accepted huge challenges to develop new areas of work and new ways of working.

It was vitally important for us to understand how I influence the team, as knowledge empowers people and demystifies the experience. It has enabled team members to use my skills to help them to move on.

My professional opinion appears to hold great weight within my organisation and in the local professional scene. My critical friend has helped me to understand that I am perceived as a very principled person with high moral values, with the courage of my own convictions and high regard for the capacity of the human spirit. West-Burnham (2007) referred to 'a dimension of the human experience that motivates, sustains and nourishes over and above the normal patterns of working [which] makes their leadership authentic and enduring'. She explored the notion of spirituality, which lurks in the background of my self-reflection. I was certainly inspired by the concept of servant leadership, especially Jaworski's personal story (1996). I am certainly committed as a leader to 'follow first' (Sergiovanni, 1992, p.72). I see my leadership as a service to children, families and practitioners, holding them in high regard as we work together to improve our lives. Exploration of this concept, together with deeper understanding of the psychology of groups and their leadership are outside the parameters of this study, but do intrigue me.

It seems important to provide a safe and supportive environment for others to explore their inner fears and take next steps in becoming who they want to be. Many people use the opportunity that I give them to do so. It is unreasonable to expect practitioners to be able to support vulnerable children and families to believe in themselves if they are not supported to do so themselves. This is now being explored in a much wider arena within our local authority, under the heading 'Every Adult Matters'.

Staff members report closer relationships with me and other members of the teams, with a growing understanding of others' roles, including mine. We are all much more comfortable with each other, which means that issues are so much easier to discuss and solve. One member wrote 'I don't know whether I am more tuned in or whether Gill's style has changed . . . but it is more pleasurable'.

This research reinforced the importance of three specific aspects of our practice that complement and facilitate our deepening relationships between adults, between adults and children and between children:

1   Our problem-solving approach to our work with each other, with children and with families. It is helpful to agree systems that everyone can use to put those principles into practice. All practitioners are expected to implement our well-documented steps to conflict resolution, which use the High/Scope model (Hohmann and Weikart, 1995, p.405). They receive training and support to do so, as do parents.

    •   At the first sign of any conflict, approach calmly – conflict is an opportunity for growth and creative problem solving.
    •   Encourage all feelings to be expressed in a safe way, allowing time for active listening.
    •   Discover the real problem together.
    •   Explore all possible solutions, until one that is acceptable to all is found.
    •   Support participants to implement the solution.

    There is an expectation that people will express their feelings and needs and listen to the needs of others. It is agreed that anyone who wishes to express an opinion, feeling, or need does so, with the help of a third party if necessary. This is made explicit to parents and children, visitors and prospective staff members during recruitment.

2   Having an agreed practice about acknowledgement of individual's learning and development is also helpful. As a team we agree to acknowledge development in a way that is meaningful to the recipient, adult or child. Judgements and empty praise are not given, but evident learning and development is specifically acknowledged. Individuals are expected to self-acknowledge in ways that are meaningful to them. Self-deprecation is always challenged. This leads to greater self-belief, which in turn encourages people to take responsibility for further learning.

3   We publish our agreed way of working together and all staff members are expected to accept its principles:

We celebrate diversity and work collaboratively with families and professionals.

We are one team that has at its heart the well-being and best outcomes for children, families and staff.

We:

- respect each other
- trust each other
- assume good intentions
- maintain confidentiality
- encourage each other
- express and acknowledge our own and each other's feelings
- accept honest feedback
- are willing to take risks
- use a solutions-oriented approach to situations.

'The whole is greater than the sum of the individual parts.'

My enrolling on a Masters degree course entitled 'Integrated Provision for Children and Families' (the purpose of our organisation) made a difference to the team. I am the leader and oldest member of the organisation, hitherto seen as 'the expert'. It enabled me to demonstrate that being a lifelong learner is fundamental to successful leadership. Undertaking practitioner research about my role afforded a great opportunity to share power and control within the team. The questionnaires and dialogues put team members firmly in control: what they thought mattered and resulted in changes in my behaviour. That it was being documented as part of an academic study added to its validity. Being valued encourages people to take risks. Acknowledgement of their role in this way led members to reflect on their part in the team. The Johari house is a very useful tool to help understand the complexity of who we are and how we are viewed. Opening Johari windows required trust that others would receive the information in good faith. When they clearly did, it led to greater trust and further risk taking.

Inviting team members to reflect on and articulate our relationship and its effectiveness gave it enormous credibility. Almost without realising it, team members became engaged in deep level thinking about my role and consequently about theirs. They found their voice to articulate some sensitive personal reflections. Expressing one's own needs and having them met carries a huge responsibility for hearing and meeting the needs of others. I believe that focussing on relationships enables conflict resolution procedures to be practised in depth, with adults and with children. Expressing one's own feelings may result in an escalation of the issue as the person to whom the feeling is expressed reciprocates. What then appear to be trivial events become more significant and people wonder if it is worth the hassle it causes.

Bruce Nixon pointed out that feelings of hopelessness are often articulated as criticism, complaint and blame. The trick is not to be pulled down by negativity, but to utilise its energy to solve the problem, which is motivating (Nixon, 1994). What is personally quite uncomfortable can easily become one's comfort zone, because it is familiar. To take up the challenge to change requires courage because personal exposure makes one vulnerable and new territory can be unnerving. If relationships are to develop, one has to give a little of oneself in order to gain. Team members have taken those brave steps and reaped the benefit. There has certainly been an increase in creative team problem-solving. It appears to have occurred in a natural and unspectacular fashion. It has resulted in a tangible sense of satisfaction and comfort within the team; members are beginning to take initiatives, hearing each other without appearing threatened by what they hear. It is natural to follow up on anything that any member feels could be improved. This contrasts sharply with teams or individuals who are not able to face their own feelings and opinions or those of others, remaining at best stuck in their learning, or defensive or even offensive about their own position. If they are heard, people are able to hear others. They can then begin to work collectively to understand more about their world. Person centred learning may, however, be threatening to the learner as they take on the responsibility for the issues they identify as needing solutions. It may also be threatening for the leaders as they share the power and control, not knowing where the learning may lead (Rogers in Kirschenbaum and Henderson, 1989, p.328). It is, however, enduring and meaningful, and creates the capacity for further learning.

The development of group relationships that enables sustainable learning is a process that has to evolve. Learning to trust takes time as well as love. Policy makers should accept that we are getting to the heart of what will make a real difference to people's lives; the leaders and practitioners involved need to be nurtured and supported to take the slow, deep route. The capacity to learn is what singles us out as a species. It pervades our lives, cannot be confined to a classroom, occurs through our experiences and is tremendously affected by the social context. It is therefore incumbent upon each practitioner to understand how he or she learns and affects the learning of others, adults and children. This self-knowledge, in turn, creates the capacity to lead one's own and group learning. It is especially important for those who are designated leaders of organisations, to facilitate individual and group reflection. Maybe a glimpse into some of the stages of one organisation's reflective journey could help in some small way to normalise the process for others. It is safe to observe the steps taken by others; one does not have to commit to the journey for oneself. Once on the way, it is comforting to know that others have been on a similar journey. One's own experience is sometimes illuminated by that of others.

What made the whole project worth all the time and effort was epitomised in one short sentence written in a questionnaire response, 'My life changed with the centre'. Intrinsic learning endures. Leadership requires people to be able to have the confidence to bring all of themselves to each situation and to do the best that they can. Working with a critical friend, who is caring yet prepared to reflect deeply is invaluable and mutually supportive. Integrating personal depth in professional contexts encourages deeper learning.

The national agenda of integrating expertise to provide for the holistic development of children and families is to be applauded. But it will not be successful without putting a huge investment into quality provision, especially human resources. Hope can only be offered to children and families by workers who themselves have hope. Self-belief can only be fostered by those who have the means to develop it in themselves. Responsibility for making this happen has to be shared by the whole community of learners. Nor will it succeed without a shift away from the old order of reward by amount of knowledge attained by pupils, where 'It is not so much what the school can do for its students but what the students can do for the school' (Ball in Fielding, 2006, p.357). The organisation's raison d'être must become 'the development of the learning community' (Fielding, 2006, p.360), rather than academic attainment. This requires a different kind of leadership, which is perhaps better described as facilitation, because of the connotations of leadership as something that is usually done by one person and usually from the front. 'To facilitate' is derived from *leitum faciles*, which in Latin means 'to make easy'. It requires interpersonal intelligence, 'the authentic range of intuitive behaviours derived from sophisticated self-awareness, which facilitates effective engagement with others' (West-Burnham, 2001, p.2). However, to be able to sustain the level of integrity and deep personal commitment necessary requires ongoing support for one's own development and emotional well being: 'Unless reformers and policy makers care for leaders' personal and professional lives, they will engineer short term gains only by mortgaging the entire future of leadership' (Hargreaves and Fink, 2004, p.8).

The pre-condition for person centred learning to take place is that:

a leader in the situation is sufficiently secure in herself and in her relationship with others that she experiences an essential trust in the capacity of others to think for themselves, to learn for themselves.

(Rogers in Kirschenbaum and Henderson, 1989, p.327)

Reflections and questions

Gill seemed to be brave and to take some huge risks during this journey with the staff team in her organisation.

*   How aware are you of how you behave as a newcomer to a group?
*   How honestly are you able to express your feelings in your staff team?
*   How important is it to you to reflect on and to understand your own experiences, as a child?

Applying learning to practice

*   Although Gill did not mention it, many leaders find reflection is facilitated by regularly writing down thoughts and feelings in a journal.
*   Reflecting with colleagues on a 'critical incident' can help us all learn from both positive and negative experiences.
*   Anyone can experiment with behaving differently. If you are always the person to lead with your opinion in meetings, a great deal can be learned from holding back and listening to others.

References

Cooper, Joanne E. (2002). Constructivist leadership: Its evolving narrative, in Lambert, Linda, Walker, Deborah, Zimmerman, Diane P., Cooper, Joanne E., Lambert, Morgan Dale, Gardner, Mary E. and Szabo, Margaret, *The Constructivist Leader*. Oxford: National Staff Development Council.

Elliott, John (1999). *Action Research for Educational Change*. Maidenhead: Open University Press.

Fielding, Michael (2006). Leadership, personalization and high performance: Schooling, naming the new totalitarianism. *School Leadership and Management*, 26 (4): 347–369.

Goleman, Daniel (2002). *The New Leaders*. London: Little Brown.

Gronn, Peter (2008). The future of distributed leadership. *Journal of Educational Administration*, 46 (2), 141–158.

Hall, Valerie (1996). *Dancing on the Ceiling*. London: Paul Chapman Publishing.

Halton, William (1994). Some unconscious aspects of organizational life: Contributions from psychoanalysis, in Obholzer, Anton and Roberts, Vega Zagier (eds) *The Unconscious at Work, Individual and Organizational Stress in the Human Services*. London: Routledge.

Handy, Charles (1990). *Inside Organisations*. London: BBC Books.

Hargreaves, Andy and Fink, Dean (2004). The seven principles of sustainable leadership. *Educational Leadership* 61 (7): 8–13.

Hohmann, Mary and Weikart, David (1995). *Educating Young Children*. Ypisilanti, MI: High/Scope Educational Research Foundation.

Huffington, Clare (2004). What women leaders can tell us, in Huffington, Clare, Armstong, David, Halton, William, Hoyle, Linda and Pooley, Jane (eds) *Working Below the Surface, The Emotional Life of Contemporary Organizations*, Tavistock Clinic Series. London: Karnac.

Jaworski, Joseph (1996). *Synchronicity, the Inner Path of Leadership*. San Francisco: Berrett-Koehler.

John, Karen (2000). Basic needs, conflict and dynamics in groups. *Journal of Individual Psychology*, 56 (4): 419–434.

John, Karen (2007). Sustaining the leaders of children's centres. The role of leadership mentoring. Presentation at 'Sustainable leadership' conference, Pen Green Research, Development and Training Base and Leadership Centre.

Kirschenbaum, Howard and Henderson, Valerie (eds) (1989). *The Carl Rogers Reader*. Boston: Houghton Mifflin.

Lambert, Linda and Walker, Deborah (2002). Constructing school change – School stories, in Lambert, Linda, Walker, Deborah, Zimmerman, Diane P., Cooper, Joanne E., Lambert, Morgan Dale, Gardner, Mary E. and Szabo, Margaret, *The Constructivist Leader*. Oxford: National Staff Development Council.

McNiff, Jean and Whitehead, Jack (2002). *Action Research for Teachers*. London: David Fulton Publishers.

Nixon, Bruce (1994). Facilitating empowerment for organisations. *Learning and Organisational Development Journal*, 15 (4): 3–11.

Obholzer, Anton and Roberts,Vega Zagier (eds) (1994). *The Unconscious at Work, Individual and Organizational Stress in the Human Services*. London: Routledge.

Piaget, Jean, (1997). *The Development of Thought: Equilibration of Cognitive Structures*. New York: Viking.

Senge, Peter (1992). *The Fifth Discipline*. London: Century Business.

Senge, Peter, Cambron-McCabe, Nelda, Lucas, Timothy, Smith, Bryan, Dutton, Janis and Kleiner, Art (2000). *Schools that Learn: A Fifth Discipline Fieldbook for Educators, Parents, and Everyone Who Cares About Education*. London: Nicholas Brealey Publishing.

Senge, Peter, Jaworski, Joseph, Scharmer, C. Otto and Flowers, Betty Sue (2005) *Presence, Exploring Profound Change in People, Organizations and Society*. London: Nicholas Brealey Publishing.

Sergiovanni, Thonas J. (1992). *Getting to the Heart of School Improvement*. San Francisco: Jossey-Bass Publishers.

Stokes, Jon (1994). The unconscious at work in groups and teams: Contributions from the work of Wilfred Bion, in Obholzer, Anton and Roberts, Vega Zagier (eds) *The Unconscious at Work, Individual and Organizational Stress in the Human Services*. London: Routledge.

West-Burnham, John (2001). *Interpersonal Leadership*. Nottingham: National College for School Leadership.

Woods, Ronnie (2003). *Enchanted Headteachers*. Report for National College of School Leadership, Nottingham.

West-Burnham, John (2007). Think piece from National College for School Leaders. In presentation by John Yates to Wokingham headteachers and local authority officers conference, Surviving, thriving and enjoying the job, Cheltenham.

Chapter 9

Learning to return

What supports adults to return to learning?

Anne Gladstone

In this chapter you will find:

- An account of a small study involving eight parents returning to learn as adults.
- An exploration of the concepts of 'resilience' and 'social and emotional capital'.
- A discussion of the importance of relationships, both past and present, in enabling adults to return to learning.

The start of the journey

The inspiration for this research was the work I carried out in a children's centre supporting parents and carers on their learning journeys. I was interested in those adults who choose to actively become learners again through accessing what McGivney (2001: 71) calls 'organised learning'. I was curious to discover from some of these adults what it was that had enabled them to begin a new phase of learning. I was aware that for many people, actually taking the step to return to learning was a time that was frequently fraught with difficulties and anxiety.

I was not so much interested in the very real barriers which adults (particularly parents of young children) face when they return to learning such as childcare funding, difficulty with access and financial constraints, all of which are well documented (Cullen and Lindsay, 2005: 49–52; Gledhill, 2002: 3–16; Fitzgerald *et al.*, 2003: 38–45). What I was interested in investigating were the things that empowered and supported adults as they took the sometimes enormous step back into the world of education, often surmounting many barriers on the way. I have used the phrase 'step back' consciously even though in reality the step could be seen as a forward one. This is because I have observed that for many people, the decision to start formal learning again begins with a swift return to a raft of attitudes and beliefs about themselves which influence their transition into the new (and perhaps unknown) phase of their life. I was interested to find out what supports adults through this change in their life and where the resilience (that I had observed) of many adults, often in the face of numerous difficulties, emanates from.

Recent government initiatives and policies in both early years and adult education (Sure Start, 2003: 6; Secretary of State for Education and Skills, 2003) would appear to be creating the possibility for everyone to have the opportunity to achieve self-fulfilment through education and employment. However, Diane Reay (2001: 334) argues that our current education system 'retains remnants of . . . past elite prejudices' and that it is 'an explicit example of the use of schooling by a dominant class to secure hegemony over subordinate groups' (ibid.: 333). In her view this state of affairs makes the transition, particularly into higher education, a difficult prospect for many working-class men and women.

The impact of adult learning on families

There are many benefits of returning to learning, other than simply gaining knowledge or perhaps employment, which impact positively on parents and children and, in the long term, on society. Research (Aldridge and Lavender, 2000; Feinstein *et al.*, 2003; Feinstein and Hammond, 2003; Hammond, 2004) has demonstrated that for many adults engaged in learning there were wide-ranging benefits in terms of improved physical, emotional and mental health, including increased confidence and self-esteem.

Parents' relationships with their children are also positively affected through involvement in learning. Hammond believes that the positive impact of learning on the psychological health of adults 'will contribute to positive family functioning and social cohesion' (2004: 566). The links between infants' mental health and the mental health of their parents are well known particularly in the area of attachment theory based on the work of John Bowlby and Mary Ainsworth (Goldberg, 2000: 1–12). The caregiver's own mental health profoundly affects the nature of the attachment between the caregiver and the child and thus, the infant's mental health. If the parent enjoys good mental health, a healthy attachment relationship between the parent and the infant is much more likely to be developed. This clearly has implications then not just for children's mental health, but also their developing intellect.

In addition children's learning and emotional well-being can be positively affected through their relationship with a parent who is directly involved with the child's learning (Arnold, 2001: 97; Horne and Haggart, 2004: 55–56; Whalley, 2001: 9). Parents have reported that as a result of their involvement in Family Learning programmes they noticed that their children were doing better at school, that their behaviour had improved and their confidence had increased.

A time of change

Returning to learning is a time of change, which for human beings, can be a profound and extremely difficult experience but can also be very positive and can provide 'the opportunity for learning' (Smith, 2002: 11). I perceived my role in the children's centre as supporting individuals through a time of change as they returned to learning.

Contemplating change involves thinking about the future and predicting or imagining what it might look and feel like. This can be 'a very demanding learning effort for many people' (Rogers and Tough, 1996: 491) involving 'the heart as well as the mind' (ibid.: 493). Rogers and Tough liken this emotional response to 'being like a roller-coaster' where extreme and opposite emotions such as depression and elation, fear and courage fluctuate constantly.

Fundamental to the understanding of change is the notion of transition. Change is seen as external, whilst transition is viewed as internal and described as 'a psychological orientation that people have to go through before the change can work' (Bridges and Mitchell Bridges, 2000: 2). Change happens relatively quickly, but the process of transition can take much longer and is typically protracted and difficult (Bridges, 2003: 8). Bridges and Mitchell Bridges (2000: 2) argue that when change occurs, transition is not an automatic process and unless transition is understood and managed, the anticipated change is very unlikely to happen as planned (Bridges, 2003: 3).

The transition process involved in returning to learning then, is potentially problematic and even when the decision to change – to become a learner again – is a positive one, the transition process has associated negative components. These can include grief, a loss of self-identity, fear, anxiety and even ill health. For some people, although the transition process may be uncomfortable, they will emerge relatively unscathed but for others the transition process may not be completed, leading to abandonment of the change itself, accompanied by a sense of personal failure. However, many adults do make a successful transition back into learning. Tough (1982: 14–15) tells us that 'men and women are remarkably successful at choosing, planning and implementing intentional change'. It would seem that successful change requires the ability to weather that change, in other words, to be resilient.

Resilience and change

Research around resilience traditionally focussed on babies and children in the context of infant mental health (Hartley-Brewer, 2001; Stein et al., 2000) as well as special education (Lewis, 2000). More recently, resilience has been a key concept in health, education and social work policy research (Bartley, 2006; Newman and Blackburn, 2002) and in considering the needs of students in higher education (Walker et al., 2006). Resilience is now seen not just as applying to individuals, but also as something which organisations and communities can promote and develop, or of course inhibit (Lewis, 2000: 1). Walker et al. (2006: 251) assert that resilience not only describes the ability to recover rapidly from difficulties, but also 'the ability to endure ongoing hardship in every perceivable way'. They see resilience generally as a very important concept in terms of education in 'formal and informal learning contexts' (ibid.: 252) and suggest that resilience (or more specifically the lack of it) should be considered in both pedagogy and student support.

In the opinion of Stein *et al.* (2000: 283), 'resilience is best regarded as an interactive process that unfolds over time' and which is 'continually influenced by ongoing changes in context'. Risk factors have been identified that might adversely affect the development of resilience such as material disadvantage and difficulties in family life (Bartley, 2006: 2). However, Stein *et al.* (2000: 282) note that, paradoxically, adversity does not necessarily prevent the development of resilience and can actually promote it. Nevertheless, according to Newman and Blackburn (2002: 3), transitional periods (such as returning to learning) are particularly risky times in terms of resilience to adversity.

Protective factors have been identified which have the capacity to promote resilience. Secure attachment is a powerful protective factor in developing resilience in the earliest years and beyond (Hartley-Brewer, 2001: 9). Other factors include those within an individual's social environment such as 'relationships with family members, peers, teachers and social institutions' (Stein *et al.*, 2000: 282). Support from a partner or confidante is identified as being key to developing resilience in adulthood. It would seem then that relationships with others, from the earliest attachment relationship with a caregiver, to those within the family and in the wider community are key factors in acquiring resilience.

The value of relationships

The transition involved in change, requires resilience which is strongly associated with relationships with others. The nature of these relationships, which are fundamental to being human, is central to my enquiry. From the minute they are born human beings are innately social – an infant's development and learning is mediated by social relationships (Gerhardt, 2004: 18). Dewey (1897: 77–80) and later Bruner (Wood *et al.*, 1976: 90) and Vygotsky (1978: 87) saw social relationships as crucial to the process of learning. More recently Rogoff (1990: 39) describes the learning process as one of apprenticeship where 'novices advance their skills and understanding through participation with more skilled partners in culturally organized activities'.

This theme is developed by Colwyn Trevarthen (2002: 3) who asserts 'a desire to know more and to gain skill in ways that other trusted people recognise and encourage is the defining feature of young human nature'. Daniel Siegel (1998: 5) discusses how mental processes 'may be fundamentally influenced by interpersonal experience' and although these influences are greatest during infancy 'the socially dependent nature of our brains suggests that interpersonal experience may continue to influence neurobiological processes throughout the lifespan'.

The importance of relationships accords with the philosophy of Paulo Freire, who sees the way for people to move forward as a process of 'transforming action' in which both themselves and others are involved (1993: 29). In order for this process to happen people have to analyse and understand their situation through dialogue with themselves and with others and then develop strategies to move forwards. The idea of learners being in control of their own learning through a reflective process involving other people is congruent with the thinking of Malcolm Knowles (1975). Knowles considers that adults need to understand their own learning and to be able to make their own decisions about it with the support of another person who is sensitive to their needs (Knowles, 1975: 18). Jack Mezirow (1999: 1), when discussing adult learning, talks about transformative learning or 'perspective transformation', the process of which emphasises 'contextual understanding, critical reflection on assumptions and validating meaning through discourse'. According to Mezirow (1991: 5), 'transformative learning develops autonomous thinking'.

Relationships and social capital

Relationships are not only important in supporting individuals to develop resilience, to cope with change and to learn and move forward. There are also wider benefits for individuals and communities that accrue from social networks and relationships. Social capital is a concept which has been identified in this respect. According to Feinstein *et al.*,

> there is strong evidence that adult learning contributes to changes in attitudes and behaviours that promote social capital and, possibly, social cohesion.
>
> (2003: vi)

Morrow, in common with many others, sees social capital as an 'elusive concept', which refers to 'sociability, social networks and social support' together with 'trust, reciprocity, and community and civic engagement' (1999: 744). Diane Reay (2002: 2) asserts that 'social capital is generated through social processes between the family and the wider society and is made up of social networks'. Seaman and Sweeting (2004: 173), looking at the role of families in 'the production and garnering of social capital', suggest that social capital can be described as 'a characteristic of the relations between people'. They go on to say that 'advantage is found where trust and reciprocity enable access to resources such as human and cultural capital that already exist' (ibid.).

Coleman describes social capital as being 'significant primarily as a way of understanding the relationship between educational achievement and social inequalities' (Schuller *et al.*, 2000: 5). Morrow (1999: 760) proposes that social capital might be conceptualised 'not so much as a measurable "thing"', but as a 'set of processes and practices that are integral to the acquisition of other forms of capital'. Coleman asserts that 'social capital is productive, making possible the achievement of certain ends that in its absence would not be possible' (Coleman, 1988: S98). So, it would seem that social capital is a desirable commodity that can be accrued through social interaction both within and outside families and as part of the educational process and can subsequently be 'cashed in terms of social mobility' (Silva and Edwards, 2004: 3).

Methodology

Thinking about the research process

The process of reflecting on methodology in the design of my research was at times frustrating and confusing but also forced me to understand 'where I was coming from' as a researcher and to use this realisation as the basis for designing and carrying out the research project from start to finish. Roberts-Holmes (2005: 21) tells us that methodology 'informs the entire research process' because it is concerned with principles and values.

There are two research traditions that can be used to understand 'the world and human behaviour within it' (ibid.: 38–39). The positivist tradition is the more traditional scientific approach that attempts to seek a particular truth, assumes a stable reality and is usually associated with the use of quantitative research methods. Alternatively, in the interpretivist tradition 'theories and concepts tend to arise from the enquiry' (Robson, 1993: 19). This tradition is concerned with 'the complexity and diversity of human interactions' (Roberts-Holmes, 2005: 38–39) and knowledge is seen as valid if it is 'the authentic and true voice of the participants' (ibid.: 40). The use of qualitative research methods is generally associated with this tradition. Robson (1993: 20) takes the view that the differences between the positivist and the interpretivist traditions are best seen as 'technical rather than epistemological'. He argues that this stance, which I found helpful, allows the researcher to select research methods that are most appropriate to their particular study. According to Brookfield (1983: 7), it is widely believed that 'a full appreciation of adult learning in the community' (which is broadly my area of investigation) is only possible if the 'traditional canons of scientific methodology' (ibid.) are abandoned.

Ethical considerations

According to Roberts-Holmes (2005: 8) ethics should be considered as a central feature of any research and must 'continuously permeate all aspects of the research process'. Robson (1993: 29) tells us that ethics generally involves conforming to a set of principles or a code of conduct that are explicit for many professionals who work directly with adults and children. I referred to the code of ethics in my own workplace regarding expected conduct when working with families. I was also guided by the principles and rules referred to by Kent (2000: 61–67) which were developed by ethicists in the early twentieth century. The four principles are autonomy, beneficence, non-malificence and justice. The four rules, which are seen as necessary in order for the researcher to develop trust with the research participants, are veracity, privacy, confidentiality and fidelity.

Choosing a research tool

Bell (1992: 4) states that 'different styles, traditions or approaches use different methods of collecting data, but no approach prescribes nor automatically rejects any particular method'. Rubin and Rubin believe that 'the experiences and perspectives of those being studied' can be captured, analysed and reported in 'rich and realistic detail' (2005: 2) through interviews. An interview is simply a conversation with a purpose which is 'initiated by the interviewer for the specific purpose of obtaining research-relevant information' (Robson, 1993: 229). Steinar Kvale suggests 'if you want to know how people understand their world and their life, why not talk to them?' (1996: 1). Interviews are extremely adaptable and allow the interviewer to probe into the responses received and gain an insight into the feelings, issues and interests of the interviewee. A disadvantage of interviewing is that it is extremely time-consuming, involving not only the interviews but also transcribing any tapes used.

According to Bell (1992: 70), interviewing is also a 'highly subjective technique' and as such is open to bias. However, in my experience the similarity of responses which has emerged in interviews I have carried out in the past has given real validity to the research. A strength of qualitative data in the form of words is that they 'have a quality of undeniability which lends verisimilitude to reports' (Robson, 1993: 370). Kvale describes the qualitative research interview as 'a construction site of knowledge' (1996: 2) and uses the metaphor of the 'interviewer as traveller' (ibid.: 4) to explain the nature of the interview process, seeing the interviewer themselves as the research instrument (Kvale, 2006: 1–2). The journey of the interviewer as traveller is thought about not only as one that leads to new knowledge, but also one which instigates reflection. This process of reflection can lead to 'new understanding and insight' (Kvale, 1996: 4).

Deciding who to interview

Since I was using the interpretivist paradigm for my research, where the focus is 'specific, local and contextual' (Roberts-Holmes, 2005: 39), I felt an approach in line with purposive sampling was appropriate when deciding who to interview. This method is where 'a sample is built up which enables the researcher to satisfy her specific needs in a project' (Robson, 1993: 142). I decided to interview just eight individuals, using semi-structured interviews, to ensure the amount of data collected was appropriate to the size of the study. Robson (ibid.: 370) warns us, with respect to data collection in qualitative research that 'overload is a constant danger'. The eight interviewees comprised two men and six women and included parents of different ages ranging from early twenties to people in their thirties.

Designing the interview schedule

According to Bell (1992: 70), wording questions for interviews is demanding, but precision is not absolutely vital because of the flexibility of the interview process. However, I needed to have some basic questions which would guide the interview and keep it 'focussed on the research subject' (Roberts-Holmes, 2005: 110). I knew from experience, both of teaching adults and working with them individually, that when I started to talk with them about their experiences of learning I could be opening up the proverbial 'can of worms'. Because of this, I had to be clear in my own mind about what particular areas I wanted to explore to ensure that I kept the interview 'on track'. I was also aware that when devising the interview questions I would need to make them straightforward and open-ended. This would give the interviewee plenty of scope for answering (within my chosen framework) and give me the opportunity to probe further and hopefully gain more insight into the responses.

When deciding on the actual wording of my questions I asked myself what it was specifically about the main question of 'what supports adults returning to learning?' that I wanted to know about. I was very interested in any memorable relationships that people had experienced with respect to learning (positive or negative), both as children and as adults. I wanted to discover if these relationships had influenced the person's attitudes to learning and to themselves as learners. I also wanted to know why people had decided to return to learning, how confident they felt about carrying out that decision and what influenced their level of confidence. The next issue I was interested in was to find out if the individuals had experienced any difficulties when they were in the process of returning to learning. If difficulties had been experienced I wanted to find out what support strategies individuals had used to overcome them and what they had experienced as helpful in this process. Although part of my interest in the subject of supporting adults into learning was about my own role, I did not want to focus on this specifically. I felt that if I did this it might well lead to 'interviewees seeking to please the interviewer' (Robson, 1993: 232) because of the personal relationship which already existed between us. I hoped that in broadening out the questions, this kind of bias would be minimised, but aspects of my role which had affected participants would be elucidated. The questions I used to guide the interviews were as follows:

Thinking of yourself as a child/young person:
- What experiences of learning (as you were growing up) come into your mind?
- Why are they memorable?

- Who were the key people who most influenced you as a learner?
- What influence did they have?

Thinking of yourself as an adult:
- What learning have you taken part in since leaving full-time education?
- What made you decide to return to learning?
- When you decided to return to learning, how confident were you in yourself as a learner?
- What do you think influenced your level of confidence?
- What difficulties (if any) did you have when you were returning to learning?
- How did you overcome them?
- What (other) support was available to you to when you were returning to learning?
- What (other) things were helpful to you when you were returning to learning?
- What would you identify as the most important factors which enabled you to return to learning?

Analysing the data

As I conducted the interviews, my initial feelings were that my collection of data was as 'rich, full and real' as Robson (1993: 370) tells us is the nature of this type of qualitative data. Robson (ibid.: 377) suggests that there is no 'right way' of analysing qualitative data and that the most important ingredient is 'clear thinking on the part of the analyst' (ibid.: 374). I made the decision that my analysis would involve grouping and regrouping the data to identify categories and themes. I realised it would be necessary to reflect on the data over a period of time to ensure that I did not jump to immediate conclusions or miss or exclude data which could be extremely meaningful.

Thoughts on my findings

First thoughts

As I reflected on the data, I was struck by the poignancy of many of the responses and the depth of feeling associated with experiences which were remembered by individuals. These feelings related both to happy memories and to less happy and sometimes distressing ones. Each person I spoke to had a unique story to tell about their learning journey, but there were striking similarities which emerged with respect to returning to learning.

The significance of relationships

Much more emphasis was placed by interviewees on relationships than on the more concrete forms of support. People were asked directly about key relationships with respect to learning in childhood and so these relationships were obviously discussed. However, relationships were again much alluded to in responses around the kind of support which was helpful when returning to learning. Individuals seemed to be making use of supportive relationships to help them through this time of transition.

Two interesting aspects that emerged with respect to relationships were first, relationships in the past, particularly in childhood, and, second, more recent and current relationships. I found that whilst individuals drew directly on relationships in the present, such as those with friends, family and professionals, they also relied on remembered relationships and the experiences associated with them. It seems to me that these different experiences interact with each other to create the emotional climate within each person that affects them very noticeably when they return to learning. Both sets of experiences, past and present, often evoked feelings of competence, confidence and a sense of self-efficacy. In the same way both memories and recent experiences also gave rise to feelings of failure, fear and alienation. The effects of remembered relationships seemed to be at least as powerful, if not more so, than more recent experiences. For all but one person, experiences within the family had positive effects. However, outside the family there was a greater proportion of negative experiences generated, all of which related to school days. McGivney (2001: 71) describes the grim reality of some adults' experiences of school when she tells us that 'one of the strongest inhibitors to engagement in organised learning is negative self-perceptions in relation to learning arising from earlier school experiences'. It seems then that experiences related to learning both during childhood and whilst growing up can have a profound effect on returning to learning as an adult.

Relationship with self and others

Part of the findings, pertaining to positive relationships, which emerged very strongly, was the ability of people to rely on their own internal resources to get them through the transition back into learning. I think this gave an insight into the resilience I have seen so often in many of the people I have worked with. I realised that each respondent's most influential relationship was the one with themselves. In this relationship it appeared that both remembered and recent experiences of interactions with others were very important. It seemed as if these factors combined to determine the level of internal support the individual could draw on when returning to learning. This internal support appeared to enable individuals to find their way through emotional issues as well as to solve the more concrete problems they faced. There are echoes here of Freud's concepts of id and ego which are seen to be important in the development of the self and the self in relationship with others (Wilderdom, 2004: 1). In this theory the id equates to the child within us and is related to the emotional parts of the mind. The ego represents the adult and relates to the rational part of the mind.

It is suggested by Siegel with respect to the learning of both children and adults that 'there are no discernible boundaries between our thoughts and our feelings' (1998: 6). Piaget (1964: 5) also believed that 'affectivity and intelligence are indissociable'. Taking these ideas of the individual's thoughts and feelings being intimately linked and inseparable, Siegel proposes a neurobiology of interpersonal experience. He explains that 'human relationships shape the brain structure from which the mind emerges' (1998: 2). Siegel suggests that interpersonal experience 'may continue to influence neurobiological processes throughout the lifespan' (ibid.: 5). It would seem then that our relationships with others and how these make us feel about ourselves, fundamentally and profoundly shape our minds both at the psychological and the physiological level. The positive or negative effects of these relationships, whether in childhood or in adulthood, leave a lasting imprint on individuals and affect their relationship with themselves.

Whatever their personal, internal resources, all respondents still appeared to need (and indeed accessed) support from friends, family, children's centre staff or other professionals during their transition back into learning. It seems that this transition period triggered some loss of personal efficacy and confidence. This corresponds with feelings commonly experienced by individuals who are in the neutral zone of the transition process (Bridges and Mitchell Bridges, 2000: 2–3). This time is generally experienced as being very confusing, with individuals often losing sight of their sense of identity. Research has indicated that even people who are 'ready and prepared' to return to learning 'often need input from other people' (McGivney, 2001: 86). My research demonstrated for all those interviewed that input and support from other people gave reassurance as well as renewing confidence and determination. According to Bennetts, 'those whose lives are at a transitory stage do appear to be particularly open to the effect of others and these alliances may be transformative and profound, leading to self-actualisation' (2001: 2).

The quality of relationships

The quality of relationships with other people also emerged strongly as an extremely important theme. This was expressed as the way relationships affected people's feelings about themselves as well as how relationships made people feel supported. One of the areas associated with quality of relationships was being enabled to move forward with returning to learning. I see moving forward as again linking in closely to change and transition. In order to move forward individuals need time to take stock, to gather information, to reflect on available choices and to make decisions. It is very hard to think about all this if people's minds are distracted by their feelings, which are often in a state of confusion during transition. Nicholson (1990: 96) suggests that in order to manage change, relationships should be formed that 'cultivate a sense of competence' for individuals. Much of the data revealed aspects of relationships which enabled individuals to deal with the emotional ups and downs and the very real difficulties which change and transition created in their lives.

The research also demonstrated that individuals experienced being listened to and understood. I think these perceptions relate to emotional containment and reciprocity which are features of supportive relationships. The space individuals need to think about change is created by the emotional containment offered through a supportive relationship. I see this as relationships enabling the individual to obtain a balance between their rational and emotional thoughts. 'I can learn' as opposed to 'I'm scared'. This thinking can be developed through a relationship with another person, but has the potential to be used eventually by the individual themselves. The relationships people described appeared to allow people to express their fears safely and then to confront and deal with them rationally. Philip and Shucksmith (2005: 1) report that successful mentoring relationships are those which involve 'trust and reciprocity'.

Emotional capital

Many of the respondents described how interactions with a variety of other people had enabled them to get to grips with their learning as well as dealing with the frustrations of finding and accessing learning opportunities. It seemed that individuals were building up a body of knowledge and a range of strategies that were enabling them to take advantage of available opportunities. It appears that through supportive relationships, individuals were able to accrue social capital which is seen as a necessary commodity for success in the educational system.

Another aspect of this building up of personal reserves is related to emotions. In this respect I have conceptualised the effect of relationships on individuals as either filling or depleting an emotional reservoir that each person has within themselves (see Figure 9.1). The level in the emotional reservoir determines an individual's levels of confidence, self-belief and resilience. The reservoir is filled or depleted by the individual internalising positive or negative aspects of relationships with others. In other words our emotional reservoirs can be filled up or drained according to our experiences when interacting with others.

I think this resonates with the concept of emotional capital that was introduced by Helga Nowotny (1981), who sees emotional capital as 'a variant of social capital' (Reay, 2002: 5) which is dependent on the existence of social relationships. Emotional capital is defined by Patricia Allatt (1993: 143) as 'emotionally valued assets and skills, love and affection, expenditure of time, attention, care and concern'. Reay (2002: 6) sees emotional capital as being

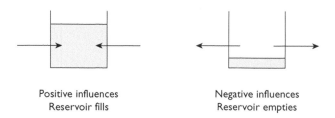

Positive influences   Negative influences
Reservoir fills   Reservoir empties

Figure 9.1 Diagram to illustrate the concept of emotional reservoirs

built up over time and comprising a 'stock of resources' which can be drawn on. Examples of these resources are 'support, patience and commitment'. These assets and resources are very similar to the aspects of positive relationships that the research demonstrated individuals experienced as supportive when returning to learning and also that respondents used in their relationships with themselves. In times of adversity, such as the transition into becoming a learner again, it is as if people use positive relationships to top up their reservoir of emotional capital. People who have accrued high levels of emotional capital through early supportive relationships may still need a small re-fill at times of stress when levels are lowered. However, people who have not had their share of emotional capital as children have a greater need to fill their reservoir in order to move towards their chosen goal with confidence and a sense of self-efficacy.

I think the fact that people talked about positive and negative experiences, both past and present, demonstrates the dynamic nature of emotional capital. It would seem to be the case that it is not only possible to accrue emotional capital, but also to have it depleted both as a child and as an adult. It is not a once and for all commodity that we each get our share of in childhood, but something which we can add to throughout our lives, given the right environment. Nowotny sees emotional capital as being 'developed in adverse circumstances' (Reay, 2002: 5). I think this very much equates to the paradox which exists in the concept of resilience where risk factors, which have the potential to inhibit the development of resilience, can actually promote it.

According to Reay, 'poverty is not an environment in which emotional capital can normally thrive' (ibid.: 17) and living in poverty is 'an emotionally draining experience'. So, it would seem that individuals who suffer disadvantage in their lives, particularly as children but also as adults, may well have decreased chances of accruing emotional capital. Disadvantage, in terms of emotional support from parents, did indeed emerge from the research. For those individuals this was associated with long-standing and entrenched negative feelings about themselves as learners. On a more positive note, the research demonstrated that even the individuals who identified negative experiences in childhood were able to draw on supportive relationships in the present for emotional support in order to support the process of returning to learning.

Aspiration versus access

It was very clear from the interviews that despite varying levels of confidence, the parents I talked to had very clear aspirations about returning to learning. Individuals also demonstrated high levels of personal motivation, whatever their previous experiences of learning, which helped them through adversity. This was not a surprise to me because my experience in working with parents mirrors these findings. However, these facts do not bear out the view which is often reflected in policy documents about adults returning to learning, and in particular those adults who live in areas which are defined as being deprived (Burke, 2006: 719–733). Policies around widening adult participation in education 'have been fixed on "raising aspirations"' (ibid.: 719). Burke believes that this assumption is 'atheoretical' and has not been 'critically examined, problematised or addressed, often exacerbating social exclusions and inequalities' (ibid.). The assumption that people's aspirations need to be raised leads to a deficit model of the potential learners which policies are supposedly designed to support. Tom Nesbit (2006: 177) also observes that within educational institutions, which are 'generally a middle-class domain', the policies as well as the practice are 'weighted strongly in favour of middle-class values', thus further contributing to exclusion and inequality that make access to these institutions difficult for working-class people.

In addition there was an underlying notion in people's responses that there was a feeling of not fitting in – that learning is 'not for the likes of them' (McGivney, 2001: 70). McGivney calls this 'a denial of imagined possibility' (ibid.). This echoes the words of Paulo Freire who writes,

> self deprecation is another characteristic of the oppressed . . . so often do they hear that they are good for nothing, know nothing and are incapable of learning anything . . . that in the end they become convinced of their own unfitness.
>
> (Freire 1993: 45)

Linked to feelings of not fitting in were notions of fear and risk in relation to returning to learning. This was expressed as fear of the unknown and fear of failure. McGivney (2001: 73) describes anxieties around returning to learning which relate to 'leaving familiar territory'. This is associated with fear of alienation from family and friends when individuals come from a background where 'there is no tradition of participation in organised education' (ibid.). Diane Reay (2001: 337) also suggests that there is an underlying fear for people of losing themselves in the process of returning to learning. For some adults, when re-entering the world of higher education, 'the threat of losing oneself . . . is as likely a prospect as finding oneself' (ibid.: 338). For Reay, there is a difficult balance to be negotiated between 'investing in a new improved identity and holding on to a cohesive sense of self' (ibid.: 338). Bennetts (2001: 2) tells us that an individual's existing sense of identity is an important factor in adult change and learning situations. Paradoxically then, the process of entering organised learning (which is seen as a positive thing to do), can itself compromise and erode an individual's sense of self.

The feelings experienced in such a transition are likened to those experienced during grieving (Williams, 2005: 2). As Marris (1986: x) puts it, 'social changes which disrupt our ability to interpret and respond to our world of experience are a form of bereavement'. This bereavement-like experience calls for a process of recovery in order that 'the underlying structure of emotion and purpose can disengage itself from irretrievable assumptions and circumstances without losing its ability to generate meaning' (ibid.). It is at this time when people will most need support to 'recover' and regain their perspective and ability to move forward. In this process of recovery the emotional capital gained through past and present relationships can be drawn on. If individuals are short of support and thus a top-up of emotional capital, then the process of recovery may well not happen. In the case of returning to learning this could well result in failing to make that transition. This would almost inevitably result in the individual experiencing failure, frustration and perhaps anger that will further deplete their emotional reservoir.

Nicholson (1990: 93), considering the effects of transition, asserts that 'there is important work to be done in the design of education, training and careers counselling to help people target future change'. McGivney (1990: 128) found there was much evidence of 'the urgent need for accessible advice and guidance systems for people who have little post-school educational experience'. When individuals are considering returning to learning McGivney also reports that 'scant attention is given by institutions to assisting individuals in their first contacts with them' (ibid.: 150). It seems that, as Nicholson tells us, 'in too many cases it is apparent that organizations are as unready for . . . transitions as are [the] newcomers' (1990: 94).

Unseen adults

An area of particular interest was the amount of post-school learning that people had already undertaken before they accessed me for support. All the participants had either successfully accessed, or attempted to access, adult learning. Many had achieved qualifications along the way. Only one person had not been successful in accessing learning prior to engagement with the children's centre. This seems to be an indicator that few people with little educational success were accessing my services within the children's centre. However, it should be noted here that the people I interviewed were currently accessing educational opportunities that many of their peers in more affluent areas may well have been able to access straight from school.

Much of my research sheds light on the very real difficulties experienced by a majority of relatively confident and experienced learners. In the light of these difficulties, I suppose it is not surprising that less confident and inexperienced learners did not make use of my services, even when I went out to meet them in the community. Hammond and Feinstein (2006: 31) tell us that 'poor attainment and disengagement at [secondary] school' are linked to a reduced likelihood of accessing courses as an adult. Fitzgerald *et al.* (2003: 26) found that the highest level of learning by adults with no qualifications was 29 per cent in their 'any learning' category and fell to as low as 11 per cent in their 'non-vocational learning' category. In the ward in which I worked, the percentage of individuals achieving qualifications at Levels 4 and 5 is 5.1 per cent. In a more affluent ward of comparable size and demography, the percentage is 31.0 per cent (Ward, 2007: 3). The implications are worrying for the world of education and for practitioners supporting adults to re-enter education.

There are numerous local and national policies and initiatives which purport to encourage and support adults back into education and training, particularly those who missed out first time round. In the document Pursuing Excellence (QIA, 2006: 16) a government priority is identified which states that learners should have 'equality of access to high quality learning opportunities that are tailored to each individual's needs'. From my experience the reality of people's experience is quite different from the rhetoric. Although the difficulties that exist for adults returning to learning are well researched, these are not always taken into account either by policy makers or learning providers when they are thinking about how to promote and deliver learning opportunities. Nesbit (2006: 183) maintains that adult education is a 'function of the state' and as such is 'regulated according to certain economic, political and cultural interests and pressures'. Nesbit goes on to say that 'the system encourages its victims to regard themselves as responsible for their failure to be successful' (ibid.: 173). McGivney, researching into adult participation in organised learning, reaches the conclusion that

> people working in education tend to regard non-participants as the 'problem', rather than exploring how the system has failed to be relevant and attractive to a large proportion of the adult population.
>
> (1990: 175)

In conclusion

It appears that whilst individuals need practical help to access learning such as funding and information about courses, emotional support is the commodity which they most value when making the transition back into learning. Since this support from positive relationships appears to be so vital to enable adults to successfully return to learning, the possibility to access such relationships needs to be available. Supportive relationships may well already exist for adults within their families and their social networks. However, within organised learning these relationships will only happen by chance unless the environment for supportive relationships to develop is created and forms a part of the process of returning to learning.

It appears from the research that in relation to returning to learning, our early relationships in childhood, both within and outside the family are extremely influential in adulthood. Children's centres are places where there is an opportunity to support relationships both in childhood and in adulthood. Through relationships with parents we can work with those who need support to get things right for their children's learning and development, particularly emotional development, on which a fulfilled and happy life is founded. If we take care to do this, we will also get things right for the adults those children will become. In addition, through positive relationships we can create an environment that encourages and supports parents themselves to return to learning with all the benefits that can bring to themselves and their families. In helping parents 'learn to return' we are not just benefiting them, but also their children.

As children's centres develop, it is important that changes that inevitably happen do not alter the local landscape to the extent that the possibility to support parents when they decide to return to learning is diminished. This is the challenge for those leading the expansion of children's centres. Lownsborough and O'Leary (2005: 84), writing about the reformation of children's services, suggest that everyone involved in children's services, 'from nursery assistants to government ministers', should learn from local success stories when leading the way in reform.

The opportunity to work with both parents and their children to promote supportive relationships needs to be grasped if we truly want them all to have fair and equal access to learning. The words of John Dewey (1897: 77–80) are as pertinent now as they were in the nineteenth century when he wrote, 'I believe that all education proceeds by participation of the individual in the social consciousness of the race' and it is through this education that the individual 'becomes an inheritor of the funded capital of civilization'.

Reflections and questions

Anne has come up with the concept of an 'emotional reservoir' which she claims can become filled or depleted according to our experiences when interacting with others.

- How does this concept work for you, in relation to your own resilience?
- What sorts of observations have you made of others around you, in relation to their resilience in the face of adversity?
- How could we apply this concept to young children?

Applying learning to practice

* A good starting part might be a discussion, as a staff group, about all of the things that help adults return to learning, from the practical to the emotional.
* Sharing stories, as staff, of our own journeys can also give us insights into understanding how parents using our settings might feel.
* Another way in could be a discussion group with parents who are planning to return to learning, which might serve as a sort of support group offering ideas and emotional support from peers.

References

Aldridge, F. and Lavender, P. 2000. *The Impact of Learning on Health*. Leicester: NIACE.

Allatt, P. 1993. Becoming privileged: the role of family processes. In Bates, I. and Riseborough, G. (eds), *Youth and Inequality*. Buckingham: Open University Press.

Arnold, C. 2001. Persistence pays off: working with 'hard to reach' parents. In Whalley, M. and the Pen Green Centre Team, *Involving Parents in their Children's Learning*. London: Paul Chapman Publishing.

Bartley, M. (ed.) 2006. *Capability and Resilience: Beating the Odds*. London: UCL Department of Epidemiology and Public Health.

Bell, J. 1992. *Doing Your Research Project: A Guide for First-Time Researchers in Education and Social Science*. Milton Keynes: Open University Press.

Bennetts, C. 2001. Introducing the Fellowship Scheme Research Project: understanding the processes of adult learning and self-directed change. *Research Brief Series (Number 1)*. University of Exeter: Research Centre for the Learning Society.

Bridges, W. 2003. *Managing Transitions: Making the Most of Change*. London: Nicholas Brealey Publishing.

Bridges, W. and Mitchell Bridges, S. 2000. Leading transition: a new model for change. *Leader to Leader*, Vol. 16, Spring, 30–36. http://www.pfdf.org/leader books/121/spring2000/bridges.html (accessed 24/04/06).

Brookfield, S. 1983. *Adult Learning, Adult Education and the Community*. Milton Keynes: Open University Press.

Burke, P.J. 2006. Men accessing education: gendered aspirations. *British Educational Research Journal*, Vol. 32, No. 5, 719–713.

Coleman, J.S. 1988. Social capital in the creation of human capital. *American Journal of Sociology*, Vol. 94, Supplement: Organization and Institutions: Sociological and Economic Approaches to the Analysis of Social Structure, S95–S120.

Cullen, M. and Lindsay, G. 2005. *Sure Start Chelmsley Wood: Report of the Local Evaluation 2004, Section 3, Supporting Adults Returning to Learning*. Coventry: Centre for Educational Development, Appraisal and Research (CEDAR), Warwick University.

Dewey, J. 1897. My pedagogic creed. *School Journal*, Vol. 54, 77–80, http//:www.dewey.pragmatism.org/creed.htm.

Feinstein, L. and Hammond, C. 2003. Health and social benefits of adult learning. *Adults Learning*, June, 22–23.

Feinstein, L., Hammond, C., Woods, L., Preston, J. and Bynner, J. 2003. *The*

Contribution of Adult Learning to Health and Social Capital. London: The Centre for Research on the Wider Benefits of Learning.

Fitzgerald, R., Taylor, R. and LaValle, I. 2003. *National Adult Learning Survey (NALS) 2002.* Nottingham, National Centre for Social Research: DfES Publications.

Freire, P. 1993. *Pedagogy of the Oppressed.* London: Penguin Books.

Gerhardt, S. 2004. *Why Love Matters: How Affection Shapes a Baby's Brain.* Hove: Brunner-Routledge.

Gledhill, A. 2002. *Birmingham and Solihull Learning and Skills Council Review of Adult and Community Learning 2002. The Voice of the Learner: Focus Group Research.* Birmingham: Birmingham and Solihull Learning and Skills Council.

Goldberg, S. 2000. *Attachment and Development.* London: Arnold.

Hammond, C. 2004. Impacts of lifelong learning upon emotional resilience, psychological and mental health: fieldwork evidence. *Oxford Review of Education,* Vol. 30, No. 4, December, 554–568.

Hammond, C. and Feinstein, L. 2006. *Are Those Who Flourished at School Healthier Adults?: What Role for Adult Education?* London: Centre for Research on the Wider Benefits of Learning.

Hartley-Brewer, E. 2001. *Learning to Trust and Trusting to Learn: How Schools Can Affect Children's Mental Health.* London: Institute for Public Policy Research.

Horne, J. and Haggart, J. 2004. *The Impact of Adult's Participation in Family Learning – A Study Based in Lancashire.* Leicester: NIACE.

Kent, G. 2000. Ethical principles. In Burton, D. (ed.), *Research Training for Social Scientists: A Handbook for Postgraduate Researchers.* London: Sage.

Knowles, M.S. 1975. *Self-Directed Learning: A Guide for Learners and Teachers.* Chicago: Association Press.

Kvale, S. 1996. *InterViews: An Introduction to Qualitative Research Interviewing.* Thousand Oaks, CA: Sage Publications.

Kvale, S. 2006. *Interviewing between Method and Craft.* Community of QI2007. http://www.qi2007.org/community/files/4/papers/entry15.aspx (accessed 19.03.07).

Lewis, J. 2000. *The Concept of Resilience as an Overarching Aim and Organising Principle for Special Education, and as a Prerequisite for Inclusive Education.* International Special Education Congress 2000, University of Manchester. http://www.isec2000.org.uk/abstracts/papers_1/lewis_j_1.htm (accessed 20/12/06).

Lownsborough, H. and O'Leary, D. 2005. *The Leadership Imperative: Reforming Children's Services from the Ground Up.* London: Demos.

Marris, P. 1986. *Loss and Change.* London: Routledge & Kegan Paul.

McGivney, V. 1990. *Education's for Other People: Access to Education for Non-Participant Adults, A Research Report.* Leicester: NIACE.

McGivney, V. 2001. *Fixing or Changing the Pattern: Reflections on Widening Adult Participation in Learning.* Leicester: NIACE.

Mezirow, J. 1991. *Transformative Dimensions of Adult Learning.* San Francisco, CA: Jossey-Bass.

Mezirow, J. 1999. *Transformation Theory – Postmodern Issues.* 1999 AERC Proceedings. New York: Columbia University. http://www.edst.educ.ubc.ca/aerc/1999/99mezirow.htm (accessed 28/08/06).

Morrow, V. 1999. Conceptualising social capital in relation to the well-being of children and young people. *The Sociological Review 1999,* 744–765.

Nesbit, T. 2006. What's the matter with social class? *Adult Education Quarterly*, Vol. 56, No. 3, 171–187.

Newman, T. and Blackburn, S. 2002. Transitions in the lives of children and young people: resilience factors. *Interchange 78*, Scottish Executive Education Department. http://www.scotland.gov.uk/insight/ (accessed 18.03.06).

Nicholson, N. 1990. The Transition Cycle: causes, outcomes, processes and forms. In Fisher, S. and Cooper, C. (eds), *On the Move: The Psychology of Change and Transition*. Chichester: John Wiley & Sons.

Nowotny, H. 1981. Women in public life in Austria. In Fuchs Epstein, C. and Laub Coser, R. (eds), *Access to Power: Cross-National Studies of Women and Elites*. London: George Allen & Unwin.

Philip, K. and Shucksmith, J. 2005. Supporting vulnerable young people: exploring planned mentoring relationships, *CRFC Research Briefing 19 January 2005*. Edinburgh: Centre for Research on Families and Relationships.

Piaget, J. 1964. *Six Psychological Studies*. Reprinted 1980, Brighton: Harvester Press Ltd.

Quality Improvement Agency (QIA) 2006. *Pursuing Excellence: An Outline Improvement Strategy for Consultation*. Coventry: Quality Improvement Agency for Lifelong Learning.

Reay, D. 2001. Finding or losing yourself: working-class relationships to education. *Journal of Education Policy*, Vol. 16, No. 4, 333–346.

Reay, D. 2002. *Gendering Bourdieu's Concept of Capitals?: Emotional Capital, Women and Social Class*. Feminists Evaluate Bourdieu Conference, Manchester University, 11th October 2002. http://www.socialsciences.manchester.ac.uk/sociology/Seminar/documents/dianeraybourdieu.doc (accessed 21.11.06).

Roberts-Holmes, G. 2005. *Doing Your Early Years Research Project: A Step-by-Step Guide*. London: Paul Chapman Publishing.

Robson, C. 1993. *Real World Research: A Resource for Social Scientists and Practitioner-Researchers*. Oxford: Blackwell Publishers Ltd.

Rogers, M. and Tough, A. 1996. Facing the future is not for wimps. *Futures*, Vol. 28, No. 5, 491–496.

Rogoff, B. 1990. *Apprenticeship in Thinking*. Oxford: University Press.

Rubin, H.J. and Rubin, I.S. 2005. *Qualitative Interviewing: The Art of Hearing Data*. Thousand Oaks, CA: Sage Publications.

Schuller, T., Baron, S. and Field, J. 2000. Social capital: a review and critique. In Baron, S., Field, J. and Schuller, T. (eds), *Social Capital: Critical Perspectives*. Oxford: Oxford University Press.

Seaman, P. and Sweeting, H. 2004. Assisting young people's access to social capital in contemporary families: a qualitative study. *Journal of Youth Studies*, Vol. 7, No. 2, June, 173–190.

Secretary of State for Education and Skills 2003. *21st Century Skills: Realising Our Potential*. London: The Stationery Office Ltd.

Siegel, D.J. 1998. The developing mind: toward a neurobiology of interpersonal experience. *The Signal, Newsletter of the World Association for Infant Mental Health*, Vol. 6, Nos 3–4, 1–11.

Silva, E.B. and Edwards, R. 2004. Operationalizing Bourdieu on capitals: a discussion on 'The Construction of the Object'. *ESRC Research Methods Programme, Working Paper No. 7*. University of Manchester: Economic & Social Research Council.

Smith, M.K. 2002. Malcolm Knowles, informal adult education, self direction and androgogy. In *The encyclopedia of informal education*. http://www.infed.org/thinkers/et-knowl.htm (accessed 28/08/2006).

Stein, H., Fonagy, P., Ferguson, K.S. and Wisman, M. 2000. Lives through time: an ideographic approach to the study of resilience. *Bulletin of the Menninger Clinic*, Vol. 64, No. 2, 281–305.

Sure Start 2003. *Children's Centres – Developing Integrated Services for Young Children and their Families: Start Up Guidance – issued February 2003*. http:// www.surestart.gov.uk/_doc/0-3B81EO.doc (accessed 03.01.07).

Tough, A. 1982. *Intentional Changes: A Fresh Approach to Helping People Change*. Chicago: Follett Publishing Company.

Trevarthen, C. 2002. Learning in companionship. *Education in the North: The Journal of Scottish Education*, New Series, No. 10, 16–25.

Vygotsky, L.S. 1978. *Mind in Society*. Cambridge, MA: Harvard University Press.

Walker, C., Gleaves, A. and Grey, J. 2006. Can students within higher education learn to be resilient and, educationally speaking, does it matter? *Educational Studies*, Vol. 32, No. 3, 251–264.

Ward, N. 2007. *Family Learning – Current Drivers*. Paper presented at the Solihull Family Learning Network Conference held at Solihull College on 7th March.

Whalley, M. 2001. New forms of provision, new ways of working – the Pen Green Centre. In Whalley, M., *Involving Parents in their Children's Learning*. London: Paul Chapman Publishing.

Wilderdom 2004. http://www.wilderdom.com/personality/L8-StructureMindIdEgo Superego (accessed 09.03.07).

Williams, D. 2005. *Life Events and Career Change: Transition Psychology in Practice*. The Eos Life-Work Resource Centre, http://www.eoslifework.co.uk/transprac.htm (accessed 28.04.06).

Wood, D., Bruner, J. and Ross, G. 1976. The role of tutoring in problem solving. *Journal of Child Psychology & Psychiatry*, Vol. 17, 89–100.

Chapter 10

Concluding thoughts

Cath Arnold

My immediate thought on re-reading the preceding chapters is what a wealth of experience and knowledge is displayed in this book. Those people who possibly think that working with young children is a 'soft' or 'easy' option must reconsider their view and come to some sort of a realisation of the importance of the early years, of families and of workers.

Each chapter tells the story of a small-scale evaluative study of early years practice either at home or in an early years setting. Although none of the findings can claim to be generalisable to all homes or to all settings, they do all provide important insights about practice and beliefs; most raise awareness of issues that are significant when thinking about children and families; and all can help us improve our practice with children and families.

Sharing stories

There is little doubt that a good way of sharing information is through stories and each of these authors has provided a coherent story of practice on which to reflect. Not all writers or researchers would agree that the disclosure of personal information enhances a research study. In fact, the publishers of this book were keen that authors 'would not become too personal'. However, anyone reading Elaine's study of her child, Millie, or Gina's study of her grandson, Zack, can see that we gain more from their insights as close family members than would otherwise be possible. Similarly, Gill's is an 'insider' account of leadership that is rarely so well documented although many of us might recognise the issues of 'being a newcomer', 'being misunderstood', 'feeling inferior' and 'wanting to lead from behind'. This issue of acknowledging our personal history in an academic paper is quite delicate. We have seen some fine examples but it can go badly wrong. If we have not worked through issues and are still trying to deal with feelings of inadequacy, then our story and writing can be quite muddled. It rarely works to construct your understanding of what happened to you in early childhood in an assignment. However, if you have had opportunities, including professional counselling, to begin to understand the impact of your own upbringing on how you function, as a parent, and as an early years worker, it might be appropriate to write about the links, as Gill has done so beautifully.

Beliefs and values

Each story told in this book is underpinned by beliefs about how people (children and adults) learn. They are not all identical but are deeply felt and expressed and most are drawn from wide experiences of practice. Gina expressed some strong beliefs about learning to read, drawn from her experience as a teacher of young children and from studying for an MA in Children's Literature. Janette wrote about getting to know children and their families from the perspective of being the parent of a 4-year-old. Ana wrote about being the leader of a community nursery, having had a similar journey to her interviewees and with a firm view about what leadership meant to her.

Some writers began with anecdotes from their own childhoods and this enabled them to make links with their enquiries. Both Suzanne and Clare did this very effectively, showing how their experiences as children impacted on their beliefs and values as adult workers. This is different to sharing deeply personal information with the reader.

Practice-based evidence

A great deal of emphasis has been given in the UK in recent years to using 'evidence-based practice'. This is a medical model often transferred to other areas of practice; for example, only parent programmes that demonstrate proof that they work have been funded by government in the UK. The 'proof' comes in the form of large quantitative studies usually using a positivist paradigm. I would argue that although small-scale studies are not generalisable and, therefore, cannot offer 'proof' of an outcome, they do offer evidence based on practice and need to be considered alongside larger, narrower studies.

Beginning with a 'hunch' or a question

Most small-scale studies have some sort of connection to the practitioner leading the enquiry and begin with a 'hunch' or a genuine question. Anne's study of parents returning to learning had a connection to her own experience, as an adult learner and began with a genuine question: 'what supports adults to return to learning?' David was genuinely interested in encouraging the children's imaginative play and his question was about improving practice and making it the best it could be. Clare wanted to build 'bridges of shared understanding' between home and nursery and she had some ideas about how they could be constructed.

Minimising power differentials

Another theme that seems to permeate this book is the question of power. All of the writers, without exception, seem to be aware of the power of the institutions they are part of and the power they hold by virtue of their position or of being adults working with young children. All seemed to take steps to try to minimise the power differential, whether that was by inviting alternative views, like Gill, or listening carefully to children, like Elaine and Gina. This issue links with the sort of ethical stance we encourage, whereby adults and children feel they have the power to opt in or out of projects and to fully participate and put forward their views and be believed.

Most techniques and methods have advantages and disadvantages as you can see from Table 10.1, and sometimes advantages could also be described as disadvantages and vice versa. The main advice would be to try to use methods that enable you to gather the data that help you either address your main question or find out more about your hunch. Most beginning researchers gather far too much data and then are not sure about what to do with the information. Try to think through what will help you gain the information you are seeking.

Most studies involve collaboration and this is an advantage, in terms of working together and making changes to and improving practice, but too many collaborators can be difficult to manage and can also generate a huge amount of data. These studies were all written up as dissertations on the Pen Green MA of between 15,000 and 20,000 words. They were carried out and written up over a period of nine months.

Time is always an issue, in the sense that most of us do not have enough time to do things as well as we would like, especially when working and studying. However, we can think through and rationalise the choices that we make, when carrying out small practitioner-led enquiries. We can also do what a dear colleague, Patrick Whitaker, often advised: 'Do the best job you can in the time available' and, therefore, be satisfied with being less than perfect.

Table 10.1 Pros and cons of the different methods and techniques used

Chapter	Type of study	Techniques used	Advantages	Disadvantages
One	Child study	Observation using a journal	Study by parents, deep insights into child's understanding. Can record what happens 24/7	One perspective and method
Two	Child study	Observation using a journal	Study by grandparent. An intimate study impossible in a setting	One perspective and method
Three	Multiple qualitative methodology	Photos, video, interviews, taped conversations	Mixed methods, a 'constellation' of views, fifteen families	Time-consuming, hard to manage data in time-frame
Four	Polyvocal ethnography	Taped interviews, personal reflections	Designed to uncover cultural attitudes. Focus can be short video vignette. Dependent on others sharing personal reflections	Involved travelling to Norway. Researcher needed to facilitate discussion rather than lead
Five	Action research group enquiry	Individual and group observations Reflections/journals Well-being and involvement scales	Collaborative, most could be carried out during normal working day. Dependent on honest reflections from team	Power differential between Head and team. Keeping momentum going over time

Table 10.1 continued

Chapter	Type of study	Techniques used	Advantages	Disadvantages
Six	Practitioner action research	Questionnaires to staff and parents Diary sheets for parents Record sheets for staff Short interviews with parents	Confined to three staff and small number of families. Multi-methods for gathering data. Other parents might become interested through seeing data	Difficult to write up coherently. Parents opted in so only small number took part
Seven	Narrative enquiry	Open interview with five women leaders	Instrumental case study with purposive sample. Data gathered by one person with deep interest in subject	Large amount of data. Time to write up and check with participants
Eight	Practitioner-led enquiry	Discussion with critical friend Focus group – five to nine Questionnaire – nine nursery staff Dialogue about findings	A good way of opening out, from one view, to five to nine using different techniques involving discussion at different stages	Power differential could make it difficult for honest responses to be gathered. Ethically quite delicate in terms of how leader feels
Nine	Critical research	Taped interviews with eight people – a purposive sample	Instrumental case study with purposive sample. Data gathered and analysed by one person with deep interest in the subject	Only gathered views of people succeeding in returning to learning. Time-consuming in terms of long interviews and transcripts

Glossary

Affiliative leader – a leader who is connected to and shares power with colleagues

Agency – acting or exerting power

Androcentric – centred on a male view of the world

Apogee – the highest form of, in this case, play

Constructivist learning – the belief that human beings develop their own understanding of the world through experimenting and through their own firsthand experiences

Dispositional milieu – the learning place, what the environment offers children opportunities to do

Dispositions – the tendency to behave in certain ways, 'being ready, willing and able to participate in various ways' (Carr, 2001: 21)

Interactionist – the belief that children learn through the interaction of biology and culture

Involvement – how absorbed a person is in what they are doing

Othering – the way we tend to see people from cultures different to our own as *other*, but we too are an *other* (Harcus, Chapter 6 in this book)

Participative culture – a culture in which power and responsibility is shared

Polysemic – having a number of meanings, interpretations or understandings

Polyvocal ethnography – using filmed material from different contexts to view and to stimulate discussion and to gather data from and between settings in order to identify cultural differences

Reader response – the theory that a text gains meaning by the purposeful act of a reader reading and interpreting it through the lens of their own experiences

'Reculturing' the organisation – creating a new ethos by changing mindsets in an organisation; asking 'why?'

Schemas – 'A schema is a pattern of repeated actions. Clusters of schemas develop into later concepts' (Athey, 2003)

Self-actualisation – to become everything one is capable of becoming

Social capital – 'an individual's or individual group's sphere of contacts' (Grenfell and James, 1998: 20)

Utopia – an ideal or perfect state or place

Zone of proximal development – the difference between what a child can do with help and what he or she can do without guidance; children on the 'cusp' of learning something may be within their zone of proximal development

References

Athey, C. (2003) Conversation with Chris Athey.

Carr, M. (2001) *Assessment in Early Childhood Settings: Learning Stories*, London: Paul Chapman.

Grenfell, M. and James, D. (1998) (eds) *Acts of Practical Theory Bourdieu and Education*, London: RoutledgeFalmer.

Index

Note: Page numbers followed by 'f' refer to figures, and followed by 't' refer to tables.